Family Involvement in Early Childhood Education

Research into Practice

Family Involvement in Early Childhood Education
Research into Practice

Jennifer Prior, Ph.D. • Maureen R. Gerard, Ph.D.

THOMSON

DELMAR LEARNING

Australia   Canada   Mexico   Singapore   Spain   United Kingdom   United States

THOMSON

DELMAR LEARNING

Family Involvement in Early Childhood Education: Research into Practice
Jennifer Prior and Maureen R. Gerard

Vice President, Career Education SBU:
Dawn Gerrain

Managing Editor:
Robert L. Serenka, Jr.

Senior Acquisitions Editor:
Erin O'Connor

Editorial Assistant:
Stephanie Kelly

Director of Production:
Wendy A. Troeger

Production Manager:
J.P. Henkel

Content Project Manager:
Ken Karges

Director of Marketing:
Wendy E. Mapstone

Channel Manager:
Kristin McNary

Marketing Coordinator:
Scott A. Chrysler

Cover Design:
Joseph Villanova

Composition:
International Typesetting
and Composition

Library of Congress Cataloging-in-Publication Data

Prior, Jennifer Overend, 1963—
   Family involvement in early childhood education: research into practice / Jennifer Prior, Maureen Gerard.
      p. cm.
   Includes bibliographical references and index.
   ISBN 1-4180-1424-9
      1. Early childhood education—Parent participation. I. Gerard, Maureen R. II. Title.

LB1139.35.P37P75 2007
372.1192—dc22

2006019016

NOTICE TO THE READER

Contents

CHAPTER 2

CHAPTER 3

CHAPTER 4

CHAPTER Building a Comprehensive Program for Family
Involvement in the Early Years

Preface

Early childhood has gained considerable attention in the field of education. No Child Left Behind and its requirements for highly qualified teachers has affected the preparation of teachers in early childhood. A growing body of research also draws attention to the benefits of family involvement related to children, schools, teachers, and parents. Because the thought of family involvement can be overwhelming and even frightening to the novice teacher, this book breaks down the process and will assist you with developing your own plan for the families of your future students. It describes the current and ongoing research related to the important benefits of family involvement as it pertains to student achievement, as well as practical ideas and specific activities for students in undergraduate and graduate teacher education programs to assist them in getting parents involved in their children's education at school and at home. This book also offers ideas for the parents and teachers of infants and toddlers as well as the parents and teachers of school-age children. While the main focus is on early childhood, ideas can be applied to students in intermediate grades. The ideas and specific activities featured in this book are designed for instant use by classroom teachers with a format that is teacher-friendly.

THE DEVELOPMENT OF THIS TEXT

As practitioners who are now teacher educators, we are sensitive to the gap between research and its application to the classroom. In our university courses we have tried to bridge this gap by making the linkages from research to practice, providing students with the "why" of family involvement to encourage their exploration of the "how." An extensive review of the literature is provided throughout the chapters of this book. The most current research is examined along with seminal or classic works.

TEXT ORGANIZATION

The organization of this book stems from our experiences as classroom teachers and the most current areas of research. Presentation of this information takes the reader from knowledge to application in a variety of areas related to family involvement. It is our desire that our students and teachers have a well-grounded understanding of the research to thoughtfully and reflectively reproduce effective materials and implement strategies in the classroom.

Chapter 1, Benefits of Family Involvement in the Early Years, presents the benefits of parent-teacher partnerships and parent-child interactions related to education. There is a wealth of research on this subject; understanding these benefits is inspirational and sure to make even the most timid of teachers consider a plan for family involvement.

Chapter 2, Diverse Families: Then, Now, Tomorrow, provides a brief historical trip through the views of families. This chapter also examines the diversity of family structures today, including ethnicity, language, and economic factors.

Many school districts, administrators, and teachers don't know where to begin to get families involved. They are often overwhelmed with other tasks or feel uncomfortable communicating with parents. In Chapter 3, Challenges to an Effective Partnerships in the Early Years, we'll take a look at the barriers and differences such as culture and socioeconomic status that can prevent positive parent-teacher partnerships. This chapter will address many of the challenges to effective family involvement and offer suggestions for how to overcome them.

Chapter 4 addresses male involvement. More and more research focuses on the involvement of fathers and male mentors in a child's education. As teachers, we tend to think about moms being involved in their children's education and we don't encourage fathers and male role models. This chapter presents important research in this area and provides strategies for communicating with fathers as well as designing school activities that cater to men.

Family involvement is much more complex than helping out in the classroom; it means developing and fostering effective partnerships between teachers and parents. Chapter 5, Creating Partnerships at School in the Early Years, presents family involvement models and ideas to begin these partnerships. It also focuses on specific ways to get started with building parent-teacher partnerships. Strategies such as regular communication, providing opportunities for parents to help out at school, planning for parent help in the classroom, and scheduling for parent helpers are presented. The ideas in this chapter help to lay the foundation for building positive relationships with parents.

We know that not all parents have the freedom to be involved with their children's education at school. In fact, there is a great misunderstanding that family involvement must take place at school. Realistically, we know this isn't possible for all parents. Chapter 6, Family Involvement at Home in the Early Years, focuses on ways teachers can involve parents in their children's education at home by providing newsletters of ideas for parent-child interaction, backpack activities containing educational activities for parents and children to complete together, and a variety of activities and resources for busy parents to be involved in from home.

Chapter 7, Family Involvement with Infant/Toddler Care and Education, addresses research related to the importance of parents as children's first teachers. This chapter also gives child care providers strategies for successful parent education and collaboration.

The final chapter, Building a Comprehensive Program for Family Involvement in the Early Years, presents ways to develop school-wide programs by involving other teachers and administrators in the process of building partnerships. This chapter also provides schedules, letters, progress report forms, and activities for parent workshops that can be used to educate parents and provide them with ideas in a variety of areas concerning their children's school experience.

UNIQUE FEATURES OF THE BOOK

In addition to providing instant family involvement activities, this book also features elements that encourage individual, small group, and class reflection. Each chapter begins with a list of key terms and definitions that will be encountered. Families in Focus, which are real-life scenarios, are provided to give readers a glimpse of classroom life and diverse family experiences. At the conclusion of each chapter, review questions and exercises are provided to encourage reflection and application of the featured topic. The authors' intent is that this book be used initially as coursework material and later becomes a teacher resource. The eight chapters can easily be used as the foundation of an 8-week modular format or a component of the course material in a 16-week semester.

ANCILLARY MATERIALS

Accompanying this book are three additional resources—the Professional Enhancement Booklet, the e-Resource, and the Online Companion™.

Professional Enhancement Booklet

A new supplement to accompany this text is the Home, School, and Community Relations booklet for students. This booklet, which is part of Thomson Delmar Learning's Early Childhood Education Professional Enhancement series, focuses on key topics of interest to future early childhood directors, teachers, and caregivers. Students will keep this informational supplement and use it for years to come in their early childhood practices.

e-Resource

The new e-Resource component is geared to provide instructors with all the tools they need on one convenient CD-ROM. Instructors will find that this resource provides them with a turnkey solution to help them teach by making available PowerPoint® slides for each book chapter, the Computerized Test Bank, electronic version of the Instructor's Manual, and other text-specific resources.

The computerized test bank is comprised of true/false, multiple choice, short answer, and completion questions for each chapter. Instructors can use the computerized test bank software to create quizzes for students. Refer to the CTB User's Guide for more information on how to create and post quizzes to your school's Internet or Intranet server.

Online Companion™

The Online Companion™ includes:
- Links to useful Web sites
- Downloadable forms, letters, and activity sheets featured in the book
- Suggestions for further research

- Case studies for further discussion accompanied by critical thinking questions
- The Online Companion™ can be accessed at www.earlychilded. delmar.com.

A MESSAGE FROM THE AUTHORS

Jennifer Prior

Most preservice teachers have never given much thought to working with families and little is offered in their preparation coursework to prepare them to work well with parents. They went into teaching to teach kids, right? Why do we need to talk about their parents? More than 20 years ago, I was one of those new teachers who planned on teaching children, but not necessarily working with parents. In fact, I avoided parents whenever I could. If there were a reason to talk with parents, it could only mean "bad news." But what I found was that the more I avoided, the more parents wanted to interact. And why shouldn't they? Education is important and the education of one's own child is of utmost importance.

As I look back on my teaching career, I realize that I wasn't prepared to work with families, nor did I understand the benefits of family involvement. After a few years, I decided to begin sending home a weekly newsletter to parents, informing them of what was to come in the week ahead. Little did I know that this simple form of communication would do so much to ease parents' minds about what their children were learning in my classroom. Parents appreciated it so much that I wondered why I had waited so long to begin some form of regular communication with them. What I found was that parents would approach me to discuss some of the great activities going on in the classroom. Because they were informed about what was happening in class, they were able to ask their children specific questions and hear the excitement in their children's voices as they talked about what they were learning.

Later on in my career, I made greater efforts to get to know and interact with families. At the beginning of the year, I made plans for how to get them involved (inside and outside the classroom). I sent home descriptions of parent jobs and encouraged them to sign up to help on a regular basis. At school events or after school, I would seek them out and make efforts to visit for a while. Phone calls and notes became commonplace, and I found the more effort I made, the more parents trusted me, and the more they seemed to value their children's education.

Maureen Gerard

Like most new teachers I was scared to death of parents. As a preservice teacher I'd had no coursework in family involvement and didn't know where to begin. After finding myself in an adversarial position on more than one occasion, I began looking for resources and ways to change family interactions in my classroom. I soon realized that a proactive form of communication each week went a long way in answering parents' questions. A progress report that covered multiple domains reassured parents and eased all of us into report card conferences. The parents' enthusiasm led to positive interactions, which made me feel much more comfortable to be around them. By implementing effective strategies (many of which are featured in this book) I found that parents became my greatest source of support and encouragement.

Final Message from the Authors

Family involvement or forming parent-teacher partnerships has now become a passion of ours and we realize that it is the teacher's responsibility to reach out and make efforts for the ultimate benefit of students. For this reason, we write this book to address the important issues related to family involvement, especially in the early years of a child's education. It is our hope that, after reading this book, you, too, will have new insights into building positive parent-teacher partnerships. It will take time to begin forming these relationships, but we must remember that our efforts, in the long run, serve to benefit young children.

Jennifer Prior is Assistant Professor of Early Childhood and Literacy at Northern Arizona University in Flagstaff, Arizona.

Maureen Gerard is Associate Professor of Reading and Early Childhood at Grand Canyon University in Phoenix, Arizona.

ACKNOWLEDGMENTS

We acknowledge all of the children and families who were our teachers along the way.

In addition, we would like to thank the following reviewers, whose valuable feedback helped to shape the final text:

Nancy H. Beaver, M.Ed.
Eastfield College of the Dallas County Community College District, TX

Marie Brand, M.S.
State University of New York, Empire College

Patricia J. Dilko, M.P.A.
Canada College, CA

Phyllis Gilbert, M.S., M.Ed.
Stephen F. Austin University, TX

Karen Danbom
Minnesota State University Moorhead, MN

Christie Honeycutt, M.Ed.
Stanley College, NC

Dawn Murrell, M.A.
Baker College, MI

Cheryl Robinson, Ph.D.
University of Tennessee-Knoxville, TN

Elaine Van Lue
Nova Southeastern University, FL

Gwendolyn J. Williams, Ph.D.
Florida A&M University, FL

Please note the Internet resources are of a time-sensitive nature and URL addresses may often change or be deleted.

CHAPTER 1

Benefits of Family Involvement in the Early Years

▥ CHAPTER OBJECTIVES

After reading and reflecting on this chapter, you should be able to:

- Communicate the results of research studies related to family involvement and student achievement.
- Relate the importance of family differences when considering programs of family involvement.
- Discuss theoretical perspectives relating the importance of parent interactions with children.

▥ KEY TERMS

Constructivist

Ecological Systems Theory

exosystem

family involvement

longitudinal study

macrosystem

mesosystem

microsystem

National Association for the Education of Young Children

pedagogical perspectives

Sociocultural Theory

INTRODUCTION: DEFINING FAMILY INVOLVEMENT

One of the difficulties with addressing issues concerning family involvement is that it is so often defined in many different ways. Some think of **family involvement** as simply parents helping the child with homework. Others think of it as volunteerism with the parent coming to school to perform tasks for the teacher. Still others think of it as the parent participating in the school's parent-teacher organization and helping out with school-wide events.

While family involvement does include the above-mentioned activities, in this book those are viewed as merely parts of a much more far-reaching perspective. Family involvement, in its most successful form, involves the following:

- positive communication between teachers and parents, schools and parents, children and parents
- parents expressing interest and value in their children's education and in larger educational issues
- parents working at home with their children
- parents expressing high, yet realistic, expectations of their children's academic pursuits
- teachers providing parents with meaningful educational experiences to do at home and during vacations
- parents helping out in the classroom truly becoming part of the teaching/learning/planning cycle
- teachers engaging in regular communication with parents about school life
- teachers communicating regularly and personally with parents about their children's progress
- parents and teachers working together on school-wide, district-level, even statewide events
- schools supporting families by providing educational experiences that assist them in supporting their children
- schools helping families to find needed community services and resources
- schools serving as a year-round community resource and community resource center

Early childhood theorists have acknowledged for decades the many facets of family involvement in the early childhood experience. Let's examine some of those theoretical perspectives on the family.

THEORETICAL FRAMEWORK

When looking at children's success in school, it is important to look at the factors that lead to this success. Many theorists address the importance of adults and families in the children's development. Vygotsky (1981), Dewey (1966), and Piaget and Inhelder (1969) suggest that social interactions are inseparable from intellectual development and assist children in achieving higher levels of understanding and cognitive development.

Jean Piaget and Inhelder

Piaget's theory of cognitive development in children is based on the continual drive of young children to match their own view of the real world—internal constructions—and the external realities they encounter. With each new experience, children constantly rework and revise—assimilate and accommodate—their own internal views with the experience. The theory is based on both a child's genetically preprogrammed "hardwiring" for development and the influences of a rich, stimulating, and responsive environment. Other people and the social setting are an important influence in the environment. Social interaction and context are "indissociable" from cognitive development. The more actively involved children are with people and things in their world, the more quickly they will assimilate new learning and accommodate their own incorrect views of the world.

John Dewey

Dewey, the father of American progressive education, promoted an inquiry-based approach to education for young children. He stressed the importance of the individual child's experiences in the educational process and believed that children learn through experience. In Dewey's estimation, two kinds of experience for learning were meaningful. First, learning must interest, stimulate, and absorb the student and, second, those learning experiences must lead to further learning. Along with Piaget and Vygotsky, Dewey recognized that educational experiences were inextricably interwoven with social experiences. Learning experiences that are interesting and individually captivating are those that children are guided into by others.

Vygotsky

Vygotsky's theory (1981), in particular, focuses on the acquisition of mental functions through social interaction.

Russian psychologist Lev Vygotsky focused on the social and cultural factors involved in development and learning. **Constructivist** in nature, Vygotsky's ideas did not just address the child's need to construct meaning, but added that social interaction is an essential element in that process. He asserted that new knowledge is internalized through involvement in social activities. As expressed by Duveen (1998), "The power of Vygotsky's idea . . . is its simplicity. The child is born into a world, which is already culturally structured and this culture is mediated for the child through the activities of those around them. In this way the child comes to take their place within this culture, and eventually, through their own activities to become a mediator of the culture to successive generations" (p. 80). Simply put, Vygotsky recognizes the importance of family and culture. We are surrounded by family members and others within a particular community and are impacted by the ideologies of that culture. A child's first, most significant teacher is the family. And a child's first, most significant learning occurs in the community. We interact with those around us within our families and communities and gain knowledge about the world as we live life together. (See Figure 1–1.)

In terms of the internalization of knowledge, Vygotsky addressed the zone of proximal development. He used this concept to discuss levels of problem-solving ability. He suggested that children have one level of development that refers to what a child can achieve on his or her own. Another level refers to the child's abilities when working under the guidance of an adult or a more able peer (Vygotsky, 1978). He believed that it is not enough to understand a child's current level of understanding, but we must also understand the child's future potential.

The **Sociocultural Theory,** as a whole, emphasizes interrelatedness and interdependence of individual and social processes in development and learning, which, in early childhood education, points to the child's home life before entering school years. "[I]t underscores a fundamental principle for sociocultural **pedagogical perspectives**—the recognition

FIGURE 1–1 Vygotsky's work emphasizes the importance of family and culture.

of children's learning processes before children come to school and of the ongoing learning outside school. Vygtosky claimed that any learning a child encounters in school has a previous history" (Mahn, 1999, p. 347). From this perspective, it is easy to see how the role of the parent contributes greatly to the intellectual and academic development of a child.

Bronfenbrenner

The **Ecological Systems Theory** (also called the bioecological systems theory) focuses not only on the development of the child or his or her immediate family, but also on the influences from his or her surrounding world. According to Urie Bronfenbrenner (1979, 1995, 1998), the leading advocate of the theory, social, political, biological, and economic conditions also affect the child. Before addressing the specifics of family influences, let's take a look at the overall view of the ecological systems theory. *Ecology* refers to the settings and institutions that affect us as we grow. Bronfenbrenner proposes ecological systems or nested layers of sociocultural influence—the **microsystem, mesosystem, exosystem,** and

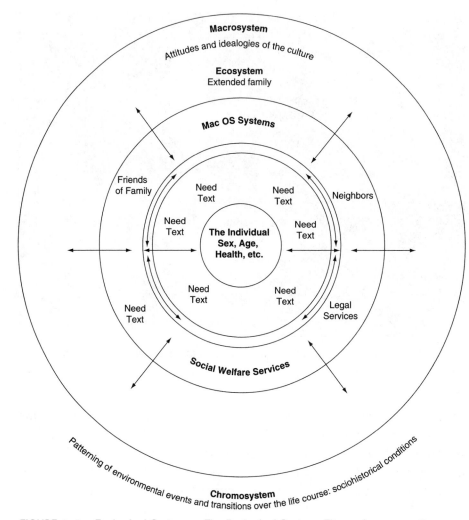

FIGURE 1–2 Ecological Systems The Ecological Systems Theory focuses on the influences from a child's surrounding world.

macrosystem. This theoretical approach examines the developing child and the child's interactions with people, objects, and symbols in "proximal processes" across multiple settings, contexts, and environments. (See Figure 1–2.)

The microsystem is the layer that most closely affects and includes the child. Within this system are settings and institutions in the child's immediate surroundings, such as family, school, teachers, church, peers, child health services, the neighborhood, and so on. The microsystem includes the pattern of activities, roles, and relationships most often experienced by the child. It is the setting where the child experiences face-to-face interaction. The child is not only influenced by these, but also has influence on them. It is a reciprocal relationship. For example, the child's family affects the growth and development of the child and, in return, the child has an influence on his or her family. Institutions within the microsystem are also affected by one another. For example, family members are influenced by the school and the school is influenced by families and the makeup of the neighborhood. A child care health professional might make recommendations to the parent, who in turn makes changes in the child's diet or exercise routines. All of these people and settings interact with one another.

The exosystem is comprised of people, settings, and institutions that indirectly touch the child's life, such as extended family members, friends of the family, neighbors, the parents' workplaces, community and social services, and the media. While these do not directly touch the child on a daily basis, they do affect the child's life. For example, a parent's workplace has an indirect effect on the child. If the parent has a positive work environment and is earning a living wage that adequately supports the family, this parent is likely to return home from work each day with a positive attitude. Conversely, a negative work environment might cause the parent to experience stress and frustration, which is likely to influence the home environment in a negative way.

The mesosystem connects the microsystem and exosystem. This system is made up of the linkages between two or more settings in which the child actively participates. For example, the child's relationships with family members in the home, friends and teachers at school, and peers and families in the neighborhood comprise the mesosystem. When the mesosystem linkages are strong and positive, the development of the child is enhanced. Likewise, weak or negative connections between the microsystem and exosystem can have a damaging impact on development.

The last ecological layer is the macrosystem, which includes attitudes and ideologies of the culture, such as laws, morals, values, customs, and worldviews. While these are not readily a part of the child's immediate world, they can have great impact. For example, the values of a particular society certainly affect parenting styles or work habits, which have a direct effect on the child's upbringing.

It is easy to see how this broad perspective on the development of a child relates to family involvement in early childhood education. From this perspective we must recognize the influences of the child's surroundings.

The school experience is not just an interaction between the school or teacher and the child, but rather is an interrelated system involving the parent, family, and community.

FAMILY INVOLVEMENT AND MODELS FOR EARLY CHILDHOOD EDUCATION

Many models for early childhood education highlight the importance of family involvement. Parent partnerships are often highly valued in programs such as Reggio Emilia and Waldorf schools. In particular, the Reggio Emilia approach builds on the importance of the parent in a child's life and in the overall community of the school (Gandini, 1997). This approach originated in Italy at the close of World War II. Parent anxieties over postwar trauma in their young children resulted in demands for municipal funding of exceptionally sensitive early education and care. The Reggio approach is well known and has been implemented in many early childhood programs in the United States. In this model, parents are encouraged to be a part of the school community to assist in supporting high-quality education for children; learning is a social and cultural process that involves children and adults—teachers, parents, community members, and political leaders—working together in the environment. The Reggio Emilia approach is based on a respect for the knowledge, capacities, and innate competencies within children to make sense of the world, and positions parents within the schools as essential in "creating a community of caring adults who value children" (Bennet, 2001, p. 6).

Waldorf Education also emphasizes family involvement and has as one of its key elements the goal of "building the school and the greater Waldorf community as networks of support for students, teachers, and parents" (Easton, 1997, p. 8). Waldorf education carefully balances academic, creative, and practical experiences to develop a child's self-assurance and independence with experiences to develop social and community responsibility. This approach typically provides learning and support opportunities for parents and values their role in the educational process.

The **National Association for the Education of Young Children** (National Association, 2004) is an organization that devotes itself to the well-being of children from birth through age eight. It focuses on quality services (both educational and developmental) for young children, and places such value on families that child care institutions seeking accreditation through the

FIGURE 1–3   The National Association for the Education of Young Children (NAEYC) emphasizes the importance of families.

NAEYC must demonstrate that families are a priority in the care and education of young children. (See Figure 1–3.) The following is the program standard for families:

The program establishes and maintains collaborative relationships with each child's family to foster children's development in all settings. These relationships are sensitive to family composition, language, and culture.

This program standard is defined by numerous criteria, including the following:

- Program staff use a variety of mechanisms, such as family conferences or home visits, to promote dialogue with families. The program staff ask adults to translate or interpret communications as needed.

- Program staff communicate with families on at least a weekly basis regarding children's activities and developmental milestones, shared caregiving issues, and other information that affects the well-being and development of their children. Where in-person communication is not possible, alternative communication practices are in place.

- Program staff communicate with families on a daily basis regarding children's activities and developmental milestones, shared caregiving issues, and other information that affects the well-being and development of their children. Where in-person communication is not possible, alternative communication practices are in place.

- The program compiles and provides information about the program to families in a language the family can understand. This information includes program policies and operating procedures.

- Program staff inform families about the program's systems for formally and/or informally assessing children's progress. This includes the purposes of the assessment, the procedures used for assessment, procedures for gaining family input and information, the timing of assessments, the way assessment results or information will be shared with families, and ways the program will use the information.

- When program staff suspect that a child has a developmental delay or other special need, this possibility is communicated to families in a sensitive, supportive, and confidential manner, with documentation and explanation for the concern, suggested next steps, and information about resources for assessment.

- Program staff encourage families to regularly contribute to decisions about their child's goals and plans for activities and services.

- Program staff encourage families to raise concerns and work collaboratively with them to find mutually satisfying solutions that staff then incorporate into classroom practice.

- Program staff encourage and support families to make the primary decisions about services that their children need, and they encourage families to advocate to obtain needed services.

- Program staff use a variety of techniques to negotiate difficulties that arise in their interactions with family members. Program staff make arrangements to use these techniques in a language the family can understand.

- Program staff provide families with information about programs and services from other organizations. Staff support and encourage families' efforts to negotiate health, mental health, assessment, and educational services for their children.

- Program staff use established linkages with other early education programs and local elementary schools to help families prepare for and manage their children's transitions between programs, including special education programs. Staff provide information to families that can assist them in communicating with other programs.

- To help families with their transitions to other programs or schools, staff provide basic general information on enrollment procedures and practices, visiting opportunities, and/or program options.
- Prior to sharing information with other relevant providers, agencies, or other programs, staff obtain written consent from the family.

The National Standards for Parent/Family Involvement are six guidelines developed by the National Parent Teacher Association to strengthen and promote parent and family involvement in schools and the community, raise awareness of effective programs, and improve existing school programs. These standards are focused on issues of effective communication and participation in school–home–community partnerships.

Standard I: Communication between home and school is regular, two-way, and meaningful.

Standard II: Parenting skills are promoted and supported.

Standard III: Parents play an integral role in assisting student learning.

Standard IV: Parents are welcome in school and their support and assistance are sought.

Standard V: Parents are full partners in making the decisions that affect children and families.

Standard VI: Community resources are used to strengthen schools, families, and student learning.

BENEFITS OF FAMILY INVOLVEMENT

So, what exactly are the benefits of family involvement? Why should teachers make efforts to build partnerships with parents and encourage them to take part in their children's educational experience? Parents play a central role in their children's academic success (Chavkin, 1993; Christenson & Conoley, 1992). This is especially the case with children in their early years of school as they adapt to the new environment and begin to form who they are as learners. (See Figure 1–4.) "It is a well-established fact that home–school collaboration benefits all children" (Raffaele, 1999). Not only do family members provide the attachment and bonding necessary in early development, but they also serve as powerful models of learning (Pipher, 1996). Family members model behaviors and provide learning opportunities as children grow (Swick, 2003).

FIGURE 1–4   Parents play a central role in their children's academic success. This is especially the case with children in their early years of school.

A look at 70 studies of parent involvement (Carter, 2002) highlights several common themes:

- Parent/family involvement has a great impact on student achievement during elementary school, middle school, and high school; parents who are involved in the schools tend to have children who do well in school.

- Variations in student achievement exist in relation to culture, ethnicity, and socioeconomic backgrounds; parents who are involved no matter what their backgrounds help close the achievement "gap."

- Parent involvement at home has greater impact on children than parent involvement in school-based activities. One-to-one time with children is the most enriching for them academically.

- Parents who involve themselves in their children's early childhood programs assist their children in more successful transitions to kindergarten and elementary school. Parent involvement makes school a less traumatic place to be.

- Assistance with homework is beneficial for students if their parents receive guidance in working effectively with their children. Parent involvement reinforces and strengthens school learning.

- There are cultural differences that impact the families that involve themselves with their children's education. Teachers/schools need to value family differences and keep them in mind when planning for family involvement.
- Mathematics and literacy skills have been shown to improve when parents are involved in the educational experience. Parent involvement sends the message that learning is important.
- When families, schools, and the community work together, greater student achievement occurs. School improvement includes parent involvement.
- Individualizing school programs is necessary for successful parent-school partnerships.

Some studies show that children's academic achievement correlates with home environments that support learning (Christenson, 1995; Clark, 1983). These studies suggest that homes with school-like qualities lead to smooth transitions between the two environments and ultimately lead to academic success. Henderson and Berla (1994) state that it is not income or social status that are the best indicators of a child's achievement, but rather the following:

- parents who create a home environment that encourages learning
- parents' expression of high educational expectations
- parents' interest in and willingness to participate in their children's education, both at school and in the community

These researchers further deduce that it is the time and intensity given to parent involvement that most closely correlates with student success. As teachers, we can assist parents in accomplishing the above goals by providing ideas for effective learning environments. We can help parents understand realistic goals for their individual children. We can also welcome parents into the school experience by expressing the value of their participation in their children's education both at school and at home.

Epstein (1995) states that parents can bring about improvement in school programs and in the general atmosphere of the school. They can also assist with providing services for families, connect families with one another, and assist teachers. She believes, though, that the most important reason to involve parents is to benefit the educational experiences of children. Epstein further states that regular interactions among teachers, schools, and parents benefit children by communicating positive views of school and the importance of making efforts to do well in school.

Research by Henderson and Berla (1994) suggests more benefits of parent involvement, including the following when parents participate in their children's education:

- increased student achievement
- improved student attitudes
- improved attendance
- decrease in discipline problems

Family involvement has been shown to lead to an increase in children's positive attitudes about school, improved attendance, and better homework habits. Children tend to see a connection between their home and school when their parents are involved. Children experience this connection even more when they see their teachers model their positive family values (Epstein, 1985; Epstein, 2000; Epstein et al., 1997). In addition to improvement in student attitudes, "research shows that well-designed [family involvement] programs can boost academic achievement and even raise low-income students' test scores" (Jones, 2001).

BULLYING

Educators, mental-health-care workers, parents, and community members are realizing the mounting seriousness of bullying in the schools. Some experts believe that bullying should be considered a peculiar form of child abuse. One of the primary prevention techniques for bullying problems is parental involvement. Lack of adult supervision or parental involvement provides fertile ground for bullying in the schools. Parents and concerned adults play a key role in curtailing bullying because children who are bullied rarely are able to handle the bullying problems on their own. More than 10 years ago, Harvard University convened international experts on school violence and bullying to study prevention strategies. Sponsored by the National School Safety Center and the Federal Office of Juvenile Justice, Delinquency and Prevention, the program included prominent researchers, mental-health professionals, and school and law enforcement personnel (1998). This effort resulted in the development of a list of services, strategies, and suggested training

FAMILIES IN FOCUS

Kyle loved school. Gregarious and outgoing, he loved recess, picture books, and finger painting. He loved Legos, Clifford the big red dog, and crayons. Kyle had amazing recall and could remember minute details of the things he read and the things his teacher taught him. He was the undisputed champion of Memory in his classroom. Kyle had a great year of school in first grade. His mom stayed at home with his baby brother but often came in to help in his classroom. She was there to help with parties, to organize and to file papers, to supervise learning centers, and to work with the class in the computer lab. Kyle's mom served on the school site council and supported many school-wide functions with her time, money, and attendance. Kyle was achieving and his mother was highly involved in his learning and his school.

Things changed dramatically in Kyle's second-grade year. He hated school. Miserable and belligerent, Kyle struggled just to get ready for school each morning, and consistently lost his backpack and his homework. He hated reading anything. His classroom behavior verged on "out of control" most days. Notes and phone calls from the school became a huge source of dread and foreboding for Kyle's mother.

So what happened? What happened that made such a change in Kyle's academic achievement and attitude toward school? Two events may account for the stark contrast between first grade and second grade. Kyle's mother began attending a nearby university to complete her master of arts degree. Needless to say, her involvement in Kyle's classroom, in the school, and even in the home changed as she juggled her own schooling demands. The second event to impact Kyle was the beliefs his second-grade teacher held about parent involvement in her classroom. A very traditional, "old-fashioned" educator, this teacher discouraged parent help in her "efficient, well-run" classroom. She firmly believed that issues such as inappropriate behavior and academic achievement were the school's business and should be handled at the school. She, therefore, did not seek out parent input or collaboration as problems began to surface with Kyle. Parent–teacher conferences were tense and adversarial for Kyle's mother and the teacher as Kyle's learning and classroom behavior seriously deteriorated.

Kyle never did very well in school after that. Some years were better than others. Eventually, after dropping out of school several times, he graduated from an alternative high school. Perhaps if Kyle's mother had fully understood the impact her involvement would have had on Kyle's entire academic career, and perhaps if his second-grade teacher had viewed parents as partners in educating the children in her classroom, Kyle's story would be very different.

(Continues)

> **FAMILIES IN FOCUS (CONTINUED)**
>
> While the above study is individual in nature, these results were replicated in a meta-analysis, a statistical translation and comparison, of 25 studies on parent involvement and its relationship to student academic achievement. This analysis indicated a common thread that when parents have high, but not unrealistic, expectations for their children's educational achievement, achievement increases (Fan & Chen, 2001).

classes for addressing bullying. It also led to the recommendation that schools provide

- rules against bullying that are publicized, posted school-wide, and accompanied by consistent sanctions.
- student and adult mentors who assist victims to build self-esteem and to foster mutual understanding of and appreciation for differences in others.
- a "buddy system" that pairs students with a particular friend or an older student who is aware of the buddy's class schedule and is available if help is needed.
- an on-campus parents' center to recruit parents to participate in the educational process, volunteer, and assist in school projects and activities.
- parenting and anger management classes for adults.
- behavior contracts signed by students and parents, and written behavior codes for students, teachers, and staff members.
- discipline policies that emphasize positive behaviors rather than punishments for wrong behaviors.
- training for all adult supervisors in cafeterias, playgrounds, or other "hot spots" where bullying is known to occur.
- classroom and school-wide activities designed to build self-esteem (for those who are bullied) by spotlighting special talents, hobbies, interests, and abilities of all students.

Think about the impact of these studies and how our schools might look, as a whole, if we all made the effort to involve parents and families in education. Increased student achievement and attitudes? Improved attendance? Fewer discipline problems? It sounds like utopia, doesn't it?

And yet, these kinds of advantages don't have to remain as lofty dreams in a perfect world. They are within our reach, if only we would begin to connect with parents.

BENEFITS RELATED TO CURRICULAR AREAS

There is a great deal of research related to family involvement and student achievement in specific curricular areas and grade levels. In this section, we'll address this achievement in the areas of reading and math, as well as grade bands of early childhood and elementary through high school.

Reading

The following studies focus on reading benefits as a result of school efforts to involve parents.

After participating in an education program involving parent-child communication, parenting, and home learning activities, third graders in Los Angeles exhibited greater improvement in reading skills (Quigley, 2000). In addition, West (2000) reports increased reading achievement with elementary school students whose parents read to their children five minutes per night, three nights a week.

A study of parent involvement in a Title I program with second- through eighth-grade students revealed that student gender and socioeconomic status had less to do with achievement than parent education (Shaver & Walls, 1998). Children whose parents attended sessions about effective parent involvement exhibited greater achievement in both reading and mathematics skills.

Faires, Nichols, and Rickelman (2000) report a study of struggling readers in first grade. Parents in the experimental group received Reading Recovery training sessions for involvement in reading lessons with their children. Children of these parents experienced significant gains on informal assessments performed by the teacher.

Hewison (1998) also reports that children have greater gains in reading when their families use teacher-suggested reading activities to help them at home.

Mathematics

While families may not realize it, the home is saturated in mathematical learning opportunities as well. Children are exposed to the use of mathematics in stores. They see and often recognize geometric shapes in their surroundings. They readily count and sort materials in the home. Children enjoy real-life problem solving. All of these are natural and very real parts of the everyday home lives of children. As teachers, we must communicate to parents how much they have already participated in their children's mathematical knowledge merely by living life with them and serving as examples. Research, of course, also supports parent interest and involvement in children's acquisition of math concepts.

In two case studies by Galloway and Sheridan (1994) [seeking to improve students' math skills related to accuracy and task completion], students showed improvement after parents implemented information from a self-instruction manual provided by teachers.

Mathematics skills improved, as well, in a parent involvement program with families of seventh graders (Mendoza, 1996). The program involved parent education workshops to increase involvement, improve parent and student attitudes toward mathematics, and increase student math achievement. Improvement was reported in all areas by 35 to 40 percent.

Starkey and Klein (2000) report two studies of interventions with mathematics. In both studies, effective interactions between mothers and children led to student improvement in mathematical knowledge.

Early Childhood

While parent involvement has been shown to be effective at all levels of a child's school experience, many researchers suggest that the benefits are greater and farther-reaching when it begins in the early childhood years. Goldberg (1989) states that "the earlier in a child's school career his/her parents become involved, and that involvement is sustained, the bigger the payoff."

Kreider (2002) discusses the results of a study of parents from low-income, ethnically diverse backgrounds in urban and rural areas. It was found that families who were involved in their children's early education programs were more likely to read to their children, visit the school, and interact with other parents.

A study (Marcon, 1999) of 708 four-year-olds, primarily from low-income families, revealed that parent involvement led to increased development of children's communication and motor skills. These benefits were particularly noticeable in boys. The researchers suggest that it is the connection between parents and schools that led to children's greater academic success.

A **longitudinal study** of an early intervention program in Chicago (Miedel & Reynolds, 1999) also showed correlations between parent involvement and student achievement. This study revealed that parent involvement during children's preschool and kindergarten years is associated with higher levels of achievement in reading, fewer grade retentions, and fewer children placed in special education programs.

Another longitudinal study by Izzo, Weissberg, Kasprow, and Fendrich (1999) compared the relationship between parent involvement and overall school performance. The study followed more than 1,200 primary-grade students over a three-year period. Involvement with the students' parents focused on the (1) regularity and (2) quality of parent/teacher interactions, (3) parent interaction with learning activities at home, and (4) participation in activities at school. All four variables correlated to some degree with overall school achievement. The third variable, parent interaction at home, was a stronger predictor of school improvement than the others.

These studies indicate just how important it is that we, as early childhood educators, begin the process of involving parents early in the schooling years. If we sit back and wait for parents to make the first move, we are likely to be disappointed as many parents aren't sure how to get involved, must "make" the time for participation, or lack the confidence to ask. In the next section, you will see the long-term effects of family involvement and how efforts with parents of children in the early years reap long-range benefits.

Long-Term Benefits: Elementary through High School

By limiting the discussion of family involvement benefits to early childhood, we fail to see the whole picture. Children benefit when parents show interest in and value the educational process throughout their educational years, as indicated in the following studies.

Gains in homework, behavior, and overall academic achievement were reported in a study of third graders (Quigley, 2000) after a parent participation project involving parenting, communication, and at-home learning. The parents and teachers also reported greater understanding of their responsibility in student success.

West (2000) studied an elementary teacher's increased parent-teacher communication efforts. This study revealed student improvement with homework and test scores when parents worked with their children at home.

Middle school students showed improvement in science in the areas of class preparation and ability to participate in classroom activities when they participated in interactive science homework activities with their parents (Van Voorhis, 2001). This study also revealed that students had improved relationships with their parents and, in addition, parent-teacher communication improved.

The benefits of family involvement appear to lead to future student success, as well. In *Attainment in Secondary School* by Feinstein and Symons (1999), it was found that when parents spend time with their children early in the school experience by reading to them and assisting with homework, and by expressing interest in education, greater academic success is evident years later.

TEACHER AND FAMILY BENEFITS

Family involvement not only benefits children and schools, but also brings about benefits for teachers and parents. Teacher benefits include improved morale, higher parent ratings, and increased support from families. Additionally, teachers notice higher student achievement levels and teacher reputations in the informal community "grapevine" are improved (Faucette, 2000). Teachers who encourage family involvement are more likely to report that they have a greater understanding of the cultures of their students' families and recognize and value parents' interests in helping their children (Epstein, 2000). These teachers also tend to be well received by parents, requested as teachers by parents for younger children, and are often recognized for their family involvement efforts.

Parents experience personal gains from this involvement as well. Epstein (1983, 1984) reports that when teachers make the effort to increase family involvement, parents tend to help their children at home more often and have an increased understanding of what their children are learning in school. They also tend to be more positive about interacting with teachers and have greater confidence in the teaching abilities of their children's teachers. Ames (1995) also found that when teachers made efforts to improve communication with parents, the parents became more comfortable with the school and involvement with activities at school.

Parents who become involved in their children's educational experience report a personal responsibility in helping their children at home and also tend to have greater knowledge of how to assist their children in positive ways. They express a greater understanding of the school program and are more supportive of their children's schoolwork (Epstein, 1984, 1985, 2000). Additionally, involved parents exhibit higher confidence levels in parenting. They also tend to have a greater understanding of child development and of home environments that promote increased learning (Epstein,

2000). We must be sure, however, to encourage a proper balance in family involvement as these efforts should result in supporting academics rather than putting stress on children to excel beyond realistic expectations. Elkind (1990) cautions, "While the encouragement of early competence can have beneficial effects, say by enhancing self-esteem, it can have negative ones as well. The pressure for early competence is tied up with competition. And competition entails failure as well as success. Children are not always prepared to deal with the ups and downs of competition, and parents who urge their children to compete may not be sensitive to the frustrations and anxieties a child may suffer in the vagaries of competition. The demands on children for early competence thus confront them with the potential for an array of emotional problems that we in the helping professions must begin to recognize and respond to" (p. 8). This should not in any way hinder our efforts in encouraging family involvement, but rather should be a reminder that the most successful family involvement focuses on encouraging a child's academic pursuits, valuing each child's educational process, and working together to support the whole child. (See Figure 1–5.)

FIGURE 1–5 Parents who become involved in their children's educational experience report a personal responsibility in helping their children at home.

▨ CONCLUSION ───────────────────────────

With the evidence stacked in favor of family involvement, we must keep in mind that parent empowerment is key. It is our role as teachers to demonstrate for parents how much power and influence they exert in the academic success of their children. It is our responsibility as teachers to express to parents their value in the educational process. As Bronfenbrenner (1979) discusses in his Ecological Systems Theory, the family most closely impacts the child. It is imperative that the parent feels empowered—that he or she is a necessary part of the child's ongoing development and education. The teacher must create an environment that is supportive, not only of children, but of their families (Swick, 2003). It is clear from decades of research that the benefits of family involvement are far-reaching and even stronger when begun in the earliest years of a child's education. All too often, though, schools and families encounter challenges that prevent smooth transitions into what would otherwise be effective programs.

▨ SUMMARY OF IMPORTANT POINTS ─────────────

- Addressing family structure and background is important as we begin to think about how best to involve parents in their children's educational experiences.
- Each American family is unique. Teachers must think about family differences when planning for family involvement.
- Differing family situations impact decisions about forming parent/teacher partnerships.
- We must acknowledge the difference between our own backgrounds and those of our students. This acknowledgment will assist us in understanding families' differing perceptions about educational experiences.
- Failure to address family structure and background may hinder efforts at building successful partnerships.
- Vygotsky asserted that knowledge is internalized through involvement in social activities.
- The Sociocultural Theory emphasizes the interrelatedness of individual and social processes in development and learning.
- The Ecological Systems Theory focuses on the institutions that impact a child's development. These include the social, political, and economic conditions that affect the child.

- The microsystem is the layer of the Ecological Systems Theory that most closely affects the child, including family, school, teachers, and peers.

- The exosystem is the layer of the Ecological Systems Theory comprised of people, settings, and institutions that indirectly touch the child's life, including extended family, neighbors, parents' workplaces, and social services.

- The mesosystem is the layer of the Ecological Systems Theory that connects the microsystem and exosystem.

- The macrosystem is the layer of the Ecological Systems Theory that has distant impact on the child, such as the ideologies of the culture.

- The school experience is not just an interaction between the school/teacher and the child, but rather is an interrelated system involving the parent, family, and community.

- Family involvement is defined in many ways, but in a broad sense includes parent/teacher communication and collaboration, parents expressing high expectations and the value of education, parents working with children at home and at school, and schools/teachers working to support families.

- Studies of family involvement overwhelmingly suggest that student achievement increases when parents are involved in their children's educational experience.

- When parents get involved in their children's education early on, the benefits to the child are far-reaching.

- Both teachers and parents benefit from family involvement programs.

■ CHAPTER REVIEW QUESTIONS

1. In your own words, define family involvement. Write down your definition.

2. In this chapter, how is family involvement defined?

3. How does the work of Vygotsky (and the Sociocultural Theory) address the importance of social interactions in the internalization of new knowledge?

4. How do ideas of the Sociocultural Theory relate to the issue of family involvement in education?

5. How does the Ecological Systems Theory relate to the issue of family involvement in education?

6. What are general benefits to children resulting from family involvement?

7. From the research on family involvement, what common threads do you see in terms of benefits to children?

■ APPLICATION AND REFLECTION

1. Review the theories of development and education addressed in this chapter. Which ideas have caused you to rethink your perspectives on the involvement of family in the educational experiences of children? Journal your thoughts.

2. When imagining yourself as a teacher, how do you feel about working directly with parents/families? Do you have fears and uncertainties? Journal your thoughts and feelings about the idea of working with parents.

3. Interview a teacher of young children. Ask how he/she encourages parents to be involved with their children's educational experience. Does this teacher encourage parents to participate at school and/or at home?

■ FURTHER READING

Arnette, J. L., & Walseben, M. C. (1998). *Combating fear and restoring safety in schools.* Washington, DC: Office of Juvenile Justice and Delinquency Prevention, U.S. Department of Justice.

Briggs, C., & Elkind, D. (1973). Cognitive development in early readers. *Developmental Psychology, 9*(2), 279–280.

Bronfenbrenner, U. (1979). *The ecology of human development.* Cambridge, MA: Harvard University Press.

Clark, M. M. (1984). Literacy at home and at school: Insights from a study of young fluent readers. In H. Goelman, A. Oberg, & F. Smith (Eds.), *Awakening to literacy* (122–130). Portsmouth, NJ: Heinemann.

Dauber, S. L., & Epstein, J. L. (1993). Parents' attitudes and practices of involvement in inner city elementary and middle schools. In N. F. Chavkin (Ed.), *Families and schools in a pluralistic society* (53–71). Albany, NY: SUNY Press.

Durkin, D. (1966). *Children who read early*. New York: Teachers College Press.

Fuller, M. L. (1994). The monocultural graduate in a multicultural environment: A challenge to teacher education. *Journal of Teacher Education, 43*(4), 269–278.

Gambrell, L. B. (1996). Creating classroom cultures that foster reading motivation. Distinguished Educator Series. *The Reading Teacher, 50,* 14–25.

Goodman, Y. (1980). The roots of literacy. In M. Douglas (Ed.), *Claremont reading conference forty-fourth yearbook*. Claremont, CA: Claremont Reading Conference.

Guthrie, J. T. (1996). Educational contexts for engagement in literacy. *The Reading Teacher, 49*(6), 432–443.

Heath, S. B. (1980). The functions and uses of literacy. *Journal of Communication, 30,* 123–133.

Heymann, J. (2000). *The widening gap: Why America's working families are in jeopardy and what can be done about it*. New York: Basic Books.

Leichter, H. P. (1984). Families as environments for literacy. In H. Goelman, A. Oberg, & F. Smith (Eds.), *Awakening to literacy*. Portsmouth, NJ: Heinemann.

Mason, J. (1977). *Reading readiness: A definition and skills hierarchy from preschoolers' developing conceptions of print* (Technical Report 59). Urbana: University of Illinois, Center for the Study of Reading.

Moles, O.C. (1993). Collaboration between schools and disadvantaged parents: Obstacles and openings. In N. F. Chavkin (Ed.), *Families and schools in a pluralistic society* (21–49). Albany, NY: SUNY Press.

Morrow, L. (2004). *Literacy development in the early years: Helping children read and write*. Boston: Allyn and Bacon.

National PTA (2004). *National standards for parent/family involvement programs*. National Educational Service.

Smith, F. (1976). Learning to read by reading. *Language Arts, 53,* 297–299.

Teale, W. (1982). Toward a theory of how children learn to read and write naturally. *Language Arts, 59,* 555–570.

Wise, A. E., & Gollnick, D. M. (1996). America in demographic denial (National Council for Accreditation of Teacher Education). *Quality Education, 5*(2).

For additional information on research-based practice, visit our Web site at http://www.earlychilded. delmar.com.

Additional resources for this chapter can be found on the Online Companion™ to accompany this text at www.earlychilded.delmar.com. This supplemental material includes Web links, downloadable forms, and Case Studies with critical thinking applications. This content can be used as a study aid to reinforce key concepts presented in this chapter and to conduct additional research on topics of interest.

■ REFERENCES

Ames, C. (1995). *Teachers' school-to-home communications and parent involvement: The role of parent perceptions and beliefs* (Report No. 28). East Lansing, MI: Michigan State University, College of Education, Center on Families, Communities, Schools, and Children's Learning.

Bennet, T. (2001, Spring). *Reactions to visiting the infant-toddler and preschool centers in Reggio Emilia, Italy.* Early Childhood Research & Practice: An Internet Journal on the Development, Care, and Education of Young Children.

Bronfenbrenner, U. (1995). The bioecological perspective from a life course perspective: Reflections of a participant observer. In P. Moen, G. H. Edler, & K. Luscher (Eds.), *Examining lives in context* (599–618). Washington, DC: American Psychological Association.

Carter, S. (2002). *The impact of parent/family involvement on student outcomes: An annotated bibliography of research from the past decade.* Eugene, OR: Consortium for Appropriate Dispute Resolution in Special Education.

Chavkin, N. F. (Ed.). (1993). *Families and schools in a pluralistic society.* Albany, NY: SUNY Press.

Christenson, S. L. (1995). Families and schools: What is the role of the school psychologist? *School Psychology Quarterly, 10*(2), 118–132.

Christenson, S. L., & Conoley, J. C. (Eds.). (1992). *Home-school collaboration: Enhancing children's academic and social competence.* Silver Spring, MD: National Association of School Psychologists.

Clark, R. M. (1983). *Family life and school achievement: Why poor black children succeed or fail.* Chicago: University of Chicago Press.

Dewey, J. (1966). *Democracy and education*. New York: Free Press (original work published 1916).

Duveen, G. (1998). Psychological development as social process. In L. Smith, J. Dockrell, & P. Thomlinson (Eds.), *Piaget, Vygotsky, and Beyond: Future issues for developmental psychology and education* (67–90). New York: Routledge.

Easton, F. (1997). Educating the whole child, "head, heart, and hands": Learning from the Waldorf experience. *Theory Into Practice, 36*(2), 87–94.

Elkind, D. (1990). The child and society: Essays in applied child development. New York: Oxford University Press.

Epstein, J. (1983). *Effects on parents of teacher practices in parent involvement*. Baltimore, MD: Center on Families, Communities, Schools and Children's Learning, Johns Hopkins University.

Epstein, J. L. (1984). School policy and parent involvement: Research results. *Educational Horizons, 62*(2), 70–72.

Epstein, J. L. (1985). Home-school connections in schools of the future: Implications of research on parent involvement. *Peabody Journal of Education, 62*(2), 58–59.

Epstein, J. L. (1995, May). School/family/community partnerships: Caring for the children we share. *Phi Delta Kappan, 76,* 701–712.

Epstein, J. L. (2000). *School and family partnerships: Preparing educators and improving schools*. Boulder, CO: Westview.

Epstein, J. L. Coates, L., Salinas, K. C., Sanders, M. G., & Simmon, B. S. (1997). *School, family, and community partnerships: Your handbook for action*. Thousand Oaks, CA: Corwin.

Faires, J., Nichols, W. D., & Rickelman, R. J. (2000). Effects of parent involvement in developing competent readers in first grade. *Reading Psychology, 21,* 195–215.

Fan, X., & Chen, M. (2001). Parental involvement and students' academic achievement: A meta-analysis. *Educational Psychology Review, 13*(1), 1–22.

Faucette, E. (2000, November/December). Are you missing the most important ingredient? A recipe for increasing achievement. *Multimedia Schools, 7*(6), 56–61.

Feinstein, L., & Symons, J. (1999). Attainment in secondary school. *Oxford Economic Papers, 51,* 300–321.

Galloway, J., & Sheridan, S. M. (1994). Implementing scientific practices through case studies: Examples using home-school interventions and consultation. Journal of School Psychology, 32(4), 385–413.

Gandini, L. (1997). Foundations of the Reggio Emilia Approach. In J. Hendrick (Ed.), *First steps toward teaching the Reggio way* (14–25). Upper Saddle River, NJ: Merril/Prentice Hall.

Goldenberg, C. N. (1989). Making success a more common occurrence for children at risk for failure: Lessons from Hispanic first-graders learning to read. In J. F. Allen & J. M. Mason (Eds.), *Risk makers, risk takers, risk breakers: Reducing the risks for young literacy learners* (48–79). Portsmouth, NH: Heinemann.

Goodman, K. S., & Goodman, Y. M. (1979). Learning to read is natural. In L. B. Resnick & P. A. Weaver (Eds.), *Theory and practice of early reading* (Vol. 1). Hillsdale, NJ: Lawrence Erlbaum Associates.

Goodman, Y. (1984). The development of initial literacy. In H. Goelman, A. Oberg, & F. Smith (Eds.), *Awakening to literacy* (102–109). Portsmouth, NJ: Heinemann.

Henderson, A. T., & Berla, N. (1994). *A new generation of evidence: The family is critical to student achievement.* St. Louis, MO: Danforth Foundation; Flint, MI: Mott (C. S.) Foundation.

Hewison, J. (1998). The long-term effectiveness of parental involvement in reading: A follow-up to the Haringey reading project. *British Journal of Educational Psychology, 58,* 184–190.

Howell, G., & Stenberg, N. (2002). Dobie's blueprint for success for pre-K, K, and 1st grade students. *Education, 122*(4), 715–720.

Izzo, C. V., Weissberg, R. P., Kasprow, W. J., & Fendrich, M. (1999). A longitudinal assessment of teacher perceptions of parent involvement in children's education and school performance. *American Journal of Community Psychology, 27,* 817–839.

Jones, R. (Nov. 2001). Involving parents is a whole new game: Be sure you win! *The Education Digest,* 67(3), 36–43.

Kreider, H. (2002). *Getting parents "ready" for kindergarten: The role of early childhood education.* Amherst, MA: Harvard Family Research Project. Retrieved January 23, 2005, from http://www.gse. Harvard. edu/hfrp/projects/fine/resources/research/kreider.html.

Mahn, H. (1999). Vygotsky's methodological contribution to sociocultural theory. *Remedial and Special Education, 20*(6), 341–350.

Marcon, R. A. (1999). Positive relationships between parent school involvement and public school inner-city preschoolers' development and academic performance. *School Psychology Review, 28,* 395–412.

Mendoza, Y. (1996). *Developing and implementing a parental awareness program to increase parental involvement and enhance mathematics performance and attitude of at-risk seventh grade students*. Maters Final Report. Ft. Lauderdale, FL: Nova Southeastern University (ERIC Document Reproduction Service No. ED 400971).

Miedel, W. T., & Reynolds, A. J. (1999). Parent involvement in early intervention for disadvantaged children: Does it matter? *Journal of School Psychology, 37*(4), 379–399.

National Association for the Education of Young Children (2004). *Program standard 7—Families: Final draft accreditation performance criteria.* Retrieved January 28, 2005, from http://www.naeyc.org/accreditation/naeyc_accred/draft_standards/fam.html.

Piaget, J., & Inhelder, B. (1969). *The psychology of the child.* New York: Basic Books.

Pipher, M. (1996). *The shelter of each other: Rebuilding our families.* New York: Ballantine.

Quigley, D. D. (2000, April). *Parents and teachers working together to support third grade achievement: Parents as learning partners.* Paper presented at the annual meeting of the American Educational Research Association, New Orleans, LA.

Raffaele, L. M. K. (1999, March 28). Improving home-school collaboration with disadvantaged families: Organizational principles. *School and Psychology Review,* 448+.

Shaver, A. V., & Walls, R. T. (1998). Effect of Title I parent involvement on student reading and mathematics achievement. *Journal of Research & Development in Education, 31*(2), 90–97.

Starkey, P., & Klein, A. (2000). Fostering parental support for children's mathematical development: An intervention with Head Start families. *Early Education and Development, 11,* 659–81.

Swick, K. J. (2003). Working with families of young children. In J. P. Isenberg and M. R. Jalongo (Eds.), *Major trends and issues in early childhood education: Challenges, controversies, and insights* (69–79). New York: Teachers College Press.

Van Voorhis, F. L. (2001). Interactive science homework: An experiment in home and school connections. *NASSP Bulletin, 85*(627), 20–32.

Vygotsky, L. (1978). *The mind in society: The development of higher psychological processes.* Cambridge, MA: Harvard University Press.

Vygotsky, L. (1981). The genesis of higher mental functions. In J. J. Wertsch (Ed.), *The concept of activity.* White Plains, NY: M. E. Sharpe.

West, J. M. (2000). *Increasing parent involvement for student motivation*. Armidale, New South Wales, Australia: University of New England (ERIC Document Reproduction Service No. ED 448411).

Yaden, D. B., Rowe, D. W., & MacGillivray, L. (2000). Emergent literacy: A matter (polyphony) of perspectives. In M. L. Kamil, P. B. Mosental, P. D. Pearson, & R. Barr (Eds.), *Handbook of reading research* (425–454). Mahwah, NJ: Lawrence Erlbaum Associates.

2

Diverse Families: Then, Now, Tomorrow

■ CHAPTER OBJECTIVES

After reading and reflecting on this chapter, you should be able to:

- Understand the changing historical perspective on childhood and family involvement in education.
- Review key programs and policies that have mandated family involvement in schools.
- Consider the factors that affect family involvement in early childhood education.
- Assess personal attitudes and beliefs about diverse family structures and family needs.
- Understand the impact of language and culture on families' involvement in their children's education.

■ KEY TERMS

chattel   extended family

Enlightenment   family structures

federal poverty level   John Locke

Industrial Revolution   nuclear family

Jean-Jacques Rousseau   tabula rasa

HISTORICAL VIEWS OF FAMILY INVOLVEMENT

Historically, little emphasis has been placed on children or family involvement with children since no real distinction existed between home, education, and work life. Children and their education merged seamlessly into the fabric of the family. Working to survive, raising children, and daily living tasks blended together in day-to-day existence. Children worked along with other family members to care for crops, tend to animals, and to complete the tasks of daily life. Many children apprenticed in trades by working closely with a parent, family member, or master craftsman through their adolescent years. Then, considered to be adults, they began having children of their own.

Children were considered "infants" until weaned at approximately ages four to six. As infants, children were nonpersons, receiving no special consideration or protection. Infants and young children were regarded as **chattel** or the property of the parents. As nonpersons, children were bought and sold, traded, or disposed of at the will of the family. Infanticide was a common practice throughout the world, and in Europe and Western society well into the seventeenth century. Infants were frequently drowned or abandoned whether boy or girl, healthy or unhealthy. Once weaned from their mothers, children were treated as if they were miniature adults. Their roles, functions, and responsibilities in the ancient social order were the same as adults; children went directly from infancy to adulthood without a childhood.

Once the power of the Roman Catholic Church was firmly entrenched, the view of children in Western cultures evolved along with church teachings. Children came to be thought of as unique human beings tainted by original sin from birth and, therefore, inherently evil. Childhood became a unique period of life. Unique demands were placed on parents and the family. From this perspective on childhood, children were believed to enter the world corrupt, so adults were responsible for training them in the ideology of the church to drive the "devil" out. This view of the child emerged in early Protestant teachings about children as well and can be found in other fundamentalist religions throughout the world. This training into goodness and piety could be harsh, abusive, and even deadly.

The writings of **John Locke** and **Jean-Jacques Rousseau** ushered in a period of enlightenment in the affairs of government and in the social perspectives on children. These and other contemporary social philosophers

FIGURE 2–1   According to Rousseau, a responsive, nurturing upbringing allowed a child's natural desire to learn to unfold.

made important assertions about young children that influenced Western thought. John Locke's contributions to views of the child were centered in the notion of the **tabula rasa;** children are blank slates at birth. Environment and experiences "write upon" the slate of the child. Authoring *Émile* in 1762, Jean-Jacques Rousseau first proposed the notion that children are naturally good and that the purpose of education is to provide for the natural unfolding development of the child. (See Figure 2–1.) For Rousseau, "goodness" or "badness" necessarily resulted from the upbringing and guidance a child received. A responsive, nurturing upbringing allowed a child's natural tendencies to unfold. Approaches that viewed children as "down-sized" adults could not allow children to blossom in their own unique way. Thus, a new, unusual emphasis on proper socialization and education of children emerged from the philosophical positions of **Enlightenment** thinkers.

With the **Industrial Revolution** and its enormous demand for human labor, huge stresses ripped the social fabric of the Western world. Working-class children were left unattended while their parents labored long hours; or worse, children themselves were pressed into laboring 12 to 14 hours a day. Poverty, poor nutrition, epidemic illness, and illiteracy resulted in high rates of childhood mortality. Health, education, and basic care concerns led to reforms at the end of the late nineteenth century that drastically reduced childhood mortality and changed the public view of children. Some of these reforms have included universal public schooling, child care programs, and specialized health care for children. Care and concern for the welfare of all young children has emerged in the past century of Western history as a societal and cultural expectation. Only in the very recent past has society come to view children as unique human beings with unique needs, deserving the respect and consideration due to all human beings (deMause, 1974).

What has been the perspective on childhood in non-Western, non-European cultures? Strong tribal traditions and family bonds in African cultures indicate the continuing involvement of extended families in the lives of children. The same can be said of Asian and Native American cultures. A strong tradition of family and clan weaves through the histories of many cultures and societies. Strict norms for the collective "good" exist, and socialization begins at the moment of birth. **Extended family** units— elders, siblings, aunts, and uncles—carry the responsibility of rearing children, socializing the young, and transitioning children into adulthood. Within these traditions, mothers, grandmothers, nannies, maids, or wet nurses serve as the nurturer and caregiver. Education and the transmission of culture to the young has traditionally rested with women.

FAMILIES TODAY

These perspectives on children, however strange they may seem to us today, persist in some form throughout the modern world. There remain all too frequent occasions where children are treated as if they were expendable nonpersons. In some societies today, infanticide is still used to resolve issues surrounding family size, gender, and resources. Opponents of abortion contend that the *Roe* v. *Wade* decision has objectified millions of unborn children and begun the practice of infanticide in utero. Trafficking in young children in the sex trade is an international concern that ripples across many nations.

Children continue to be regarded as miniature adults in more than a few modern societies. David Elkind (1981) began sounding the alarm about the stresses and pressures placed on children growing up in today's world in *The Hurried Child*. These unrealistic expectations have children assuming adult-like responsibilities, behaviors, and values long before they are socially, cognitively, or emotionally developed. Children continue to be economically exploited and are forced to work under debilitating circumstances. Child labor is forced by parents and employers in many parts of the world and may be the slim thread of survival for poverty-stricken families in the Third World. According to the Children's Defense Fund (2006), children disproportionately make up the numbers living in poverty. Divorce, substance abuse, domestic violence, and parental unemployment/underemployment have created unprecedented numbers of children living in poverty, living without proper care and nutrition, and experiencing stunted development.

There exist as many forms of family today as there are individuals making up those families. The social, economic, and political context of our world influences family structure just as families influence our social, economic, and political orders (Bronfenbrenner & Morris, 1998). "Research using a range of data sets and analytic approaches consistently shows that children's well-being is associated with family structure, usually defined as the number, type, and marital status of parents or guardians" (Childstats.gov, 2005). More children than ever before are raised in family structures other than the nuclear family, with 32 percent of children living in nonnuclear families (Childstats.gov, 2005). The most common nonnuclear family structure in the United States today is the one-parent family. More children are of other than white Eurasian descent, with more than 40 percent of children in the United States coming from racially and ethnically diverse heritages. (See Figure 2–2.)

As the landscape of the American family changes, the numbers of governmental, nonprofit, and for-profit agencies to support and work with the modern family are proliferating at an incredible rate. Local, state, and federal initiatives direct more resources toward addressing the problems faced by today's families. The role of the federal government in families and in education has also grown dramatically in the past century as well.

FIGURE 2–2   More children than ever before are raised in family structures other than the nuclear family.

The Lanham Act of 1941 provided federal funds to communities in order to build and operate child care centers during World War II. Two thousand centers operated in forty-one states (Hurwitz, 1998).

Brown v. Board of Education of Topeka, 1954, establishes the equality of all students in public schools. Early childhood education is included in this Supreme Court decision.

Project Head Start began as a key component of Lyndon Johnson's War on Poverty in 1965. Great Society programs for young children were designed to provide high-quality, comprehensive early education to low-income children. The heart of the local Head Start program is the parent policy council. Made up of parent volunteers, the council chooses educational curricula and directs the local program. Parents are trained and employed by the local program as well. The goals for parent involvement in Head Start programs are:

1. Parental involvement in decision making as well as operation of the program
2. Parental participation in the classroom as volunteers while becoming paid employees of Head Start

FIGURE 2–3   IDEA impacts the rights of parents of children with disabilities in relation to the school.

3. Encouragement of parents to plan support and education activities of their own
4. Parents will work with their own children with the coaching and encouragement of the Head Start staff (Gestwicki, 2000)

Public Law 94-142, signed into law in 1975, provided for a free education for all children regardless of their disability from birth to age 21. The entire process of serving children with special needs from diagnosis to litigation if needed is controlled by the child's parent or guardian. Parents of the child must approve and sign off on every step of the process.

The Individuals with Disabilities Education Act (IDEA, 1991) defines major parental rights. (See Figure 2–3.) IDEA impacts the rights of parents of children with disabilities in relation to the school in specific ways:

1. The right to be informed of their parental rights
2. The right to be informed of their parental rights in their native language

3. The right to be informed prior to any assessment being conducted if placement in special education may be the outcome of the assessment
4. The right to be referred to outside evaluators and to no- or low-cost legal services
5. The right to be involved in determining educational goals, services, and placement through membership on an interdisciplinary Individualized Education Plan (IEP) team
6. The right to be informed prior to any change in placement, educational goals, or services provided to the child
7. The right to review the child's school records
8. The right to initiate a due process hearing
9. The right to receive a transcript of the hearing and the decision
10. The right to appeal through the court system

Family literacy programs have evolved in the past several decades based on the belief that parent learning and literacy levels are key to the child's academic success. It is assumed that in order to break the cycle of poverty and illiteracy, an education program is necessary. Interactions between the parent and child are an essential strategy for parenting-skills instruction while addressing the needs of the whole family system. A wide range of initiatives and funded programs in the field of family literacy fall into two distinct categories: (1) home-school partnerships designed to involve parents in literacy activities and events that support the school and its goals, (2) intergenerational literacy programs designed to improve the literacy development of adults and children involved as co-learners of basic skills.

No Child Left Behind legislation of 2001 was passed by Congress to "ensure that all children have a fair, equal, and significant opportunity to obtain a high-quality education" (U.S., 2002).

No Child Left Behind guidelines provide for parental involvement in the following ways:

1. Itemized score analyses to be produced and reported by schools . . . so that parents . . . can interpret and address the specific academic needs of students as indicated by the students' achievement on assessments.
2. Each state plan must include an assurance that agencies will coordinate and collaborate . . . with agencies providing services to children, youth, and families.
3. The state will encourage local educational agencies and individual schools participating in a program assisted to offer family literacy services.

4. The state will encourage effective parental involvement that fosters achievement to high standards for all children; and be geared toward lowering barriers to greater participation by parents in school planning, review, and improvement experienced.

Federal legislation in education continues to encourage the involvement of families in the education of their children. Parents' and family involvement helps to foster academic achievement. Barriers at the school level in policy and programming must be addressed and improved.

Family Structures in a Changing Society

Our rapidly changing society has brought about a change in **family structures,** family organization patterns, functions, and interrelatedness due to social and economic expectations (Swick, 2003), which result in challenges for teachers and schools in terms of involving parents in their children's education.

Addressing family structure and background is important as we begin to think about how best to involve parents in their children's educational experiences, as these family structures and backgrounds often dictate the efforts and concessions we must make in reaching them and developing partnerships. In this ever-changing world, we find an ever-changing family structure. From a traditional standpoint, we often view the **nuclear family** as mother, father, and a few children living under the same roof. The father typically works outside the home, while the mother may or may not work outside the home, but either way, tends to the children. In reality, the typical American family is quite different from this traditional image.

American families today are unique and very different from one another. It is essential that, as teachers, we think about the range of family differences when planning family involvement that is realistic and workable for all. (See Figure 2–4.) While some children come from traditional homes with a working father and a stay-at-home mother, most children have different family structures. Many children come from families with two working parents or from single-parent families where the parent works outside the home. We find more and more children from blended families, that is, families who have experienced divorce and remarriage. Some children have an absent parent or divorced parents who may or may not have amiable working relationships in raising their children. With so many different kinds of families, we must take the time to address these differences. These varying situations inevitably impact our decisions about forming parent-teacher

FIGURE 2–4 It is essential that teachers think about the range of family differences when planning for family involvement.

partnerships. A one-plan-fits-all attitude concerning family involvement will most likely foster an exclusionary approach that leads to frustration rather than success.

Socioeconomic Status

More than 13 million children live in poverty in the United States today (Childstats.gov, 2005). The **federal poverty level** is $19,350 for a family of four (Federal Register, 2006). Families living in poverty lack the where-withal to provide food, shelter, clothing, medical care, child care, and time to the children in those families. Children of poverty lack the most basic survival needs. This reality holds sobering consequences for schooling in America. Upon entering school, children of poverty start "behind" in the readiness skills, social skills, and physical development necessary for academic achievement as defined by middle-class norms and expectations. The lives of these children are frequently marked by crime and unrest. They will grow up in deteriorating neighborhoods marred by violence. Resolving disputes aggressively through physical force will be the pattern they observe and learn.

Poverty and its associated conditions are the most common environmental risk factors for childhood abuse and neglect. Lack of income contributes in direct and indirect ways to the risk of neglecting education as well. If a parent is socially isolated while living in poverty, alternatives for school involvement are minimal. Schools can offer hope and strengthen learning outcomes of children whose parents are struggling with economic conditions. First, a safe haven for the child of poverty with before- and after-school care is essential to mitigate the risk of childhood violence. Supervision and assistance with learning in this setting also helps the child to achieve. Social skills and positive peer relationships can be encouraged by the school personnel. In addition, nutritional demands, another risk factor for children of poverty, can also be addressed by the school. Again, the school can help struggling families by providing at least two nutritionally balanced, subsidized meals for the child away from home. Teachers cannot expect good learning and attention from a poorly fed or malnourished child. Finally, family-based services and health care can also be offered through the school. It is important for you as a teacher to be aware and informed of the various programs and agencies in your community that offer services to children and families.

It is equally as important that you consider what you have believed about families in poverty. Stereotypes concerning the poor persist in our society. Poor people are not all people of color who are lazy and shiftless. In fact, the percentages of white working poor are as high as those of color. Not all the poor live in the inner city; many poor children are living in rural settings. Families in poverty are not all living on welfare or too lazy to work. According to the Children's Defense Fund (retrieved 2006), more than 7 out of 10 poor children live in a family where someone worked for at least part of the year. More than 1 in 3 poor children lived in families with full-time year-round workers.

Lack of resources does not mean lack of care or commitment. Teachers who do not blame the families living in poverty for their dire circumstances will be better able to communicate with and support them. You must gather basic information about the family to forge a bond for working together. Communicate with low-income families enthusiastically and positively, even if the communication is persistently one-way. Show respect for the low-income family just as you would a middle-income family or a colleague on your campus. Be involved in the community surrounding your school so that any perceived threat from you or the school environment is reduced. Be sensitive to the extreme limitations of families living in poverty. School just cannot be "done" the same way when parents have no money or time for field trips, class parties, special materials, or registration fees.

FAMILIES IN FOCUS

She could be the teacher across the hall from you. She could be your neighbor or someone you see regularly at the grocery store. Her story is not uncommon. Ellen was a typical wife and mother in a typical middle-class neighborhood in a typical suburban area. One day her world came apart at the seams when her husband arrived home from work early, began packing up his belongings, and asked her for a divorce. The story he offered was ridiculously trite. He had met someone at the office. She was younger, fun to be around, bright and full of energy . . . and so on and so on.

Ellen received the house and child support in the divorce settlement. She was given full custody of the children and all the bills and all the heartaches, too. She was thankful to have the house; she could never afford rent payments on the meager salary she earned at her re-entry job. However, the house was starting to need some costly repairs; the washing machine was on its last leg; and the child support payments didn't adequately cover the costs of raising three school-age children who needed clothes, lunch money, and orthodontia. Ellen constantly struggled with teetering at the brink of financial ruin. She didn't qualify for assistance from the state, but she sure needed some help. Health insurance premiums took a huge part of her monthly paycheck, but she couldn't possibly afford to be without the health insurance. Ellen needed someone in her community to assist her in finding some resources to help keep her kids healthy, clothed, and in school.

School involvement!! Ellen couldn't possibly get away from her job to make it to parent-teacher conferences. It wasn't that she didn't care about how the children were doing in school, but there wasn't any hope that her employer would give her the time for three conferences in one week. Early morning conferences were out of the question. It was hard enough for her to get the kids out the door in the morning and herself off to work without complicating the morning chaos with parent-teacher conferences. She needed some creative approaches to conferences that would work with her life. She wanted to stay as involved with her children's schooling as she had been in years past, but she needed some creative ways to be involved now.

Working with the kids on homework could sometimes be a nightmare. She barely had the energy after her commute home in the evenings to feed everyone and get them off to bed without spending hours on homework. She had already been through school and didn't want to feel like she was relearning math, science, or U.S. history. Ellen liked the assignments that forced her and the kids to spend time together playing games and activities meant for the whole family. She liked the assignments that forced her to stop and really talk with her children or brought them to the kitchen table when she was making dinner. She needed the children's teacher to assign homework creatively so that the family was strengthened, not strained to its limit.

Language and Culture

To most teachers, it is no surprise that we live in a society of growing diversity. In their book, *Multicultural Education in a Pluralistic Society* (1998), Gollnick and Chinn project that, by the year 2010, 40 percent of America's schoolchildren will come from diverse racial backgrounds. They estimate that underrepresented groups will exceed the white population by the year 2020. This issue becomes increasingly pressing to address in light of the fact that the majority of teachers today are from white, middle-class backgrounds (Fuller, 1994). Regardless of our own race, culture, and ethnicity, we must acknowledge and affirm that our students' backgrounds are likely to be very different from our own, which means that our students' families are also likely to have very different perceptions about the educational experience. They are also likely to have very different expectations of teachers and schools. Failure to address family structure and background may very well hinder our efforts at building successful partnerships and, ultimately, hinder the academic success of our children and our students.

> Enough research has been done on cultural differences in home socialization practices with regard to school learning that we know these differences exist. We have, however, almost no information about these issues for many of the ethnic groups that are now well represented among America's language-minority children. (August & Hakuta, 1997, p. 103)

In order to better serve diverse families, education professionals must address the barriers that exist and provide support. (See Figure 2–5.) Because all families differ from one another, it is the teacher's responsibility to take the time to understand the background, expectations, and needs of each family in order to best offer support. Zhang and Bennet (2003) cite factors that impact the parent-teacher relationship, such as cultural background, cultural sensitivity, aligned expectations, language, and cultural identities. Having an understanding of these factors assists educators in developing partnerships with diverse families.

Communication is the key to positive interactions. Educators have much to consider when communicating with families from diverse backgrounds, including tone of voice, body language, and use of educational jargon (Zhang & Bennet, 2003). Misunderstandings can, in fact, hinder parent-teacher partnerships if we do not recognize cultural differences. In some cultures, for example, it is considered rude to ask clarifying questions

FIGURE 2–5   In order to better serve diverse families, education professionals must address the barriers that exist and provide support.

or express opinions. A teacher might interpret this as a lack of interest rather than an expression of respect.

It is important for teachers to understand that culture impacts the structure of families. Extended family members, for example, may be the primary caregivers and may need to be included in the educational decision-making process (Shu-Minutoli, 1995).

In the United States, we are bound by time, and completing tasks in a timely manner is valued. This orientation can contribute to cultural misunderstandings with diverse families. Many cultures value personal interaction and are not bound to Western time constraints. For this reason, it may be necessary to interact on a more personal level with families and allow adequate time for parents to consult extended family members when making decisions about their children's academics.

From a study in a Southeast Asian community in New England (Collignon, Men, & Tan, 2001), three themes emerged from school discussions with community focus groups. Community members did not have a clear understanding of the U.S. educational system. They felt the need to know the district administrators and how they were appointed to their positions and wanted to know their responsibilities. They felt that not enough attention was placed on language differences. The people in the community wanted interpreters and materials translated into their languages. They felt this was important in order for them to provide input on children's educational experiences. They felt that the school had low expectations of them and expressed concern that the school felt they were not interested in their children's education. They also wanted to understand the definition of parent involvement and what was expected of them. The outcome of these discussions reflects the need to make special efforts to address the concerns of diverse families and communities. It is important to note that similar concerns were expressed by families in other immigrant communities, as reported by Al-Hassan and Gardner (2002).

Greene and Nefsky (1999) promote a family-centered approach where educators recognize and appreciate the uniqueness of individual families and assist them in receiving the necessary resources in order to provide children and families with the best possible experiences. They also emphasize the importance of encouraging active participation, participation in parent support groups, and development of teacher-family collaboration.

Because such a wide variety of cultures are represented in our school systems, teachers need to learn to understand the cultures of their students, which affect families' understanding of the educational system. For example, Hispanic culture typically holds the belief that schools and teachers hold positions of authority. Parents from these countries would feel uncomfortable entering into the culture of the school as this would be considered an invasion of the educational community (Espinosa, 1995). It is the belief of many parents that their job is to nurture their children while academics are the responsibility of the school.

In working with any family, but with those from diverse cultures in particular, the following suggestions (Espinosa, 1995) should be considered:

- Whenever possible, communicate in person.
- Show respect and withhold judgment.
- Utilize translators and translated materials whenever possible.
- Create a friendly, welcoming atmosphere.

FIGURE 2-6   A community liaison can help to bridge the gap between families and schools.

Srebalus and Brown (2001) point out that Native American family members may be reluctant to express personal information. They typically avoid direct eye contact and attempt to avoid public shows of emotion.

In addition, Martinez and Velazquez (2000) suggest the following for working with migrant families:

- Understand families' perceptions of the purpose of education. (Many migrant families place more importance on morals, respect, responsibility, and manners than on academics.)
- Be sensitive to the family lifestyle.
- Provide community liaisons. (See Figure 2–6.)
- Provide child care, food, and transportation.
- Create curricular activities that reflect the culture of the community in order to help parents relate to children's work at school.
- Be open to collaborating with parents about their contributions to their children's academic experiences.
- Provide Spanish-language books for reading at home.
- Provide parent workshops and allow parents to teach others special skills they have.

FAMILIES IN FOCUS

Danny Fuentez beat the odds. His family immigrated from Mexico. He learned English as his second language. His father provided for the family as an occasional day laborer. Eventually, his mother deserted the struggling family and returned to Mexico. Danny's father tried to keep the family together in a ramshackled trailer home in a weed-infested park several blocks from the school. Danny worked hard. He rarely seemed able to succeed at learning. Danny beat the odds because of Mr. Pace.

Mr. Pace was one of the rare male faculty members at Danny's elementary school. He taught sixth grade. Other than the P.E. teacher and the custodians, there were few male role models on the campus. Like many elementary schools, the principal was female, virtually all of the teachers were female, and the support staff were female. A school-wide student mentoring program had been put into place by the time Danny arrived in first grade. A wide range of interventions and services were marshaled to support Danny as he struggled with language adjustments, emotional needs, and some basic survival needs, and Mr. Pace was assigned to be Danny's mentor. Mr. Pace went beyond the surface ways of mentoring, though he did those things, too. Danny received treats, encouraging notes, and visits from Mr. Pace. But more than that, he received Mr. Pace's time and his heart. Mr. Pace often made home visits to Danny and his father. He would shoo away all of his sixth-grade students to tutor Danny after school. He would regularly appear at the classroom door with a McDonald's bag and ask if Danny could get away for lunch. The two of them could be spotted at a picnic table, reading through Danny's primer book together or working on multiplication flashcards or practicing the states and capitals. For four years, Mr. Pace mentored Danny through elementary school. In his middle-school years, Mr. Pace kept up the connection with Danny; he went to all of his wrestling matches, and continued to send him notes and treats. Danny struggled with learning in middle school and even through high school, but he was an incredible wrestler. He was a strong team member and his team took the state championships during his senior year of high school. The flow of Danny's life was forever changed because one man made the effort to be involved with him as a strong role model. Thank you, Mr. Pace.

- Think about "family" involvement, rather than merely "parent" involvement.

There are a vast number of cultures represented in the United States and families within each culture are, in themselves, unique. Given this fact, it becomes increasingly important for teachers not to rely on generalizations about cultural differences, but rather to expend the effort and take the time to get to know each individual family.

CONCLUSION

If current demographic trends continue, we can only expect greater diversity in family structures, language, and cultural backgrounds in the future. Likewise, if current policy trends continue, mandates will make it necessary for teachers and schools to have improvement programs in place that emphasize family involvement. It is more important now than ever before that teachers and schools establish the practices and hone the skills necessary to partner with all families.

SUMMARY OF IMPORTANT POINTS

- In the past, little emphasis was placed on family involvement.
- Children were viewed as "nonpersons," and received no protection or special consideration.
- With the evolution of church teaching came a new view that children were unique human beings tainted by original sin.
- John Locke's contributions to views of the child were centered in the notion of tabula rasa: children are blank slates at birth.
- Jean-Jacques Rousseau first proposed the notion that children are naturally good and that the purpose of education is to provide for the natural unfolding development of the child.
- There exist as many forms of family today as there are individuals making up those families. More children than ever before are raised in family structures other than the nuclear family.
- As the landscape of the American family changes, the numbers of governmental, nonprofit, and for-profit agencies to support and work with the modern family are proliferating at an incredible rate.
- Family literacy programs have evolved in the past several decades based on the belief that parent learning and literacy levels are key to the child's academic success.
- More than 13 million children live in poverty in the United States today.

- Regardless of our own race, culture, and ethnicity, we must acknowledge and affirm that our students' backgrounds are likely to be very different, which means that our students' families are also likely to have very different perceptions about the educational experience.

- Communication is the key to positive interactions.

▪ CHAPTER REVIEW QUESTIONS

1. What are the perspectives that have historically been held regarding family involvement?

2. What are the ways that a teacher can address poverty and the effect it has on education?

3. Why is it important to address family structure and background when considering programs for family involvement?

4. What are the possible drawbacks of not acknowledging your own family background when considering family involvement programs for your students?

▪ APPLICATION AND REFLECTION

1. Reflect on your personal family structure and background. Keep a journal about the details of your culture, ethnicity, and upbringing. How do your experiences impact your perspectives and expectations about the school experience? How do you think your background impacts your thoughts on family involvement in your classroom?

2. In a small group, brainstorm a list of some of the ways the historical views of the child and childhood—child as nonperson, child as chattel, child as miniature adult, child as born evil, child as a unique human—are evidenced in modern culture.

3. Reread Ellen's story carefully. Think of some creative options for Ellen that might keep her involved with her children and their school.

▪ FURTHER READING

Dickenson, G. E., & Lenning, M. R. (1990). *Understanding families: Diversity, continuity, and change.* Boston: Allyn & Bacon.

Kendall, F. E. (1996). *Diversity in the classroom: New approaches to the education of young children* (2nd ed.). Williston, VT: Teachers College Press.

Hanson, M. J. (1998). Ethnic, cultural, and language diversity in intervention settings. In E. W. Lynch & M. J. Hanson (Eds.), *Developing cross-cultural competence: A guide for working with young children and their families* (3–22). Baltimore, MD: Brookes.

For additional information on research-based practice, visit our Web site at http://www.earlychilded. delmar.com.

Additional resources for this chapter can be found on the Online Companion™ to accompany this text at www.earlychilded.delmar.com. This supplemental material includes Web links, downloadable forms, and Case Studies with critical thinking applications. This content can be used as a study aid to reinforce key concepts presented in this chapter and to conduct additional research on topics of interest.

■ REFERENCES

Al-Hassan, S., & Gardner III, R. (May/June, 2002). Involving immigrant parents of students with disabilities in the educational process. *Teaching Exceptional Children.*

America's children in brief: Key national indicators of well-being, 2005. Retrieved July 28, 2005. http://www.childstats.gov/

August, D., & Hakuta, K. (Eds.). (1997). *Improving schooling for language minority children: A research agenda.* Washington, DC: National Academy Press.

Bronfenbrenner, U. & Morris, P. (1998). The ecology of developmental processes. In Damon (Ed.) Handbook of child psychology (pp. 993–1028). John Wiley & Sons. Inc.

Collignon, F. F., Men, M., & Tan, S. (2001). Finding ways in: Community-based perspectives on Southeast Asian family involvement with schools in a New England state. *Journal of Education for Students Placed at Risk,* 6(1&2), 27–44.

deMause, L. (1974). The evolution of children. In deMause (Ed.) The history of childhood. New York, NY: Pyschohistory Press.

Elkind, David. (1981). The Hurried Child. Reading, MA: Addison-Wesley.

Espinosa, L. M. (1995). Hispanic parent involvement in early childhood programs. *ERIC Digest.*

Federal Register (January 24, 2006). Vol. 71, No. 15. pp. 3848–3849. Retrieved March 20, 2006, http://aspe.hhs.gov/poverty/06fedreg.htm.

Fuller, M. L. (1994). The monocultural graduate in a multicultural environment: A challenge to teacher education. Journal of Teacher Education, *43*(4), 269–278.

Gestwicki, Carol (2000). Home, School, and Community Relations: A Guide to Working With Families. 4th edition. New York. Delmar Thomas Learning.

Gollnick, D., & Chinn, P. (1998). *Multicultural Education in a Pluralistic Society*. Upper Saddle River, NJ: Prentice-Hall.

Greene, G., & Nefsky, P. (1999). Transition for culturally and linguistically diverse youth with disabilities: Closing the gaps. *Mutiple Voices for Ethnically Diverse Exceptional Learners, 3*(1), 15–24.

Hurwitz, S. (1998). War nurseries: Lessons in quality. Young Children. v3 n5, p 37–39.

Individual with disabilities act (1990) Pub. L. No. 105-17, 20 U.S.C. 1400.

Martinez, Y. G., & Velazquez, J. A. (2000). Involving migrant families in education (ERIC Document Reproduction Service N. ED 448010).

No Child Left Behind (2002). U.S. Department of Education Retrieved January 16, 2006. http://www.ed.gov/nclb/

Shu-Minutoli, K. (1995). Family support: Diversity, disability, and delivery. *Yearbook in Early Childhood Education, 6,* 125–140.

Srebalus, D. J., & Brown, D. (2001). *A guide to the helping professions*. Boston: Allyn & Bacon.

Swick, K. (Summer, 2003). Communication concepts for strengthening family school-community partnerships. Early Childhood Education Journal, *30*(4), 275–280.

The state of America's children (2005). Children's Defense Fund. Retrieved January 16, 2006, http://www.childrensdefense.org.

Zhang, C., & Bennett, T. (2003). Facilitating the meaningful participation of culturally and linguistically diverse families in the IFSP and IEP process. *Focus on Aautism and Other Developmental Disabilities, 18*(1), 51–59.

CHAPTER 3

Challenges to Effective Partnerships in the Early Years

■ CHAPTER OBJECTIVES

After reading and reflecting on this chapter, you should be able to:

- Recognize and identify personal attitudes and perceptions that can hinder establishment of parent partnerships.
- Identify common challenges related to effective partnerships with parents.
- Create a plan for dealing with anticipated challenges.

■ KEY TERMS

cultural barriers	ESL
diverse backgrounds	language barriers
educational system	logistical barriers
ELL	noncustodial parent

CHALLENGES TO EFFECTIVE FAMILY INVOLVEMENT

If family involvement leads to such important benefits for children, teachers, and parents, why are parent-teacher partnerships such a challenge to implement? For most, it is due to fear—fear of criticism; fear of making a mistake; fear of not knowing what to say or do to develop positive relationships with families. Most teachers, especially new teachers, share these fears, and rather than deal with them they choose to avoid. As mentioned in the introduction to this book, avoidance can be a favorite strategy at the beginning of a teaching career. But what is often found is that the more a teacher avoids parents, the more they pursue. After all, they care about their children and simply want to be assured that their children are in the best possible environment for learning.

Most new teachers never consider having to interact with parents. They plan to simply be outstanding instructors who are fun and caring and motivating—teachers every child would love. So, when parents walk through the door on the first day of school and want to ask questions, these teachers are often fear-stricken. But when a teacher faces his or her fears and makes efforts to connect with parents, he or she will most likely find much more acceptance than criticism, more successes than mistakes, and more ways to connect than ever imagined. Then the benefits of working with parents will become evident.

This book is about creating positive relationships and partnerships with parents and families, but before we begin to make a plan for forming these partnerships we must first address the challenges that get in the way—the important issues that make connecting with parents difficult. In this chapter, we'll address difficulties with perceptions; parents' knowledge or lack of knowledge of the educational process; language, cultural, and socioeconomic barriers; and conflicts with time, scheduling, and commitment. While these challenges may seem overwhelming, they can be overcome. Hopefully, by addressing these issues your fears will begin to subside and you'll be truly inspired to make efforts to connect with parents.

PERCEPTIONS

The first roadblock to overcome is our perception of parents. Teachers often enter the field expecting challenging relationships with parents. We expect conflict and judgment and so adopt a defensive attitude. Many teachers feel that they must "educate children 'in spite' of their parents, rather than in partnership with them" (Baum & McMurray-Schwarz, 2004, p. 58).

Not only do many teachers expect judgment from parents, but they, in turn, pass their own judgment when they feel that children are not coming to school fully prepared to learn. Rather than trying to understand the reasons behind this perceived unpreparedness (such as poverty, family stress, or other factors), they tend to criticize.

There are differing perceptions, as well, in terms of what teachers and parents think family involvement means. Many teachers see involvement as parents assisting in the classroom, attending school events, and being involved in parent organizations, while parents may define it as helping with schoolwork, reading to children at home, and instilling the value of education. According to Ascher (1988),

> Parent involvement may easily mean quite different things to people. It can mean advocacy; parents sitting on councils and committees, participating in the decisions and operation of schools. It can mean parents serving as classroom aides, accompanying a class on an outing or assisting teachers in a variety of other ways, either as volunteers or for wages. It can also conjure up images of teachers sending home notes to parents, or of parents working on bake sales and other projects that bring schools much needed support. Increasingly, parent involvement means parents initiating learning activities at home to improve their children's performance in school: reading to them, helping them with homework, playing educational games, discussing current events, and so on. (p. 109)

Without communication between teachers and parents, unspoken perceptions and expectations can lead to misunderstandings and disappointment.

Another perception that forms barriers to positive relationships is related to teacher and parent roles. Parents often feel that parenting is their job, teaching is your job, and the two are not related. Some perceive that teachers are the experts and parents are not. Parents raise their children for years at home and then send them off to school to "learn" for the first time. In reality, children enter our classrooms with much knowledge that will help them in school. Let's take a brief look at the wealth of literacy knowledge children glean from their home environments.

Upon entering school, most children have gained extensive knowledge about written language from their experiences with literacy in everyday life. They see print in the environment; they are often read to by family members; and they observe literacy routines in the home (newspaper reading, list making, etc.). They construct their own ideas about the function, structure, and conventions of written language (Sulzby & Teale, 1991) and imitate literacy behaviors based on their interpretations of the acts of reading and writing they observe. They often understand the "alphabetic nature" of print, how to handle books, and are aware that print is read from left to right. They use various cueing systems and have observed that the writings of others have meaning (Goodman, 1984).

Families influence the development of literacy in their children through physical environment, interpersonal interaction, and the emotional and motivational climate (Leichter, 1984). Leichter explains that the physical environment refers to economic and educational resources available, visual stimulation, and physical family arrangements. Interpersonal interaction involves the literacy opportunities available to a child while interacting with parents and siblings. The emotional and motivational environment refers to relationships within the home that affect a child's experiences with literacy.

Numerous studies have focused on the homes of early readers and writers. Briggs and Elkind (1973) studied five-year-old children (readers and nonreaders) to determine why some children read earlier than others. Their results revealed that the early readers had more educated mothers and fathers who read to them more frequently than the nonreaders.

In a study of 20 reading five-year-olds, Clark (1984) found similarities in the home environments that she attributes to early reading success. She concluded that many of the parents were professionals and had a wide range of books in the home. (See Figure 3–1.) Many of the children had older siblings (also early readers) who acted as teachers and models. These homes exhibited positive adult-child interactions and the parents conveyed genuine interest in their children's experiences. Clark also found that the parents of these early readers frequented their local libraries for personal use and assisted the children in making their book selections.

Likewise, Teale (1984) describes the homes of early readers as "rich literacy environments" that very naturally include reading and writing activities, such as reading books and newspapers, writing letters, and making lists. The children living in these homes interact positively with others who model involvement with literacy materials.

The availability of reading materials in the home has also proven to be a significant factor in early reading success, according to Durkin (1966) and Morrow (1993). These homes often have library corners for children and a wide variety of books made available throughout the house. Children who are frequently read to by parents and siblings show a greater interest in books and ultimately become better readers (Briggs & Elkind, 1973; Clark, 1984).

FIGURE 3–1   Older siblings often act as teachers and learning models in the home.

Studies of early readers also report the significance of writing materials in the home, which leads to an increased interest in writing activities. The children are encouraged to scribble and develop writing skills naturally, which enhances the reading process (Morrow, 1993). The home environments of early readers are also characterized by interactive adults. (See Figure 3–2.) Parents in these homes are responsive to their children's interest in literacy and provide literacy experiences and discussion.

Merely by looking at the literacy practices that many children experience before entering school, it is essential that we recognize the importance of parents and the home environment and how much children have gained before beginning formal education.

With this in mind, it is easy to see why our perceptions of parents must change to encompass the value of what they have already contributed to their children's learning before they enter our classrooms. Additionally, when we do recognize family practices that are interfering with a child's development and educational success, we must provide ideas and assistance to help parents work more effectively with their children. Most importantly, we must express our value of parent contributions to children's development and learning and communicate with families about the roles we hope they will play in their children's educational experiences related to the classroom.

FIGURE 3–2   The home environments of early readers are characterized by interactive adults.

SCHOOLING EXPERIENCE

Knowledge of the **educational system** factors into the level of family involvement at school and at home. In my experience, it was the parents who were teachers or former teachers who asked the most questions and made the efforts to obtain information about their children's learning experiences. These parents understood the way schools "worked" and how their own involvement benefited their children. Other parents made commitments early on in their children's school careers to be involved in the classroom or in school events and organizations. While they asked fewer questions and challenged teachers less, they understood the system and, for the most part, supported it.

In sharp contrast were the parents who felt detached from the school environment. They tended not to ask specific questions, only showed up at major school events or conferences, and seemed somewhat intimidated by the school environment. In many cases, these parents just accepted their lack of information rather than seeking out answers to their questions. Of course, there were also families who had other obstacles to being involved in their children's school careers. Those who did not speak English or came from diverse cultural backgrounds (discussed later in this chapter) had obvious challenges with connecting to the school environment. Unfortunately, most parents do not typically have high comfort levels with the school system. Most parents have not previously worked as teachers in a school, which means that they need us, the teachers, to help them understand the way school "works" and what they can do to be involved.

The younger the children with whom you work, the less familiar their parents will be with helping out at school or understanding what they can do at home to assist their children. Many parents feel intimidated by the school setting because of their own schooling experiences or lack of experiences. For some, this intimidation stems from insecurities from lack of higher education. They see the teacher as the educated one who knows best and feel that they have nothing, educationally, to offer their own children. "Not only do parents with a lower level of education have difficulty in assisting with home learning, they tend to feel intimidated when communicating with teachers and school administrators and thus may avoid getting involved with the school" (Tinkler, 2002). Intimidation can also stem from a nonwelcoming classroom environment. The teacher isn't unfriendly, per se, but rather remains standoffish and does not attempt to make meaningful connections with parents. In these situations, parents and teachers have difficulty communicating and the insecurities on both sides prevent the development of effective partnerships.

LANGUAGE BARRIERS

In our changing society, teachers find their classrooms filled more and more with children from **diverse backgrounds,** children whose home language is not English. This presents a problem for the typical Euro-American, English-speaking teacher. How do we communicate with parents who do not speak English? It is difficult enough to communicate effectively about their children's progress, let alone determine ways to involve them in the educational process.

Most teachers truly want to communicate effectively with these families, but what are they to do when language differences stand in the way? Even years of foreign language classes can leave the typical teacher with limited vocabulary for discussing the details of a child's progress in school. Gibson (2002) states that "the total number of foreign born residents has tripled" in the last 30 years, so facing **language barriers** is a reality for today's teachers. Not only does this create difficulties in communication between teachers and parents, but parents experience difficulty in assisting their children with homework that is in a language they do not understand (Aspiazu et al., 1998).

Fortunately, these days, it is more and more common for school districts to have translators available to assist during parent-teacher conferences. New teachers should not be afraid to request translators for these meetings with parents. I, personally, feel that it is too much to ask a young child to translate for his or her parents, particularly when the topic of discussion entails the child's progress in school.

When working with families who have limited English skills, it is useful to make frequent contact with your school's **ESL/ELL** teacher for suggestions. This teacher at your school can often offer assistance with providing written communication in a specific native language. This teacher will also be knowledgeable about resources offered through the school district. If there are limited district resources, Web sites for translation purposes (such as http://www.babelfish.com) can help to provide you with some assistance in written communication.

While you may feel uncomfortable trying to communicate with a parent with limited English, it is often necessary to make an even greater effort to involve this parent in your classroom. This gives the parent an opportunity to observe the classroom environment and activities, firsthand, while picking up on the language a bit through interaction with you and the other students. Be sure to communicate this parent's value to the educational process and the importance of speaking and reading to the child in his or her first language to provide a rich foundation in that language. Research tells us that children who have a solid foundation in their first language make a smoother transition to their second language. Parents with limited English need to understand the importance of a rich first language and we can express to them that speaking this language at home is an asset rather than a deficit to their children.

FIGURE 3–3 Involving parents with diverse backgrounds is exciting and allows parents and children to share fascinating experiences, traditions, and customs.

CULTURAL BARRIERS

Differences in cultural background can create **cultural barriers** to effective communication between parents and teachers; however, this can be one of the least troublesome challenges. Involving parents with diverse backgrounds is exciting and allows parents and children to share fascinating experiences, traditions, and customs with the class. (See Figure 3–3.) However, there can be obstacles to involving parents from diverse backgrounds in that many do not understand the classroom "culture" in U.S. schools. This can lead to the feeling of inferiority and insecurity about how to participate in children's learning experiences.

It is important to consider that your understanding and willingness to embrace a child's culture leads to his or her academic success. If we truly want to be the best possible teachers, this is not something we can avoid. Even the very noble perspective that "all my students are equal" or "there is no color in my classroom" doesn't "cut it" in today's classrooms. Particularly if you are a white, middle-class teacher, adopting this kind of attitude simply means that

FIGURE 3–4   With the increasing number of minority students in U.S. schools, it is necessary to focus on all cultures represented by the families of students.

the dominant culture prevails in your classroom. With the increasing number of minority students in U.S. schools, focus on only one culture is no longer acceptable if we truly want to meet the needs of all children. (See Figure 3–4.)

Let's take a particular look at academic achievement among Latino children. Hispanic youth are considered to be the "most under-educated major segment of the U.S. population" (Inger, 1992, p. 1). Portales (2000) maintains that second-, third-, and fourth-generation Hispanic students are less successful academically because school expectations for both children and families remain low. His research reveals a lack of encouragement or challenge for Hispanic youth to achieve in schools, to complete school, or to attend college. These students also have the highest dropout rate (Gibson, 2002), and yet, in a study by Aspiazu et al. (1998), researchers found that when Hispanic parents were assisted in strategies for helping their children with schoolwork, the children's academic achievement improved.

Understanding views of education among parents of diverse cultural backgrounds is "key" for teachers. For example, many teachers view a lack of involvement at school as an expression of lack of interest, yet, in Latino culture teacher respect is emphasized and parents typically don't "interfere" with the work of the teacher. While teachers in the United States view parent interest in schoolwork as "caring for their child's education, Latino parents may view this as a sign of disrespect" (Trumbull et al., 2001).

Numerous studies (Cairney & Munise, 1994; Delpit, 1994; and Ladson-Billings, 1994) suggest that when teachers partner with parents and caregivers from minority cultures, teachers gain cultural understanding and are better able to lead students to academic success. Delpit (1995) "urges Anglo teachers to invite parents and community spokespeople to come to school to share stories of home and community life so the teachers will be better prepared to teach 'other people's children'" (Lazar & Slostad, 1999, p. 206). Rather than adopting an "us-them" attitude, we must come together in understanding and partnership for the benefit of each child.

DIVORCE

Elkind (1994) describes today's family structure as "more fluid, less stable, and more vulnerable to outside pressures than previous generations." The situation of divorce is commonplace in the teacher experience. In fact, "fully half of the nation's first-graders can now expect that before they graduate their parents will divorce" (Evans, 1998, p. 2). The pressure of divorce is difficult enough for the children who often experience anger, abandonment, loneliness, and anxiety (Frieman, 1997), not to mention the parents, who must find ways to help their children through the experience.

The tensions between divorced parents can create tensions in parent-teacher partnerships. The teacher is all too often caught in the middle of an emotional war over an innocent child. While these kinds of situations may make relating to parents uncomfortable, a child of divorce needs an advocate all the more.

In some cases, you may find that the father is absent and your primary parent contact is the mother. You may find, as is sometimes the case, that both parents want to be involved, but that tensions exist between them. In some cases, the child may be fortunate enough to have two divorced parents who have a positive working relationship concerning their child. Whatever the situation, we must make efforts to support the child and his or her family in the best way we can. It is especially important to reserve judgment of these families and serve as a neutral party with the express purpose of supporting the child. Particularly, when a noncustodial father is isolated from the child's educational experience by the mother, it is necessary for the teacher to recognize the importance of both parents' support and make efforts to involve them both. (See Figure 3–5.) "For many of

FIGURE 3–5   It is necessary for the teacher to recognize the importance of both parents' support and make efforts to involve both mothers and fathers.

these parents, the school's passivity in reaching out to them can reinforce their feeling of not being a part of their children's lives" (Frieman, 1997). Divorce is a family crisis that affects everyone involved. Because of this, it is even more important for the teacher to make the effort to assist both parents in supporting the child in the best way they can. "If schools treat parents as unimportant, if they treat them as negative education influences on their children, or if they discourage parents from becoming involved, then they promote the development of attitudes that inhibit achievement at school" (Henderson, 1988, p. 151). This also applies to the noncustodial father whose value of his child's school experience will promote academic achievement. In situations where the **noncustodial parent** has been permitted to have contact with the child, this parent should be included in the

---

FAMILIES IN FOCUS

Alyssa, her mother, and stepfather entered the classroom on Back-to-School night, followed shortly thereafter by Alyssa's father. The three adults seemed very uncomfortable to be in one another's presence, while it was apparent that the young girl loved all three. Privately, her mother explained to the teacher, Mrs. Johnson, that Alyssa spent half the week with her and half the week with her father. "If she comes to school unprepared or doesn't have homework completed or materials needed for school, let me know because her father doesn't always do what he needs to do." Later, Alyssa's father approached Mrs. Johnson. He made it very clear that he wanted to be involved in his daughter's first-grade experience and that he did not want to be "pushed out" by her mother. He wanted separate parent-teacher conferences and to receive information from the classroom and from the school, so he could stay informed. Mrs. Johnson made a deal with him that she would mail paperwork to him on a weekly basis and make personal contact with him frequently over the phone. The tension of the situation was obvious, but the teacher admired this father's desire to stay connected with and be supportive of his daughter.

---

educational process through regular teacher communication, invitations to school events, and separate conferences to discuss the child's progress.

To overcome the possible barriers concerning parents of divorce, it is important to make a plan for communicating regularly with the noncustodial parent. If your school does not have a written policy addressing noncustodial parents, you might want to encourage this or, at least, create your own handout explaining your value of both parents in a child's school experience. (See Chapter 4 for more information about the benefits of father involvement and strategies to involve dads with their children's education.)

Provided that the noncustodial parent does not have restrictions in being involved with the child, make it a point to have all school-written communications mailed to the noncustodial parent. Be sure that the school's office personnel has the mailing address of the noncustodial parent. If your school does not routinely mail information to noncustodial parents, make the effort to do this yourself. Keep a stack of addressed envelopes in your classroom, so you can easily send information to this parent on a regular basis. Make periodic phone calls to this parent and be sure that he or she receives progress reports and has the opportunity to discuss the child's progress with you, ideally, in person. As challenging and time-consuming as these procedures may be, the benefits to the child are great and should be the focus of your efforts.

LOGISTICAL BARRIERS

There are also many **logistical barriers** to family involvement and getting to the school setting. Time, commitment, need for child care, and transportation are all issues to be considered when trying to involve parents. Remember that time is an important commodity for all of us. Many parents juggle jobs, children, children's activities, and other commitments. Even stay-at-home mothers often have other children at home who keep them from spending time at school. "With the rise of two-breadwinner families, one-parent families and the need for family members to hold more than one job, families may have demands on their time that prevent them from being as involved as they might like to be" (Kauffman et al., 2001). Low levels of commitment to children's education can be another barrier. Often parents, due to numerous commitments, do not make educational involvement a priority. Merely sharing the benefits of family involvement and offering simple suggestions for ways they can be involved at home (see Chapter 6) can assist parents in shifting their priorities and making a commitment to their children's academic achievement.

Keep in mind, also, that many parents may desire to volunteer in the classroom, but do not have access to child care or cannot afford it. The issue of child care creates problems for parents desiring to attend conferences or evening events at school (Tinkler, 2002). Transportation is another obstacle to volunteering in the classroom or attending school events. A two-parent family with only one car would most likely use the car for getting to work, which leaves one of the parents without transportation. For parents with child care and transportation needs, careful considerations are needed and special concessions may be necessary. (See Figure 3–6.) For example, making home visits to communicate personally with parents can help to bridge a gap, conveying to parents that they are valuable and necessary to their children's success in school.

All of these issues must be considered when encouraging parents to volunteer at school. If these were the obstacles to overcome at your school, what would you do to try to overcome them? List your ideas on a sheet of paper.

WORKING WITH DIFFICULT PARENTS

There are times when a teacher encounters difficult parents. These might be parents who would rather force the school or teacher to do what they want rather than trying to work together. They might just be critical of the school and the teachers, making everyone involved feel self-conscious and

FIGURE 3–6 For parents with child care and transportation needs, careful considerations are needed and special concessions may be necessary.

Time: _____

_____

_____

Commitment: _____

_____

_____

Child care: _____

_____

_____

Transportation: _____

_____

_____

Check Your Attitude toward Working with Parents			
Feel that parents are more hindrance than help in the classroom	☐ Yes	☐ No	☐ Wish I felt this way
Tense up when parents come to the room	☐ Yes	☐ No	☐ Wish I felt this way
Prefer to teach in my classroom all alone	☐ Yes	☐ No	☐ Wish I felt this way
Compare brothers and sisters from the same family	☐ Yes	☐ No	☐ Wish I felt this way
Feel threatened by upset or angry parents	☐ Yes	☐ No	☐ Wish I felt this way
View parents as allies and a great resource	☐ Yes	☐ No	☐ Wish I felt this way
Believe that parents of low-income children don't care as much	☐ Yes	☐ No	☐ Wish I felt this way
Enjoy collaborating with several outside persons in my classroom	☐ Yes	☐ No	☐ Wish I felt this way
Have strong feelings about certain groups of people	☐ Yes	☐ No	☐ Wish I felt this way
Feel most parents let their children watch too much television	☐ Yes	☐ No	☐ Wish I felt this way
Feel most parents are too busy for their children	☐ Yes	☐ No	☐ Wish I felt this way
Work better if there is appropriate social distance between parents and myself	☐ Yes	☐ No	☐ Wish I felt this way
Believe parents whose children dress themselves inappropriately for school are irresponsible	☐ Yes	☐ No	☐ Wish I felt this way
Feel that optimal growth happens when I work closely with parents	☐ Yes	☐ No	☐ Wish I felt this way
Am pleased when parents leave quickly	☐ Yes	☐ No	☐ Wish I felt this way
Look forward to parent-teacher conferences	☐ Yes	☐ No	☐ Wish I felt this way
Believe that most parents have abdicated their role to schools	☐ Yes	☐ No	☐ Wish I felt this way
Like the parents of students in my class	☐ Yes	☐ No	☐ Wish I felt this way

FIGURE 3–7   Self-Assessment.

defensive. These challenging parents, themselves, can seem like roadblocks to effective partnerships. (See Figure 3–7 for a useful self-evaluation tool.)

Fortunately, there are strategies that can be implemented to help in these situations. For starters, it is important to remain respectful, open, and receptive to them. Challenging parents often expect to be treated unfairly and might be pleasantly surprised by your willingness to hear them and address their concerns. Remember to keep in mind the goal of "partnership." As you converse with a challenging parent, use language that refers to a team effort for solving problems. Take time to genuinely understand the parent's feelings and frustrations and be sure to communicate that you are empathetic. Use active listening strategies, reflecting back to the parent what you understand him/her to have said and validate the parent's feelings and concerns. Be sure to ask the parent exactly what he or she needs you to do to resolve the issue. Most importantly, reassure the parent that you care for his or her child and that your goal is for all involved to work together to bring about the most successful experience possible for the child.

■ CONCLUSION

While the benefits of family involvement are many, there are still numerous obstacles to developing effective partnerships between teachers and parents. Perceptions on the part of both teachers and parents can create misunderstandings. The educational knowledge of parents or their understanding of the education system and how schools "work" can affect parents' comfort level in being involved at school. Additionally, parents who are uncomfortable with the school environment may also feel insecurities in assisting their children at home and may feel they have little to offer in terms of their educational progress. Language and cultural barriers are fairly obvious barriers that affect the level of meaningful communication and understanding of the academic process and, specifically, the individual child's progress in school. Finally, logistics can often contribute to lack of family involvement. Time, commitment, need for child care, and transportation are all factors to be considered in connecting with parents and encouraging them to involve themselves with their children's education.

Fortunately, there are solutions to many of the challenges teachers experience when encouraging family involvement. In the next chapter, we'll address ways to foster effective partnerships with parents. Keeping in mind that the goal is to provide each child with the best possible educational experience, we'll look at successful models for family involvement and explore ideas for beginning to make connections with parents.

■ SUMMARY OF IMPORTANT POINTS

- Family involvement leads to important benefits for children, in terms of academic achievement.

- Even in light of benefits to children, parents and teachers often have difficulty working together to promote successful academic experiences.
- Perceptions of the roles of parents and teachers can interfere with effective parent-teacher partnerships.
- Teachers often expect parents not to be supportive of them and avoid making connections with parents out of fear of criticism.
- Misconceptions exist in terms of defining family involvement.
- Teachers need to value what parents have contributed to their children's early learning experiences prior to formal education.
- The level of parents' knowledge of the educational system can affect their level of involvement.
- Parents who are uncomfortable with the school environment or who have insecurities relating to their own education may feel they don't have much to offer their children academically.
- Many parents are intimidated by the school environment and teachers.
- Language barriers make parent-teacher communication difficult and may lead to decreased family involvement.
- Making efforts to provide translators or translated written materials helps to involve parents whose first language is not English.
- Inviting parents with limited English to visit and participate in the classroom helps them to better understand their children's school experience.
- Parents from diverse cultural backgrounds may have difficulty understanding the culture of U.S. schools.
- Embracing children's home culture leads to academic success.
- Parents from diverse backgrounds may perceive involvement in the classroom or questioning of classroom activities as signs of disrespect to the teacher.
- Divorce is often a barrier to involvement by noncustodial parents.
- Efforts to communicate with noncustodial parents may be challenging, but lead to greater benefits for the child.
- Parents often experience challenges related to lack of time, commitment level, need for child care, and transportation. These should be taken into consideration when encouraging parents to participate at school.

CHAPTER REVIEW QUESTIONS

1. Why is it important to consider challenges to effective relationships between parents and teachers?

2. Why do you think teachers fear criticism and judgment from parents?

3. How can perceptions become barriers to parent-teacher partnerships?

4. What kinds of educational experiences have most children had before entering school for the first time?

5. How does the educational knowledge of parents or knowledge of the school system affect family involvement?

6. What challenges exist in terms of language and culture?

7. How can teachers and schools assist parents from diverse backgrounds in feeling valued and being involved in their children's academic experience?

8. What problems related to parent-teacher partnerships arise with divorced parents?

9. What can teachers do to involve noncustodial parents in their children's education?

10. How do logistical factors affect family involvement?

APPLICATION AND REFLECTION

1. What are your personal fears related to parent-teacher partnerships? Write a journal entry addressing your fears, concerns, and expectations.

2. Interview a parent of a school-aged child. Ask the parent to discuss how he or she feels about relating to teachers. How does the parent define family involvement and what challenges does he or she experience in this area? What does the parent see as being the benefits of working closely with the teacher?

3. What are your ideas related to overcoming language and cultural barriers? Write a journal entry addressing your ideas for valuing language and culture and involving parents from diverse backgrounds.

4. Review Families in Focus on page 65. Dialogue with another student to discuss ideas for respecting divorced parents and involving both parents in the child's educational experience.

5. Make a plan for overcoming logistical barriers to family involvement. How will you deal with parents' time constraints? What will you do to encourage parents to make their children's education a priority? How will you connect with parents who have challenges concerning child care or transportation?

■ FURTHER READING

Bermudez, A. B., & Marquez, J. A. (1996). An examination of a four-way collaborative to increase parental involvement in the schools. *The Journal of Educational Issues of Language Minority Students,* Special Issue, 16. Retrieved May 8, 2005, http://www.ncela.gwu.edu/pubs/jeilms/vol16/jeilms1601.htm.

Crouter, A.C. (2004). *Work-family challenges for low-income parents and their children.* Mahwah, NJ: Lawrence Erlbaum Associates.

Halfon, N. (2002). *Child rearing in America: Challenges facing parents with young children.* Cambridge, MA: Cambridge University Press.

Hart, B. (2005). *It takes a parent: How the culture of pushover parenting is hurting our kids and what to do about it.* Putnam Adult.

Yaden, D. B., Rowe, D. W., & MacGillivray, L. (2000). Emergent literacy: A matter (polyphony) of perspectives. In M. L. Kamil, P. B. Mosental, P. D. Pearson, & R. Barr (Eds.), *Handbook of reading research* (425–454). Mahwah, NJ: Lawrence Erlbaum Associates.

For additional information on research-based practice, visit our Web site at http://www.earlychilded.delmar.com.

Additional resources for this chapter can be found on the Online Companion™ to accompany this text at www.earlychilded.delmar.com. This supplemental material includes Web links, downloadable forms, and Case Studies with critical thinking applications. This content can be used as a study aid to reinforce key concepts presented in this chapter and to conduct additional research on topics of interest.

▧ REFERENCES

Ascher, C. (1988). *Improving the school-home connection for low-income urban parents.* New York: ERIC Clearninghouse on Urban Education (ERIC Document Reproduction Service No. ED293973).

Aspiazu, G. G., Bauer, S. C., & Spillett, M. D. (1998). Improving the academic performance of Hispanic youth: A community education model. *Bilingual Research Journal, 22(2,* 3, and 4), 1–20.

Baum, A. C., & McMurray-Schwarz, P. (August, 2004). Preservice teachers' beliefs about family involvement: Implications for teacher education. *Early Childhood Education Journal, 32*(1), 57–61.

Briggs, C., & Elkind, D. (1973). Cognitive development in early readers. *Developmental Psychology, 9*(2), 279–280.

Cairney, T. H., & Munsie, L. (1995). Parent participation in literacy learning. *Reading Teacher, 48,* 392–403.

Clark, M. M. (1984). Literacy at home and at school: Insights from a study of young fluent readers. In H. Goelman, A. Oberg, & F. Smith (Eds.), *Awakening to literacy* (122–130). Portsmouth, NJ: Heinemann.

Delpit, L. (1995). *Other people's children.* New York: New Press.

Durkin, D. (1966). *Children who read early.* New York: Teachers College Press.

Elkind, D. (1994). Ties That Stress: The New Family Imbalance. Cambridge, MA: Harvard University Press.

Frieman, B. B. (April, 1997). Two parents—two homes. *Educational Leadership,* 23–25.

Gibson, M. A. (2002). The new Latino diaspora and educational policy. In S. Worthem, E. G. Murillo, & E. T. Hamann (Eds.), *Education in the new Latino diaspora: Policy and the politics of identity.* Westport, CT: Ablex Publishing.

Goodman, Y. (1984). The development of initial literacy. In H. Goelman, A. Oberg, & F. Smith (Eds.), *Awakening to literacy* (102–109). Portsmouth, NJ: Heinemann.

Henderson, A. T. (October, 1988). Parents are a school's best friends. *Phi Delta Kappan,* 148–153.

Inger, M. (1992). Increasing the school involvement of Hispanic parents. ERIC Digest. New York: ERIC Clearinghouse on Urban Education, Teachers College, Columbia University.

Kauffman, E., Perry, A., & Prentiss, D. (2001). *Reasons for and solutions to lack of parent involvement of parents of second language learners.*

New York: ERIC Clearinghouse on Elementary and Early Childhood Education (ERIC Document Reproduction Service No. ED458956).

Ladson-Billings, G. (1994). *The dreamkeepers: Successful teachers of African American children.* San Francisco: Jossey-Bass.

Lazar, A., & Slostad, F. (March/April, 1999). How to overcome obstacles to parent-teacher partnerships. *The Clearing House, 72*(4), 206–210.

Leichter, H. P. (1984). Families as environments for literacy. In H. Goelman, A. Oberg, & F. Smith (Eds.), *Awakening to literacy.* Portsmouth, NJ: Heinemann.

Morrow, L. (1993). *Literacy development in the early years: Helping children read and write.* Boston: Allyn & Bacon.

Portales, M. (2000). *Crowding out Latinos.* Philadelphia: Temple University Press.

Sulzby, E., & Teale, W. (1991). Emergent literacy. In R. Barr, M. Kamil, P. Mosenthal, & P. D. Pearson (Eds.), *Handbook of reading research* (vol. 2). New York: Longman.

Teale, W. H. (1984). Reading to young children: Its significance for literacy development. In H. Goelman, A. Oberg, & F. Smith (Eds.), *Awakening to literacy* (110–121). Portsmouth, NJ: Heinemann.

Tinkler, B. (2002). *A review of literature on Hispanic/Latino parent involvement in K-12 education. Assets for Colorado Youth.* Retrieved April 24, 2005, http://www.buildassets.org/Products/latinoparentreport/latinoparentrept.htm.

Trumbull E., Rothstein-Fisch, C., Greenfield, P. M., & Quiroz, B. (2001). *Bridging cultures between home and schools: A guide for teachers.* Mahwah, NJ: Lawrence Erlbaum Associates.

4

Involving Fathers and Male Role Models

■ CHAPTER OBJECTIVES _____

After reading and reflecting on this chapter, you should be able to:

- Communicate the research findings related to male involvement and student achievement, especially involvement of fathers in a child's education.

- Reflect on and understand the importance of your own attitudes and assumptions regarding men in early childhood classrooms.

- Plan for making personal connections with fathers and male role models.

- Plan for participation of fathers, male family members, and male role models.

- Determine what important information is needed to communicate well with each one of a child's parents.

- Examine school policies and school climate in regard to fathers and male involvement with young children.

■ KEY TERMS _____

cognitive development   fingerprint clearance

criminal background checks   gendered

dad-friendly   male role model

father figures   student-led conferences

father involvement   verbal linguistic

You have begun to think about family involvement in your future class-room. You have also examined some of the challenges to effective family involvement in the school. This chapter focuses on the activities that you can plan for greater father involvement. Fathers have long been a hidden parent in children's school success. The delicate issues of planning for families that are single-parent families, blended families, families with same-sex parents, and marriages in legal dissolution are never easy to negotiate when trying to encourage male involvement. Recognizing the many facets of these issues, and strategically planning father involvement with this current reality is discussed in this chapter.

RESEARCH ON MALE INVOLVEMENT

Both common sense and research findings tell us that school-age children do best academically when both parents participate in the important events and activities of school life. These children have a stronger sense of self, are more emotionally secure, and have fewer social adjustment problems. Cognitive, social, and emotional development are stronger for children whose mothers *and* fathers are consistently present and engaged in their lives. The research evidence also shows that the involvement of both parents in the early childhood years has a very positive effect on children's academic performance later on (Henderson & Berla, 1994; U.S. Department of Education, 1994). In recent years, more attention has been focused on fathers and **father involvement** in school achievement. A growing body of research indicates that fathers have a very important role in the intellectual development of their children. Unfortunately, many fathers remain relatively uninvolved in their children's school, assuming that it is more important for mothers to be involved. Oftentimes, schools are unwelcoming to fathers, **father figures,** or other male family members.

The reality for most teachers today is that many of the students in their classrooms come from nontraditional family structures. You may teach many children who do not have both a mother and a father in the home. You will have students from single-parent families, from blended stepfamilies, and from families with same-sex parents. Research findings indicate that these students will be at a disadvantage in some ways. It is important for you to keep fathers, father figures, and male family members well informed and involved in your classroom. By making this effort, you will see greater gains in academic achievement, improved classroom behavior, and a happier school climate.

Fathers Matter in Children's Well-Being

The children who tend to do better in school, who are less prone to depression, and who are more successful in social relationships are the children with a father or father figure in the home. Conversely, children from single-parent homes have lower achievement and get into trouble more often than children from homes with two parents. Child psychologist Michael Lamb found that whether measuring **cognitive development,** psychosocial development, or sex-role development, children are better off when their relationship with their father is close and warm (1986). (See Figure 4–1.)

Even at a very young age when most people assume mothers dominate interactions with children, father-child exchanges have been shown to promote a child's physical well-being, perceptual abilities, and competency for social relatedness (Krampe & Fairweather, 1993). A longitudinal study of intact, two-parent families by Furstenberg (1995) indicated that children whose fathers were in the home and highly involved attained higher levels of education, were economically better off, had lower levels of delinquency, and healthier psychological well-being. Yeung, Sandberg, Davis-Kean, and Hofferth (1999) had similar findings in studying 1,000 children longitudinally. Yeung et al. found those whose families remained intact with an involved father were more successful as adults and had higher earnings in the labor market. These studies and many more with similar findings affirm for us that fathers are the "forgotten contributors to child development" (Lamb, 1975, p. 245). Fathers contribute to the healthy development of their children in a unique, essential way.

Fathers Matter in Education

School readiness and academic achievement are directly linked to the involvement of fathers and father figures with young children. A school-age child with an involved male in his or her life is more patient, curious, and

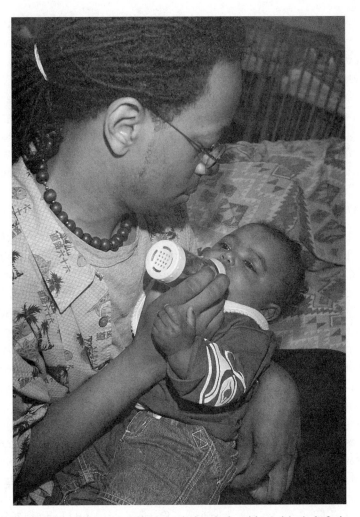

FIGURE 4–1   Children are better off when their relationships with their fathers are close and warm.

confident. (See Figure 4–2.) Using data from the 1996 National House-hold Education Survey, the National Center for Education Statistics reports that in two-parent households, children are more likely to do well academically, to participate in extracurricular activities, to enjoy school, and are less likely to have ever repeated a grade or to have been suspended or expelled if their fathers have high involvement in their schools (Nord, Brimhall, & West, 1997). Children with involved fathers are able to remain in their classroom seats, to wait patiently for others, and to sustain interest in their schoolwork (Biller, 1993). Children who have male role models

FIGURE 4–2   School-age children with involved male role models are more patient, curious, and confident.

who read to them regularly are more likely to perform better on measures of cognitive skills including those of verbal ability (Bing, 1963); they are better able to solve complex mathematical and logical puzzles and they have also been found to have a higher sustained interest in solving analytical problems (Biller, 1993). Even premature infants with consistently involved fathers born to Latino, African-American, and other minority populations living in inner-city areas have substantially higher cognitive skills than full-term infants growing up in the same areas without fathers (Yogman, Kindlon, & Earls, 1995).

The research is equally clear that male absence from the home has negative effects for young children. Parish found that the self-image of

---

FAMILIES IN FOCUS

Daniel was the only child of Mr. and Mrs. Tate, a couple who had him later in life. Mrs. Tate was actively involved in the culture of the school, attending PTA meetings, helping with school events, and assisting in his classroom. Toward the beginning of the school year, Daniel's second-grade teacher announced a volunteer opportunity that seemed to appeal to parents who could only periodically fit volunteering into their schedules. It was the job of Guest Reader—a parent who would visit the classroom a few times a year to read aloud to the class. The first to express interest was Daniel's father, a businessman with a very busy schedule. He was excited to have this opportunity to share in the academic experience of his son. Mr. Tate would arrive on his scheduled date to read, fresh from the office, dressed in a suit, and would sit down to read silly stories to the second graders as his proud son sat beside him and beamed.

---

adolescent children is dependent on how loving the fathers are toward mothers in the home (1994). Self-image suffers when there is no father or father figure in the home and when there is no intimacy with a **male role model** (Field, 1995). Children whose fathers were not involved in their education were less likely to get A's, enjoy school, and participate in extracurricular activities. They were more likely to repeat a grade (Cooksey & Fondell, 1996). For young girls, male involvement is the link to their sense of competence, especially in mathematics (Radin, 1983).

Men are essential to the healthy development of children. "Fathers do not mother" (Pruett, 2000, p. 17). They communicate differently, they play differently, they encourage children differently, and they discipline differently. There is a balance between male and female caregivers that enriches, broadens, and expands the experience and resiliency of the child. Men *need* relationships with children as well. It is essential that everyone—you, administrators, and the parents of your students—appreciate the role of males in the parenting partnership. This knowledge will help you to better meet the needs of families and your students.

BARRIERS TO FATHER INVOLVEMENT

In 1995, President Clinton recognized the importance of the forgotten parent by instructing all federal departments and agencies to make a concerted effort to include fathers in program, policy, and research agendas of the national government (Clinton, 1995). Fathers, father figures, and male role models can be a powerful, positive force in a child's education when they are involved. As classroom teachers, it is our responsibility to ensure that we are communicating regularly and clearly with both parenting partners. Some of the barriers that prevent open, two-way communication between men and schools are: (1) the myths and assumptions teachers and administrators bring to teaching, (2) the father's fears that discourage involvement, and (3) inappropriate program design and school policies which tend to exclude fathers and father figures. Overcoming these barriers will ensure stronger home-school partnerships, higher levels of male participation, and more positive contributions to child well-being.

Myths and Assumptions about Fathers

Too often teachers and administrators translate the words "parentinvolvement" to "mother involvement," and assume that fathers are the detached, disinterested parent. Men are relegated to being the breadwinners and the disciplinarians who rarely appear at school. The equally wrong notion persists that all fathers in low-income, high-risk settings are absent fathers or that children from these backgrounds have no male figure in their lives. However, research data indicate that more than 60 percent of mothers with children in Head Start programs report that their children have regular, consistent interaction with a father or a father figure (McBride & Lin, 1996). These myths and assumptions have a negative impact on children's academic achievement and cognitive development. It is important for you to begin developing your own father-involvement plan with these questions in mind. What have you believed about the role of mothers and fathers in the school lives of your students? Have you tacitly believed that the children from low-income or minority populations grow up with minimal male involvement? Check your own attitudes and feelings about the children that come to your school who are fatherless. Expect that fathers want to be involved with their children.

Fathers' Fears and Gendered Schooling

Have you looked closely at the number of men versus the number of women working in schools and considered how this may account for low male involvement? The myth continues to persist that working with young children is "women's work." Schools have traditionally been the place of women's work with elementary schools staffed by 95 percent female teachers; 60 percent of their principals are female as well (Shedlin, 2004).

The elementary school curriculum places strong emphasis on **verbal linguistic** skills, which favor girls. Behavioral expectations and classroom management plans favor girls. Compliance and quiet seat time are rewarded while active learning and overexhuberance are discouraged. Typical early childhood classroom reading corners are made up of picture books favored by girls, while there are fewer information books and nonfiction items to encourage literacy in boys. Check the environment of your classroom. Are moms represented as often as dads in textbooks, pictures, and so on? Check the climate of your school. Does it welcome male participation in the activities there? Schools do not always welcome men.

One male principal recounts an amusing yet sobering story after visiting an elementary school in New York. A chirpy first grader wanted to know why he was in her school. The principal responded that he was considering working in the school. The distressed little girl asked, "Is Mr. Ball leaving?" When assured that the P.E. teacher, Mr. Ball, was not leaving, the first grader made the next leap of logic and asked if he was taking the janitor's job. The principal was of course not going to take the janitor's job. Since both the gym and the janitor's closet were located in the basement of the school, the child reached a frustrating conclusion. "Well, if they're not leaving, how could you work here? We don't allow men above the basement!" (Shedlin, 2004, p. 28). Too many schools still keep men "in the basement."

These factors shed light on a great many of the fears that fathers may hold in relation to schools, to teachers, and to the female-dominated environments that impacted them so dramatically as young male students. Fathers may fear exposure and inadequacy in a setting which has been a traditionally female domain. Many men have grown up with an inadequate or absent **male role model** themselves. They are uncertain how to father their own children as a result and may feel inadequate to the task. Fathers do not start out on the parenting adventure with all the skills that are important to being an effective dad (Frieman & Berkeley, 2002). Teachers can help to develop fathering skills and thereby improve the academic achievement of the students in their classroom.

PROGRAM AND POLICY BARRIERS

Inappropriate program design at your school may be discouraging the involvement of fathers and father figures. Most school policies were designed for a dated society where dads went off to work 8 to 10 hours a day, where they were narrowly thought of as the sole provider for the family, and where they only interacted with their school-age children as the disciplinarian. As a result, parent-teacher conferences are typically scheduled during the business day when working fathers (and mothers) are on the job. These conferences are scheduled in short, 15-minute time slots. The teacher expects to get parents "in and out" and to "tell everything" about the child in just 15 minutes. Schools neglect fathers who are not in the home by sending out a single set of papers such as handbooks, newsletters, report cards, and parenting materials. Access to confidential files is usually limited to the custodial parent in the case of divorce. And when there is conflict or tension between divorced parents, school policies are generally sympathetic toward mothers. Before you can develop an effective classroom plan for involving fathers, you must first learn all that you can about your school and district policies. If policies are in place that discourage fathers from full involvement in either the lives of their children or in the life of the school, point out these inconsistencies to colleagues and to your building administrator. Work constructively to rewrite policies and argue for their adoption before school boards and the district superintendent. Lead the effort in making your school a **"dad-friendly"** place. You can work collaboratively at the district level to improve teaching and learning in your school.

Not everyone will be committed to the efforts you make to involve fathers. The lack of responsible male family members is often cited in the public media as an explaining factor of school failure. Many will challenge your effort to put time, energy, and resources into the men they believe cause so many of the problems facing school-age children. Many women you work with in education will be unwilling to acknowledge their resistance to men and male involvement in schools. Teachers are not generally trained to work with parents and fewer still are comfortable making a focused effort to work with fathers. Some mothers will try to act as gatekeepers of information and will block involvement of fathers in all aspects of their children's lives (De Luccie, 1995). Men must become actively involved in the education of children to help them achieve success as they progress through the educational system.

SCHOOL ACTIVITIES AND STRATEGIES FOR INCREASING MALE INVOLVEMENT

Dads and male role models are frequently missing from the family involvement picture. Fathers are sometimes considered the "hard-to-reach" school population. This is all the more disturbing when you consider that as much as half of a school's parent body may be "hard-to-reach" (Shedlin, 2004).

Most teachers and school districts talk about "family" involvement, but recognize that all too frequently it means "mother" involvement. What activities and strategies can you include as you plan for family involvement that will increase father participation in your classroom? What school and district-wide changes will maximize the benefits that men bring to the achievement of young children? We will examine scheduling options, offer communication tips, suggest ways to maximize information handling, and ways to include men more often in school activities.

As you plan for father involvement in your classroom, it is important for you to set some very specific goals. Research shows us that fathers are more likely to participate in school activities when they are provided a clear link to their child's educational progress (Hadadian & Merbler, 1995; Markowitz, 1984). Research also indicates that the highest rates of father participation will be in attending activities with other family members, activities that will help them to plan for their children's future, and activities that teach them to be better parents (Turbiville & Marquis, 2001). Be certain to make this link directly for fathers by sharing research results, articles, and information about their child's cognitive development and academic achievement. Figures 4–3 through 4–6 provide short fact sheets to copy and send home to reinforce the important role of fathers. You will need to identify the significant male role models for each one of your students. These male figures may be fathers, stepfathers, friends, neighbors, family members, church

---

You have a powerful impact on your child! Your influence improves:

- cognitive development and thinking capacities in your child's brain.
- problem-solving capacities and spatial reasoning.
- sex-role identification.
- sense of security and self-image.

You Can Learn More:

Cooksey, E., & Fondell, M. (1996). Spending time with his kids: Effects of family structure on fathers' and children's lives. *Journal of Marriage and the Family, 58*(3), 693–707.

Pruett, K. (2000). *Fatherneed: Why father care is as essential as mother care for your child.* New York: The Free Press.

Snarey, J., & Vaillant, G. E. (1993). *How fathers care for the next generation.* Cambridge: Harvard University Press.

FIGURE 4–3   Dad, Do You Know How Much You Matter?

Father involvement improves a child's well-being in so many important ways:

- improving school readiness and school behavior.

- improving academic achievement and performance on standardized tests.

- decreasing delinquency and behavioral problems out of school.

- more confident, secure, and willing to try new things.

- higher mathematical competency and interest in analytical problems.

You Can Learn More:

Biller, H. (1993). *Father and families: Paternal factors in child development.* Westport, CT: Auburn House.

Pruett, K. (2000). *Fatherneed: Why father care is as essential as mother care for your child.* New York: The Free Press.

Snarey, J., & Vaillant, G. E. (1993). *How fathers care for the next generation.* Cambridge: Harvard University Press.

FIGURE 4–4   Dad, Do You Know How Much You Matter?

Father involvement is very important to your daughters!

- Girls with involved dads have higher verbal skills.

- Girls with involved dads have more confidence in mathematics.

- Girls with involved dads do better with logical puzzles and have greater sustained interest in problem solving.

You Can Learn More:

Pruett, K. (2000). *Fatherneed: Why father care is as essential as mother care for your child.* New York: The Free Press.

Radin, N. (1983). Father-child interactions and the intellectual functioning of four-year-old boys, *Developmental Psychology,* 6, 353–361.

Snarey, J., & Vaillant, G. E. (1993). *How fathers care for the next generatino.* Cambridge: Harvard University Press.

FIGURE 4–5   Dad, Do You Know How Much You Matter?

leaders, or life partners. Don't neglect moms! Let mothers know of your plans to include fathers and male role models as much as possible in the classroom. You should inform them of your goals and recruit their cooperation in your efforts. Implement your goals one step at a time. Progress comes slowly. You must believe that your efforts will pay off over time.

Fathers are different than mothers!
And the differences are so important.

- Fathers have a distinct style of communication that challenges the child's verbal skills.
- Fathers play more with their children.
- Fathers encourage their children to push their limits.
- Fathers speak to their children in brief, direct, and to-the-point ways.
- Fathers stress justice, fairness, and duty when they discipline their children.
- Fathers tend to prepare their children for the "real" world.

You Can Learn More:

Pruett, K. (2000). *Fatherneed: Why father care is as essential as mother care for your child.* New York: The Free Press.

Snarey, J., & Vaillant, G. E. (1993). *How fathers care for the next generation.* Cambridge: Harvard University Press.

FIGURE 4–6   Dad, Do You Know How Much You Matter?

Scheduling

School schedules today don't always encourage male participation. What are the ways you can adjust your school schedule to accommodate fathers? It was suggested earlier in this chapter that parent-teacher conferences are typically scheduled during the business day when working fathers (and mothers) are on the job. These conferences are scheduled in short, 15-minute time slots in which the teacher is expected to "tell everything" about the child. Examine the ways that your school and district can reorganize the conference calendar to make it easier for fathers to be included in conferences. Some corporations and the branches of the military have instituted more father-friendly policies by giving fathers and mothers release time to participate in conferences and school activities. Many more employers will not give employees time off. Can conferences be rescheduled for early mornings, nights, and Saturdays rather than only during the school day? Can the traditional 15-minute time slot be lengthened to 30 minutes with the expectation that parents come to engage in conversation? Each and every parent deserves all of the time he or she needs during the parent-teacher conference.

Student-led conferences are alternate formats for conferences in which the child showcases his/her portfolio of work for parents. These are much more informative and richer opportunities for families than is the teacher "tell everything" style of conferencing. Why should you plan for student-led conferences? Student-led conferences:

- are child-centered; the focus is on what the child can do.
- include multiple forms of assessment to communicate student academic progress with the parents.
- provide a more holistic, complete picture of the child's learning.
- support families, children, and the process of learning.
- provide children an opportunity to evaluate their own learning.

For more information regarding student-led conferences see Figures 4–7 and 4–8.

Traditional Parent–Teacher Conference	Student-Led Conference
Before Conferences:	**Before Conferences:**
Teacher prepares the conference material to present to parents.	Students prepare and practice for conferencing with their own parents.
Students fear what the teacher may say to their parents about them.	Students are excited to showcase their learning to their parents.
Teacher reflects and reports on student learning.	Students reflect on and demonstrate their learning to their parents.
Schedule is set by building office hours in 15-minute time slots.	Schedule is set by teacher along with students in 30-45-minute time slots.
During Conferences:	**During Conferences:**
Teacher initiates the conference.	Students initiate the conference.
One conference occurs at a time.	Multiple conferences occur at one time.
Teacher controls the conference.	Students lead the conference.
Teacher "tells everything" without student input, little dialogue with parents.	Teacher talks with parents before, during, or after students have led the conference.
After Conferences:	**After Conferences:**
Parents and teacher reflect on student's learning and progress.	Student, parents, and teacher reflect together on student's learning and progress.
Teacher and/or parents set goals for the student's learning.	Students set their own goals for improvement with the teacher and parents.

FIGURE 4–7   Comparisons of Traditional Parent–Teacher and Student-Led Conferences.

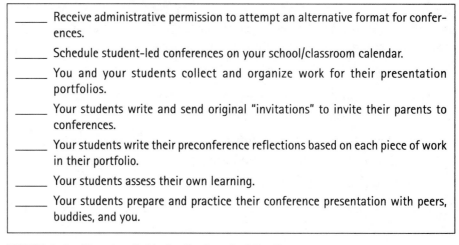

_____ Receive administrative permission to attempt an alternative format for conferences.

_____ Schedule student-led conferences on your school/classroom calendar.

_____ You and your students collect and organize work for their presentation portfolios.

_____ Your students write and send original "invitations" to invite their parents to conferences.

_____ Your students write their preconference reflections based on each piece of work in their portfolio.

_____ Your students assess their own learning.

_____ Your students prepare and practice their conference presentation with peers, buddies, and you.

FIGURE 4–8   Planning Guide for Student-Led Conferences.

Communicating with Fathers and Male Role Models

Teachers are communicators! It is part and parcel of our profession that we must find many different ways to communicate with a range of audiences. Fathers and male role models are one important audience that you must purposefully plan to address. (See Figure 4–9.) How can you specifically plan to communicate with the men that are in the lives of your students? You can begin the school year by surveying the fathers and male role models. Figure 4–10 is a general-interest survey to help you begin to understand the families and family arrangements of your students. Review the policies and practices for sending materials home in your school and district. Do forms and enrollment papers allow space for information about fathers, their place of work, their work schedules, and their contact information? If the father is not in the home, make the effort to create duplicates of all materials to be mailed to him. You must be certain that the school office also has contact information for these fathers and that the office is sending duplicate announcements and newsletters to their address as well. Duplicate copies of some documents for noncustodial parents may require deleting addresses and phone numbers. Be sure to check on these sensitive legal issues with your building administrator.

Phone calls can be a simple way to increase family involvement in your classroom. Plan to contact fathers by phone on a regular basis to make positive reports about their children. Many fathers will be unable to meet with you during the regular school day but will be able to accept a phone call from you. Your flexibility in scheduling will go a long way toward involving fathers in the education of your students. As with scheduling conferences,

FAMILIES IN FOCUS

It was Open House. School would begin on Monday morning. Parents with children-in-tow and children with parents-in-tow visited the classroom for two hours. A man wandered in the door all by himself. He quietly introduced himself as the father of a child who would be coming into the classroom for the first time on Monday morning. He explained that he had been divorced from his daughter's mother for a while and lived in an apartment near the school so that he could remain active in the lives of his three children. Pain crossed the man's face as he asked for help in keeping in touch with school events. He asked for duplicate copies of school news, progress reports, and flyers to go to his address as well. "Of course" was the answer to his request.

The week that school began was a flurry of activity. The promise to send home duplicate materials for this father was forgotten. One afternoon as the bell rang and children spilled out of classroom doors, there stood this father waiting patiently on the breezeway to collect his three children. He was genuinely committed to staying involved with them. Their greetings with him were full of hugs, kisses, and proud displays of artwork and school papers. It renewed the teacher's resolve to do everything to help him father his children. After carefully reviewing the situation with the principal, duplicate copies of everything went to him so he had continuing information from the school through the year. He received a special invitation to accompany the class on a field trip visit to the wildlife preserve. He had specially scheduled conferences during parent-teacher conference week. And he received a VHS tape of the orchestra performance he missed because of his work schedule. The school year was turbulent and full of stress for his children. Their mother actively discouraged our inclusion of their dad in school activities. The children became the rope in an emotional tug-of-war between the two parents. Despite it all, their father remained a constant presence in their lives.

plan a morning for early appointments or drop-in visits from fathers. Or you may want to plan a Saturday for visits with fathers and significant males. We have seen teachers who have very successfully organized "Breakfast Club with Dad" mornings. They provide coffee and refreshments, organize activities for father and child, and plan a brief classroom update for dads. You can plan a similar time for fathers during the school week, on Saturdays, or in the evenings. Be sure to advertise these special events in your weekly newsletter and tell fathers in your regular phone calls of their availability. Figures 4–11 through 4–13 are included as a model for planning and organizing a special family meeting with fathers in your classroom.

FIGURE 4–9   Fathers and male role models are an important audience that must purposefully be addressed.

Introduction to the Workshop

Use this opportunity to do a brief review of upcoming school and classroom events. Explain to dads and their children that books written by children help them to see the connection between spoken and written words. The children will create their own books along with their dads based on photos taken of them since birth. Children are very interested in stories of when they were babies. Sharing these stories to create the child-authored book will connect fathers with their children. The attitudes that young children hold toward books and learning are greatly influenced by what they see modeled at home. Encourage dads to Read! Read! Read! with their children. Give fathers the fact sheet on Literacy Development at Home (Figure 4–14). Refer to Chapter 6, Family Involvement at Home, for other ideas.

An Accordion Book

MATERIALS

   markers

   scissors

   glue

Name_____

Address (if different from child's)_____

Street Address

_____
City　　　　　　　　　　　State　　　　　　　　　Zip Code

Telephone_____(home)_____(work)

E-mail address_____

Is there any information you would like me to know?_____

_____

What special expertise or career backgrounds do you have to share with the school?

_____

How are you interested in volunteering at our school?

☐　　governance, site council
☐　　classroom volunteer
☐　　construction and maintenance

What kinds of fathering information are you interested in receiving?

☐　　lending library of resources
☐　　seminars, workshops, courses
☐　　Internet, Web resources for home study

FIGURE 4–10　Back to School Survey for Fathers, Friends, and Involved Others.

construction paper

index cards

WHAT TO DO

1. Fold a sheet of 8 1/2 × 11 construction paper the long way (hotdog style). Cut in half along the fold line.
2. Tape the two ends together to form one long strip of paper.
3. Fan fold like an accordion into eight sections.
4. Glue an index card on the first folded section and the last folded section to form "book covers."
5. Use the markers to print a title on the book.
6. Start with newborn photos of your child and sequence his or her growth with photos from birth to the present day. Together, write the story text to accompany each photo as dad recollects the events and special moments represented by each photo. The book will show the growth of the child from infancy and tell the child his/her

> You are Invited!!
>
> Date_____
> Time_____
> Place_____
>
> Fun! Tasty! Nutritious! Informative! Come have breakfast together.
> Who's Invited: You and your child. Bring photos of your child from infancy to present day!!
> What to Bring: Contribute your favorite _____.
> Please complete and detach the form below by _____
>
> ....
>
> _____Yes, we will attend Breakfast with Dad.
> _____Sorry, we won't be able to attend Breakfast with Dad.
>
> Child's name_____
> If you have questions about this meeting, please call _____
> Name_____
> Phone_____E-mail Address_____

FIGURE 4–11   Invitation to Breakfast Club with Dad.

> You are Invited!!
>
> Date_____
> Time_____
> Place_____
>
> Fun! Tasty! Nutritious! Informative! Come have breakfast together.
> Who's Invited: You and your child. Bring photos of your child from infancy to present day!!
> What to Bring: Contribute your favorite _____.
> If you haven't made your reservation yet, call _____.

FIGURE 4–12   Reminder Note of Breakfast Club with Dad.

own special story. If photos are not available to the father, have the two write out text to describe special events such as birthdays, vacation trips, and holidays.

7. As fathers work with their children, circulate and discuss the child's progress very informally.

Closure

Thank everyone for coming to the Breakfast Club. Tell them again how valuable they are to the healthy development and academic achievement of their children. Make yourself available for personal appointments later.

Purpose

To provide fathers with practical information and opportunities to interact with just their own child.

Note: Be aware of food allergies some children in your classroom may have. Wheat, milk and milk products, highly acidic juices, chocolate, eggs, and nuts are common foods that create allergic reactions in some children. Be sure to ask fathers if there are known allergies to foods or food restrictions before you share breakfast.

Advance Preparation

- Enlarge a piece of student artwork, a photo, or other similar item.
- Glue onto poster board. Cut into several puzzle pieces. Mix pieces up in a basket or box.

Nametags

Materials

- construction paper
- masking tape
- pencils
- patterns for nametag
- markers

Make nametags for each Breakfast Club member.

Mixer

- As fathers and children arrive, ask each to write his or her name on a tag.
- Use masking tape to attach the nametag to clothing.
- Pass the basket around and have each father take one puzzle piece. Be certain that there are enough puzzle pieces for each dad to take a piece.
- Say "Each father has a puzzle piece. Please find others with the matching pieces to assemble the picture. Fit the pieces together and introduce yourself!"

FIGURE 4–13   Plan for Breakfast with Dad.

Teachers can play a critical role in providing fathers with information about positive fathering and involvement in their children's education. Newsletters from the school and from your classroom can provide fathers with invaluable information about parenting skills. Columns contributed by male faculty members for fathers or by other fathers for fathers will more likely be read and used. Newsletters can also inform fathers of current organizations and initiatives to support fathering. Some of these helpful organizations include:

- The National Center on Fathering (1998) is a nonprofit organization, founded in 1990, that focuses on research and education

Children develop literacy skills through life experiences. This refers not only to interactions with books, but also by observing the literacy behaviors of others and being praised and motivated by family members for mimicking literacy behaviors.

Research identifies similarities in the home environments of children who read early:

- Lots of books in the home
- Siblings who act as teachers and models
- Positive adult/child interactions
- Parents who show interest in the child's experiences
- Frequent trips taken to the library
- Library corners in the home set up with numerous children's books
- Reading with parents and siblings
- Opportunities, access to writing materials

You Can:

- Read! Read! Read! daily with your child.
- Go to the library and select books together
- Read aloud to your children
- Read and draw with your children
- Read and dialogue with your children
- Read and perform the story
- Encourage your children to make lists
- Give your children writing materials as they play

FIGURE 4–14   Encouraging Literacy Development at Home.

related to fathering. The organization offers seminars, books, and a Web site; publishes a newsletter entitled *Today's Fathers*; and sponsors a biannual Father of the Year Essay Contest. And there is a strong emphasis on instructing fathers in fathering skills and on "turning the hearts of fathers back to their children."

- The National Fatherhood Initiative (1998) is a nonprofit organization, founded in 1994, that is aimed at improving children's lives. This initiative sponsors a clearinghouse and resource center, includes 2,000+ groups across the country in its resource directory, and offers a newsletter entitled *Fatherhood Today*. The organization sponsors an annual conference and has initiated an advertising campaign focusing on the importance of fathering in our society.

- The Center on Fathers, Families and Public Policy (CFFPP, 1998) is a training, technical assistance, and public education organization aimed at helping to create a society in which parents—both mothers and fathers—can support their children physically, emotionally, and financially. The organization challenges the negative public perception of low-income fathers. CFFPP publishes a newsletter entitled *Issues and Insights* and has also published other materials, including an extensive "Curriculum for Young Fathers" and "A Report on Low-Income Fathers and Their Experience with Child Support Enforcement."

Electronic communication is a marvel of technology that can help you to keep in touch with both parents! Creating a listserv of all your parents and a school Web site make communication of general information with both parents quick and easy. If you create your weekly newsletter on the computer, you can simply "cut and paste" the document into an e-mail for all the parents on your listserv. Your listserv can include e-mail addresses for dads at work, family members, or for dads who are not in the home. Links to helpful Web sites can also be a regular part of your e-mail communication. E-mail communication will also allow you to communicate quickly and effectively with many fathers when personal, face-to-face communication is impossible. Again, you must plan to send regular, positive updates on their children. Make sure to report mostly "good stuff!"

Special occasions and school events are frequently missed by fathers who are unable to take time off from work. Technology is, again, a tremendous tool to keep men involved with their children. If taking time off for a special event is impossible, video recordings of musicals, band performances, sports events, and so on, can be copied very inexpensively to DVDs and given to fathers. This is an equally effective method to keep dads who are deployed with the military involved with their children and school. DVDs can also be sent electronically to fathers. If you do not have the hardware capacity to do this, multiple copies of videotapes can be made at minimal cost. Technology can be indispensable as you keep the fathers of your students involved in your classroom.

Information Groups for Men

You can lobby your school counselor to become involved in your effort to increase the involvement of fathers in school. The counselor can organize and host a school-wide "informational" meeting for divorced fathers, whether they are the custodial or noncustodial parent. These groups must focus on information rather than "therapy" to be most successful. The kinds of information that divorced fathers most need from teachers and school counselors include:

- Educational and inexpensive activities for him and the children to enjoy together during scheduled visitation times; for example names, locations, and hours of libraries, museums, field trips, zoos (see Figure 4–15)
- Educational vacations and outings for extended visitation times
- Booklists of books to read together or for fathers to read aloud (see Figure 4–16)
- Educational toy and puzzle suggestions for fathers to buy with their children
- How to praise children for daily accomplishments they have in school (see Figure 4–17)
- How to understand, value, and put the child's needs first
- How to maintain open communication with the mother of his children
- How to listen, to admit mistakes, and to find better ways of fathering their children

Including Male Role Models in the Classroom

It is a heartbreaking reality that many fathers will consciously choose to be absent from the lives of their children. They may be physically absent and/or emotionally absent. Some fathers will be physically absent for reasons other than divorce. Military service can keep fathers away from home for as much as 18 months to 2 years during a deployment. Some professions demand that fathers travel for long periods of time. Incarceration can mean both a physical and emotional absence in fathering. The emotionally absent father may very well be in the home but take no interest in his children, and he may never connect with them emotionally.

You can help children with absent fathers by working to include male role models into your day-to-day classroom activities. As you think about bringing male volunteers into your classroom, think creatively about the resources and people in your community. We have looked closely at ways to include parents into the classroom. Who are the men that you might enlist to be regular volunteers in your room?

Museums	Location	Hours	Fees, Special Details

Libraries	Location	Hours	Children's Story Hour, Special Details

Zoos	Location	Hours	Fees, Special Details

Parks	Location	Hours	Fees, Special Attractions

Musical Events	Location	Dates	Fees, Special Details

Other Events	Location	Hours	Fees, Special Details

FIGURE 4–15 Worksheet for Local Activities in Your Area.

The Table Where Rich People Sit, by Byrd Baylor (Simon & Schuster, 1994; ISBN 0-684-19653-0). The storyteller tries to figure out just how rich her unconventional family is. The book is visually engaging. You and your children may want to start listing things you and your family value.

Yonder, by Tony Johnston (Dial, 1988; ISBN 0-8037-0277-9). This story looks at the traditions of family handed down by each generation as they plant a tree to memorialize each family member's birth and death.

Island Boy, by Barbara Cooney (Viking, 1988; ISBN 0-670-81749-X). Rich illustrations help tell a family history on an island off the coast of Maine.

The Relatives Came, by Cynthia Rylant (Simon & Schuster, 1985; ISBN 0-02 777220-9). An outrageously funny family celebration in an overpopulated house make up this picture book. The extended family enjoys each others' company for days.

Bigmama's, by Donald Crews (Greenwillow, 1991; ISBN 0-688-09950-5). This is a tale of an African-American family traveling by train to a reunion at their grandmother's home.

Mama Is a Miner, by George Ella Lyon (Orchard, 1994; ISBN 0-531-06853-6). Mother's workday in a mine is compared with her daughter's day up on top. A great discussion starter for unconventional female roles.

Owl Moon, by Jane Yolen (Putnam, 1987; ISBN 0-399-21457-7). A lovely father/child experience as the two bundle up in winter to go "owling." A starting point for your own father/child rituals and traditions.

Charlie Anderson, by Barbara Abercrombe (Simon, 1990; ISBN 0-689-50486-1). Two sisters adopt a cat that shows up each night on their doorstep at dinnertime. On weekends, the girls visit their father in the city. They find out that the cat has two homes and two families who love it just as they do! Excellent story to discuss visitation and separate residence issues.

Boundless Grace, by Mary Hoffman (Dial, 1995; ISBN 0-8037-1715-6). Grace longs to be part of a real family and is torn once she meets her father in Africa. If children feel that their unconventional family is not a real family, this book will help to discuss this.

Amazing Grace, by Mary Hoffman (Dial, 1991; ISBN 0-8037-1040-2). Grace lives with her mom and grandmother and imagines herself in many roles. A wonderful picture book to illustrate that unconventional families don't restrict children in their hopes and dreams.

Mountain Wedding, by Faye Gibbons (Morrow, 1996; ISBN 0-688-11348-6). Two large families try to meld and there's confusion and merriment all around with the 12 children, horses, and guests. Excellent start to understanding blended families.

Amelia Bedelia's Family Album, by Peggy Parish, illustrated by Lynn Sweat (Greenwillow, 1988; ISBN 0-688-07677-7). Amelia's boss' family wants to have a party with all of her relatives invited. So Amelia gets out her family album. This book is as full of language play as are all the other Amelia books.

Working Cotton, by Shirley Anne Williams (Harcourt, 1992; ISBN 0-15-299624-9). An entire family works at picking cotton in this story.

FIGURE 4–16   Brief Reading List for Fathers on Family Issues (*Continues*).

The Pinballs, by Betsy Byars (HarperCollins, 1977; ISBN 0-06-020917-8). This deserves its place as one of the favorite books for fifth and sixth graders. The dysfunctional homes the story characters come from may start your own discussion of families in need of repair.

Bobby Baseball, by Robert Kimmel Smith (Delacorte, 1989; ISBN 0-385-29807-2). This is a nice exploration of a father-son relationship which is weightier than the title suggests.

A Question of Trust, by Marion Dane Bauer (Scholastic, 1994; ISBN 0-590-47915-6). Mom has moved out and the kids are furious. Their father withdraws emotionally from them when they need him most and their mother appears not to care.

From the Notebooks of Melanin Sun, (Scholastic, 1995; ISBN 0-590-45880-9). Melanin Sun's mother, after years of being single, is now in love with a woman. A useful way to begin dialogue with children about same-sex partnerships.

The Rain Catchers, by Jean Thesman (Houghton, 1991; ISBN 0-395-55333-4). Gray is surrounded by women in her grandmother's house. This house is a retreat of safety and sanity from which the extended family gains strength.

Haymeadow, by Gary Paulsen (Dell, 1994; ISBN 0-440-40923-3). In a place devoid of family, the main character comes to understand himself, his father, and his grandfather.

The Barn, by Avi (Orchard, 1994; ISBN 0-531-06861-7). This is about fathers and sons and obsessions.

Looking Back: A Book of Memories, by Lois Lowry (Delacorte, 2000; ISBN 0385326998). A photo memoir of Lowry's family. This award-winning author will inspire your own family storytelling.

The Keeping Quilt, by Patricia Polacco. (Simon & Schuster, 1988; ISBN 0671649639). This wonderful picture book centers on a quilt passed from generation to generation in Polacco's Russian Jewish family. She describes how the quilt binds together generations of stories.

When I Was Young in the Mountains, by Cynthia Rylant and Diane Goode (Dutton, 1992; ISBN 0140548750). The author's memories of growing up in the Appalachian mountains. This beautifully illustrated, patterned, predictable story will inspire your own family memories.

Song and Dance Man, by Karen Ackerman and Stephen Gammell (Knopf, 1992; ISBN 0679819959). Grandpa looks back at his life and careers.

FIGURE 4–16 (*Continued*).

- Are there other male teachers or male staff members on your campus that could become a regular visitor to your classroom? Consider the male staff members in your district offices and at other schools in the district. Secondary schools have a much higher ratio of male teachers than do elementary or primary schools.

- Is there a retirement community or assisted living community in your school district? Retired men are frequently willing to "grandfather" young children.

		You've discovered the secret	Fun
Wow	Hurray for you	You Figured it out	You're growing up
Way to Go	You're right on target	Fantastic	You tried hard
Super job	You're on your way	Hip Hip Hooray	You Care
You are so special	How nice	Bingo	Wonderful sharing
Outstanding Work	How smart		Outstanding performance
Excellent	Good Work	Magnificent	You're a good friend
Great	That's incredible	Marvelous	I trust you to . . .
Good	Hot Dog	Terrific	
Neat Work	Dynamite	You're very important	You're special
Well Done	You're beautiful	Phenomenal	You mean so much
Remarkable	Very Unique	You're sensational	You make me happy
I knew you could	Nothing can stop you	Super Work	You make me laugh
I'm proud of you	Good for you	Creative thinking	You belong here
Fantastic	I like your . . .	Super ideas	You're my friend
Star Effort	You're a winner	Excellent thoughts	You brighten my day
Nice job of . . .	Remarkable effort at . . .	Exceptional performance	I respect you for . . .
Looking Good	Beautiful job of . . .	You're a trooper	You are my world
You're on top of it	Spectacular	You're responsible	Correct A-OK
Beautiful	You're spectacular	Very Exciting	You're a joy
Now you've got it	Darling	You understood it correctly	A+
You're catching on	Precious	What an imagination	You're a treasure
Bravo	Great discovery	Great listening	Awesome

FIGURE 4–17   90 Ways to Praise Your Child for Schoolwork.

- Does your community have a Big Brother agency? Contact the agency to find men who might be willing to volunteer in your classroom.
- Recruit classroom volunteers from the city service departments of your community. Police departments, fire departments, and health workers are often encouraged to contribute volunteer hours and there may be men in these departments who are perfect candidates.
- Recruit classroom volunteers from large corporations that encourage and provide release time for volunteerism.

Of course, great care and caution must be used in recruiting men to be volunteer workers in the schools. Appropriate **criminal background checks** and **fingerprint clearance** are ways to ensure that your male classroom helpers are safe, reliable volunteers who will do no harm. As with any parent helper, clear directions and complete training to relate to young children will be necessary. You may want to refer back to Chapter 5 as you prepare for male volunteers in your classroom. But you are the professional and must be present with your students at all times. Male volunteers in your classroom should not take on your teaching responsibilities, recess duties, or be left in your classroom with students when you are not there. Diligence on your part will go far in preventing any questions or issues from arising later on.

■ CONCLUSION

Family involvement is any activity that empowers parents and families to participate in the educational process. Father involvement empowers fathers in particular to participate in the education of their children. Educating young children is a shared responsibility between parents, teachers, and schools. Increasing father involvement will positively impact the development of the child while improving academic achievement and school climate.

Establishing a bridge to involve fathers in the classroom requires that you challenge myths and assumptions about men in the schools. Teachers must plan for personal connections with fathers and male role models, and they must purposefully prepare for their participation in the classroom. Schools must be dad-friendly places that welcome and value their contributions. Fathers contribute invaluable time, skills, and experience to the school.

■ SUMMARY OF IMPORTANT POINTS

- Research reaffirms the importance of father involvement in a child's development and academic achievement.
- Myths and assumptions about men in schools discourage father involvement.
- Purposeful planning for fathers and male role models in the classroom will increase father involvement.
- Communication is important to encourage father involvement in your classroom.
- Policies and the school climate must be kept dad-friendly to involve fathers in their children's education.

■ CHAPTER REVIEW QUESTIONS

1. How are fathers important to the school achievement of their children?

2. What are some of the modern myths and assumptions that discourage male involvement in education?

3. What are some of the barriers that prevent fathers from becoming involved in schools?

4. How can technology help you to involve fathers in your classroom?

5. Explain one strategy that will be useful when fathers do not have release time for special events.

6. Explain one communication strategy that will be useful when fathers cannot meet with you face-to-face.

■ APPLICATION AND REFLECTION

1. Reflect on your own attitudes and feelings about fathers. Engage in a small group discussion about the assumptions related to men in schools.

2. Making phone calls to fathers when face-to-face interactions are not possible is an important way to help establish communication. Plan the words you will say in your positive, encouraging phone calls to fathers. Share your ideas with a classmate.

3. Learn all that you can about the policies a local district regarding custody issue, distributing duplicate materials, and ways to involve parents not living in the child's primary home.

■ FURTHER READING

Crider, M. R. (2005). *The guy's guide to surviving pregnancy, childbirth and the first year of fatherhood.* Da Capo Lifelong Books.

McBride, B., & Lin, H. (1996). Parental involvement in Prekindergarten at risk programs: Multiple perspectives. *Journal of Education for Students Placed At-Risk.*

Poussaint, A. F., & Cosby, B. (1987). *Fatherhood.* Berkley Trade.

Pruett, K. D. (2000). *Fatherneed: Why father care is as essential as mother care for your child.* New York: The Free Press.

Snarey, J., & Vaillant, G .E. (1993). *How fathers care for the next generation.* Cambridge: Harvard University Press.

Shedlin, A. (January/February, 2004). Dad-friendly matters more than we see. *Principal, 83,* 23–25.

For additional information on research-based practice, visit our Web site at http://www.earlychilded. delmar.com.

Additional resources for this chapter can be found on the Online Companion™ to accompany this text at www.earlychilded.delmar.com. This supplemental material includes Web links, downloadable forms, and Case Studies with critical thinking applications. This content can be used as a study aid to reinforce key concepts presented in this chapter and to conduct additional research on topics of interest.

■ REFERENCES

Biller, H. (1993). *Father and families: Paternal factors in child development.* Westport, CT: Auburn House.

Bing, E. (1963). The effect of child-rearing practices on the development of differential cognitive abilities. *Child Development, 34,* 631–648.

Clinton, W. (1995, June 16). Supporting the role of fathers in families. Memorandum for the heads of executive departments and agencies. Washington, DC.

Cooksey, E., & Fondell, M. (1996). Spending time with his kids: Effects of family structure on fathers' and children's lives. *Journal of Marriage and the Family, 58*(3), 693–707.

De Luccie, M. F. (1995). Mothers as gatekeepers: A model of maternal mediators of father involvement. *The Journal of Genetic Psychology, 156*(1), 115–131.

Field, T. (1995). Adolescents from divorced and intact families. Journal of Divorce and Remarriage, *23*(3/4), 165–175.

Frieman, B., & Berkeley, T. (1998). What early childhood educators need to know about divorced fathers. *Early Childhood Education Journal, 25,* 239–241.

Frieman, B., & Berkeley, T. (2002). Encouraging fathers to participate in the school experiences of young children: The teacher's role. *Early Childhood Education Journal, 29*(3), 209–213.

Furstenberg, F. F. (1995). Dealing with dads: The changing roles of fathers. In P. L. Chase-Lansdale & J. Brooks-Gunn (Eds.), *Escape from poverty: What makes a difference for children?* New York: Cambridge University Press.

Hadadian, A., & Merbler, J. (1995). Parents of infants and toddlers with special needs: Sharing views of desired services. *Infant-Toddler Intervention, 5*(41), 141–152.

Henderson, A., & Berla, N. (Eds.) (1994). *A new generation of evidence the family is critical to student achievement.* Washington, DC: National Committee for Citizens in Education.

Krampe, E. M., & Fairweather, P. D. (December, 1993). Father presence and family formation: A theoretical reformulation. *Journal of Family Issues, 14*(4), 572–591.

Lamb, M. (1975). Fathers: The forgotten contributors to child development. *Human Development, 18*, 245–266.

Lamb, M. (Ed.). (1986). *The father's role: Applied perspectives, the changing roles of father.* New York: John Wiley & Sons, 3–27.

Markowitz, J. (1984). Participation of fathers in early childhood special education programs: An exploratory study. *Journal of the Division for Early Childhood, 8*(2), 119–131.

McBride, B., & Rane, T. (1996). Father/male involvement in early childhood programs, *Early Childhood Research & Practice, 25*(1), 11–15.

Nord, C. W., Brimhall, D., & West, J. (1997). Fathers' involvement in their children's schools (NCES 98-091). Washington, DC: U.S. Department of Education, National Center Educational Statistics.

Parish, T. and J. R. Necessary. "Parents' Actions: Are They Related to Children's Self-Concepts, Evaluations of Parents, and to Each Other?" Adolescence 29.116 (Winter 1994): 943–947.

Pruett, K. (2000). *Fatherneed: Why father care is as essential as mother care for your child.* New York: The Free Press.

Radin, N. (1983). Father-child interactions and the intellectual functioning of four-year-old boys. *Developmental Psychology, 6*, 353–361.

Turbiville, V., & Marquis, J. (2001). Father participation in early childhood education programs. *Topics in Early childhood Special Education, 21*(4), 223–241.

U.S. Department of Education (1994). *Strong families, strong schools: Building community partnerships for learning.* Washington, DC: Author.

Yeung, W. J., Sandberg, J. F., Davis-Kean, P. E., & Hofferth, S. (1999). Children's time with fathers in intact families. *University of Michigan.*

Yogman, M., Kindlon, D., & Earls, F. (1995). Father involvement and cognitive/behavioral outcomes of preterm infants. *Journal of the American Academy of Child and Adolescent Psychiatry, 34*(1), 58–66.

5

Creating Partnerships at School in the Early Years

■ **CHAPTER OBJECTIVES** _____

After reading and reflecting on this chapter, you should be able to:

- Discuss different family involvement programs teachers have implemented.
- Describe methods of regular communication with parents.
- Plan for making personal connections with parents.
- Plan the elements of a Back-to-School night.
- Create a presentation, providing information for parents.
- Understand the importance of communication through a weekly newsletter.
- Understand key components of communicating one-on-one with parents.
- Create and define a list of parent jobs in the classroom.
- Define important information to assist in training parent helpers.
- Understand the importance of expressing appreciation to parents.

■ KEY TERMS _____

Back-to-School night   parent jobs

parent communication

PLANNING FOR FAMILY INVOLVEMENT

Now that we've discussed the benefits and challenges of family involvement, it's time to begin planning for family involvement in the classroom. This chapter will describe practices used by teachers to encourage
family involvement. It will also address effective strategies for creating
partnerships with parents and ways to develop regular communication;
and strategies for providing opportunities for parents to help out in the
classroom, planning for parent help, and scheduling parent helpers.
Planning in these areas must be strategic in order for your program to be
successful.

Schools typically provide a variety of ways for parents to be involved,
such as activities to educate parents, communication between school and
home, and opportunities to volunteer (Jones, 2001). While school-wide
programs will be described later in this book, there are many things that
teachers have done over the years to build partnerships.

Davern (2004), whose responsibility it was to consult with parents of
children with disabilities, reports of the use of daily communication notebooks. These notebooks served the following purposes:

1. to provide an awareness of the child's day
2. to elicit information from home
3. to provide information about the child's active participation
4. to share information with parents about projects and events
5. to offer activity/homework ideas for parents and children at
home
6. to share health concerns
7. to report progress

Davern states, "The importance of seeking parents' perspectives on educational practices is of great benefit when designing and implementing programs for children with disabilities" (p. 22). Not only did she use this method
of regular communication, but she interviewed parents about their perceptions of the effectiveness of the daily communication notebook. Overall, she
found that parents liked this form of communication, but offered a few

suggestions. Parents wanted balanced messages, reporting areas of concern along with good news. They felt that some concerns needed to be addressed in person rather than in writing and they also wanted teachers to avoid the use of educational jargon.

Davern sees the communication notebook as one way to connect with parents, but she also suggests that teachers seek out parents to determine which form of communication they would prefer.

Moore (2002) suggests the following activities to encourage open communication between parents and teachers:

1. Begin a parent committee with the expressed purpose of addressing communication issues.
2. Survey parents, asking for suggestions for improving communication.
3. Send home a newsletter reporting special events and weekly activities.
4. Periodically send home personalized notes about children's accomplishments.

Sheryl Orman (1993) reports the use of school-to-home math backpacks as a way to connect with parents. Each backpack she created contained markers, pencils, paper and other necessary mathematics supplies, an inventory of supplies, an informational letter to parents, and a journal. Children took turns taking the backpacks home and were permitted to keep them for a few days. The purpose was for parents and children to work together to complete a math-related activity and then report their experiences in the journal. Orman explains that the use of these backpack activities helps connect parents with school activities and provides them with engaging and interactive experiences with their children.

Eldridge (2001) suggests that the basics of interacting with parents should cover several key components, including the use of regular communication, guidance for how to help children at home, and sensitivity toward each family's uniqueness. Eldridge also mentions the need to tailor involvement around the child's specific needs and to offer parents a variety of ways to participate. Gage and Workman (1994, p. 77) add, "Our understanding of parent involvement needs to be on a continuum that allows for parent participation on a variety of levels and through a wide variety of activities." There are many ways to communicate with and involve the parents of your children. The remainder of this chapter will focus on specific ways to develop and maintain effective partnerships with the parents of children in your charge.

FIRST IMPRESSIONS

Creating a welcoming classroom environment is the first thing you can do to set the stage for parents to feel comfortable and welcomed as they enter your classroom. (See Figure 5–1.) Decorate your room in a way that communicates that you are happy that students and parents will be a part of your classroom. Prepare the walls with decorations, but be careful not to clutter the walls. "A cluttered, disorganized, or dismal classroom certainly does little to encourage communication between parents and teachers" (Swick, 2003). Your room should not look too busy and should have enough open space on the walls to display students' projects. Store away materials in cabinets or on shelves in a neat and organized way. If previous teachers have left materials behind, neatly store the materials you think you will use and give away the rest. (If materials left behind are not the property of the school, consider giving them away to students.) Label seating areas with students' names, so parents can immediately sense that you are ready for their children.

FIGURE 5–1   Creating a welcoming classroom environment is the first thing you can do to set the stage for parents to feel comfortable in your classroom.

Remember that parents will develop their first impressions of you as they enter your classroom. Dress professionally and wear a smile that conveys that you're happy they're here. Take time to greet each parent personally. Make eye contact as you speak to parents and try to appear as relaxed and comfortable as you can. Also, "we need to know the rules of the culture so to speak or at least be responsive about how our gestures and eye contact are impacting the communication with parents" (Swick, 2003). These small gestures will help set parents at ease and will go a long way in developing positive relationships.

COMMUNICATION

As mentioned in the introduction of this book, the best way to begin a family involvement program is to focus on communication. Communication between school and home is the very foundation of a program's success (Moore, 2002). There are many ways to have regular communication and the more teachers make the effort to connect with parents, the stronger the partnership will be.

Making Personal Connections

At the beginning of the school year, parents are often nervous about having a new teacher for their children. Recognizing this, it is important to provide information to parents about who you are. Providing a letter telling about yourself is a great way to begin. A letter of this kind helps parents to realize that you are a real person with a family, hobbies, hopes, and dreams. Parents will likely realize that they have things in common with you and will talk to you about these commonalities. To create a letter of this kind for yourself, address the following questions:

- Where did you grow up?
- Where did you go to school?
- Who are the members of your family?
- What pets do you have?
- What are your hobbies?
- Where have you traveled?
- Why did you decide to become a teacher?
- What do you love about teaching?

- What are your goals?
- What is your favorite book?
- What is your most exciting experience?
- What are your hopes for students in the coming year?

Try drafting a letter about yourself at this time. On the lines below, list other topics you would like to cover in this letter. When you're ready to write your letter, you can use the template that has been provided in Figure 5–2.

Letter topics:

_____
_____
_____
_____
_____
_____
_____

Dear Parent,

_____
_____
_____
_____
_____
_____
_____
_____
_____
_____
_____
_____
_____
_____

Sincerely,

_____

FIGURE 5–2   About Your Child's Teacher.

Back-to-School Night

If your school has a Back-to-School or Meet-the-Teacher night, you'll have a great opportunity to make those first connections with parents. If your school doesn't have this kind of event, you may want to consider having one of your own and inviting parents to visit your classroom before the school year begins or within the first few weeks. First impressions are very important, so this is your chance to make parents feel welcome and provide them with the information they'll need as the school year begins.

Prepare for this event by sending invitations or making personal phone calls to invite parents to attend. Have a copy of your "about me" letter ready to give to parents. You'll also want to have a letter printed out that provides information about your routines and expectations. Use the following list of questions to guide your preparations.

1. Will students need special materials?
2. Are there materials you would like parents to donate?
3. Will students need to bring snacks to school?
4. Can students bring water bottles to school?
5. What is your general behavior plan?
6. What time does the school day begin and end?
7. Where will parents drop off and pick up their children?
8. What is the system for children who ride the bus?

Having a printed information sheet for parents that addresses some of these questions often eases parents' minds and lets them know that you are aware of their concerns. Be sure to create an inviting environment for parents' first visit to your classroom. While it is recommended that children's work "decorate" the walls of the classroom, it is important to have the room tastefully decorated before the first day of school. Create a "welcome back" bulletin board, label desks or tables, cubbies, and coat hooks with students' names. Give your classroom a "lived-in" feel, so parents get the idea that you have prepared for the arrival of their children.

Supplies

Parents often want to know what supplies their children will need for the beginning of the school year. Many school districts have policies that do not allow teachers to require families to provide supplies, so be sure you check with your school before preparing such a list for parents. If supply lists are not allowed in your district or if you choose not to use them, you might consider creating a list of supplies that parents are free to donate, should they so choose. This can be done in the form of a "donations table." On the table place several index cards, each labeled with a different supply item, such as pencils, markers, hand sanitizer, facial tissue, paper towels, glue, crayons, and so on. A sign beside the table reads, "Would you like to donate? Take a card or two and bring the items to class within the first two weeks." This allows parents to donate if they have the desire and the means to do so, yet takes pressure off families who are not in a position to do so.

Presentation

For your back-to-school event, prepare a short presentation for the parents in order to introduce yourself, review some of your classroom routines, and explain the handouts you have provided. Be sure to communicate the value of parents in their children's education and let them know that they will have opportunities throughout the year to visit and help out in the classroom and at home. Let them know that family involvement is a priority for you and you will communicate regularly with them through weekly newsletters, phone calls, notes, and conferences. During this presentation, let parents know that you will be available to meet with them through private appointments if they have special concerns or if their children have special considerations that you need to know about right away. Invite parents to write down these concerns and considerations that night so you can contact them for private appointments. (See Figure 5–3 for a form to use for this purpose.)

Creating the Presentation

The presentation at **Back-to-School night** is the first opportunity you'll have to make a great first impression. This means that you'll want to convey to parents that you're professional, knowledgeable, prepared, and that their children are in good hands. You can do this by creating a presentation that provides useful information in a professional manner. Use the following questions to guide the creation of your presentation. A Presentation Planner (Figure 5–4) has been provided, as well, to assist you in creating visual aids for the presentation. Questions to consider include:

1. What is your philosophy of early education?
2. What is your philosophy of classroom management?
3. What routines will you have in place in your classroom?

Child's name:

_____

Parent name:

_____

Phone number:

_____

Questions or concerns about my child:

_____
_____
_____
_____
_____
_____
_____

Would you like to schedule an appointment? _____
Would you prefer a telephone appointment? _____
Days and times available: _____

FIGURE 5–3   Special Considerations.

Use this planning sheet to help you brainstorm information you want to provide in a presentation to parents.
Information about philosophy, classroom management, and routines:

_____
_____
_____

Information about the first day of school:

_____
_____
_____

Information about parent/teacher communication:

_____
_____
_____

Information about the value of family involvement at school and at home:

_____
_____

FIGURE 5–4   Presentation Planner.

4. Where should the children go when they arrive on campus?
5. Where will parents meet their children after school?
6. What is the routine for children who ride the bus?
7. What is the schedule for the school day?
8. How will you communicate with parents?
9. How can parents help out at school?
10. What can parents do at home to assist their children?

Visual Aids

You should plan to have visual aids that will help parents to follow along with you as you present information. These visuals can be electronically created or created by hand. The information below serves as a guide to assist you with your visual presentation.

Electronic Visuals

Computer programs, such as Microsoft PowerPoint, are great for creating presentations. PowerPoint, in particular, provides slide templates that can be used to insert information for parents on a variety of topics. As you explore the program, you'll find that you have options for slide format and background graphics. Remember, though, that you don't want to present too much information on a slide. The rule of thumb is to place no more than six lines on a slide with no more than six words per line. The slide should serve as a guide to follow as you present. Plan to speak casually with the parents, rather than reading from the slide.

Overhead Transparencies

If you don't have access to a machine to project from your computer screen, you can still use computer-generated slides for your presentation.

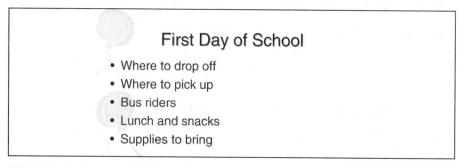

FIGURE 5–5   Computer programs, such as Microsoft PowerPoint, are great for creating presentations.

Simply create your slides and print them out on overhead transparencies. These can be equally as effective as projecting slides from your computer. Should you decide not to create overhead transparencies without the use of a computer slideshow program, remember to create them in a viewer-friendly format. Use the same rule of thumb (six lines/six words per line). If you place too much text on a transparency, it will be difficult for parents to read. If you need to provide parents with detailed information, consider creating handouts that they can take home to read.

Posters

You might decide to create visual aids by hand. These, like computer slideshows and overhead transparencies, can be created in a professional manner as well. Be sure that the text on your poster is large enough for easy viewing. Also, be sure to use a dark marker and write neatly. You might also consider typing the text using a word-processing program, enlarge the text, and print. Then cut and paste the text to your poster. Adding attractive graphics or clip art will also create visual appeal.

Be sure to allow time for a question/answer session at the end of your presentation. You might want to provide note cards to parents for writing down questions that pertain specifically to their own children, rather than to all children in the class. This allows you to address specific concerns privately, at a more appropriate time. Should a parent ask a question involving a detailed answer, such as "What will you do to challenge my child in reading," express your willingness to address this question in a meeting at a date in the near future and schedule the appointment before the parent leaves that evening. Parents should leave this event with the feeling that their children are in good hands and that you are not only prepared to teach their children, but that you have also taken the time to gather the information they will need in order to support their children at the beginning of a new school year.

Weekly Newsletters

The thought of sending a weekly newsletter can seem somewhat overwhelming. You may be afraid to make the commitment for fear that you will not keep up with this form of regular communication. However, when you begin sending a weekly newsletter, you'll find that it is one of the best things you can do to stay connected with parents. For this reason, it is strongly recommended that you make the commitment to send a newsletter

---

FAMILIES IN FOCUS

The classroom was buzzing with excitement. Parents eagerly arrived to meet their children's new teacher. Forty or more parents and children packed the classroom. Mrs. Long, a former primary-grade teacher, arrived at Parent Night loaded with questions and concerns. As the teacher, Ms. Owens, chatted with her, pleasantly, she abruptly ended the formalities and said, "Now tell me about your philosophy of teaching reading." What a question! How could she do justice to this question on a night like tonight? Ms. Owens smiled, expressing her understanding of the importance of the question, and responded, "I'd love to talk to you about this, but I would like to have the chance to discuss this with you thoroughly. Can we meet next week after school one day?" She was satisfied with this answer. On the weekend, however, it occurred to Ms. Owens that this mother would fret until they had had this conversation, so she decided to call her. "Mrs. Long," the conversation began, "this is Allen's teacher. I know you won't be able to rest easy until you've had the chance to ask questions about my teaching strategies, so fire away!" They spent about half an hour talking about school, teaching, educational philosophies, and reading. They spent another hour on the phone simply talking about life. From that phone call on, this mother was one of Ms. Owens' biggest fans.

---

to parents each and every week. Some teachers like to send newsletters at the end of the week, telling what happened in the past five days. Others choose to send the letter at the beginning of the week to tell parents what is to come. Either way is fine, just be sure to communicate regularly. Your newsletter should have a standard format with which parents become familiar. Each week they know where to look in the newsletter for specific information, such as announcements, donations, homework suggestions, and classroom activities. Figure 5–6 provides a newsletter template divided into specific sections. You can use this template or create your own on the computer. Many word-processing programs have newsletter templates that you can use to create a customized newsletter that fits your individual style and communication needs. Figure 5–7 provides a sample newsletter to give you an idea of the kinds of information you can provide to parents. The easiest way to create a newsletter is to do it right after you have completed your lesson plans for the next week, and include information from the lesson plans. Then, print out the letter and it will be ready to send home the next Monday.

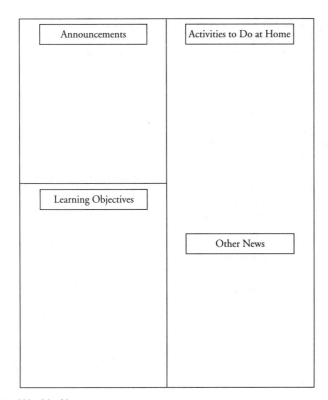

FIGURE 5–6   Weekly News.

Some teachers like to send a newsletter that is created by the children. This kind of letter is best when sent home at the end of the week; its purpose is to inform parents of weekly highlights rather than give logistical information. (See Figure 5–8 and the sample provided in Figure 5–9.) For this kind of newsletter, take a few minutes each day to ask students to suggest one or two important events from the day. Have students dictate to you what to write for that day. At the end of the week, the newsletter will be complete and you can duplicate copies of it and send it home to parents.

Why Not a Monthly Newsletter?

Some new teachers ask, "Why not send a monthly newsletter or just send one periodically?" This reasoning is understandable. Let's face it, as a teacher, one more thing to do each week can seem overwhelming. A monthly newsletter is not a bad idea, but it doesn't provide the consistency that most parents

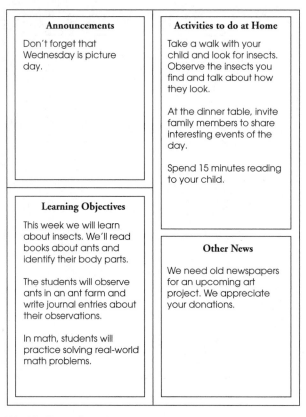

Announcements

Don't forget that Wednesday is picture day.

Activities to do at Home

Take a walk with your child and look for insects. Observe the insects you find and talk about how they look.

At the dinner table, invite family members to share interesting events of the day.

Spend 15 minutes reading to your child.

Learning Objectives

This week we will learn about insects. We'll read books about ants and identify their body parts.

The students will observe ants in an ant farm and write journal entries about their observations.

In math, students will practice solving real-world math problems.

Other News

We need old newspapers for an upcoming art project. We appreciate your donations.

FIGURE 5–7   Weekly News Sample.

desire. A weekly newsletter provides regular communication, and most importantly, gives parents something to look for each week. A newsletter sent less often is likely to be lost or forgotten. When parents know that the letter will be sent on a particular day each week, they are likely to look for it and count on it for updates about school events and classroom activities. My suggestion is to make a weekly newsletter a part of your routine. Just as you write lesson plans each week, make **parent communication** a part of your regular routine.

Parent Phone Calls

Making personal phone calls can be time-consuming, but can go a long way to develop strong parent-teacher partnerships. Try making a phone call to each parent within the first two weeks of school. This allows you to touch base with a parent before there are any problems to discuss.

Here's what happened in our class this week:

Monday:

_____

_____

_____

Tuesday:

_____

_____

_____

Wednesday:

_____

_____

_____

Thursday:

_____

_____

_____

Friday:

_____

_____

_____

FIGURE 5–8   Weekly Highlights.

Here's what happened in our class this week:

Monday:
Today we read a funny story. It was about a dog that wanted to be a bird. Kelly told us about her new puppy. We had fun in art class.

Tuesday:
We played with a big parachute in physical education class. It was hot outside, but we still had fun. We learned about solids and liquids in science.

Wednesday:
We learned a lot in computer class today. We learned how to import pictures. In reading, we learned about writing complete sentences.

Thursday:
Today we had an acting company visit our school. They performed a funny play. We decided that our class should perform a play, too.

Friday:
We did a fun experiment in science. We mixed vinegar and baking soda. It foamed up and went all over the place.

FIGURE 5–9   Weekly Highlights Sample.

FIGURE 5–10 One-on-one meetings with parents are the best times to make personal connections and build partnerships.

Simply tell the parent how much you enjoy having his or her child in your class and how you are looking forward to a great school year. Invite the parent to ask questions or address concerns. Parents appreciate these efforts and, if you should need to contact them to address behavior problems in the future, you'll find that they are more likely to be supportive of you.

ONE-ON-ONE WITH PARENTS

You'll often have opportunities to meet one-on-one with parents. These are the best times to make personal connections and build partnerships. (See Figure 5–10.) As you meet with parents, individually, whether in formal conference settings or casually before or after school, it is important to create feelings of acceptance, partnership, and trust; build confidence and show appreciation; be positive, and use active listening skills that show your value of them (Moore, 2002).

Developing Partnerships

The development of partnerships with parents need not be a covert operation. Let parents know up front that this is your goal and explain why it is important for teachers and parents to work together in order to benefit children. As you communicate with parents, continue to mention your goal of partnership (Cromer, 1997) and convey to them their value in the educational experiences of their children. You might even find it useful to survey parents about their interests. Invite them to share their concerns, and allow them to address issues related to their children and the school (Katz, 1995). Purposefully plan for opportunities to engage parents in activities with you to assist the children. Swick (1997) emphasizes the importance of collaborative parent-teacher activities as a means to empower early childhood programs. Working together is, perhaps, one of the best ways to strengthen communication (Swick et al., 1997).

Building Confidence and Fostering Appreciation

Parents often lack the confidence needed to fully engage in the educational process. For this reason, it is important to express parent value and provide guidance for how to participate. Begin by sharing your goals for each child and invite parents to share their wishes and goals for their children. "Support for each other's goals and efforts appears to empower everyone involved—including the children" (Cromer, 1997). Express to parents that you recognize the work they do with their children and what a valuable job it is. Noddings (1995) states, "Nurturance of each other creates an inviting and effective communicative relationship."

Active Listening

Couchenour and Chrisman (2000) express the importance of active listening and describe it as a process where the listener values and appreciates the other person's message. When speaking with a parent, try to listen carefully and hear what the parent is trying to communicate. Rather than jumping in to add your own thoughts, relay back to the parent the importance of his or her concern and converse *with* the parent about the concern.

Couchenour and Chrisman also mention the importance of reflecting when communicating with parents. They describe reflecting as a process of repeating back to the person what was just said. This allows you the chance to clarify your understanding of the parent's concern. They emphasize the teacher's use of a supportive and sincere tone and note that the process of reflecting empowers the relationship between parents and teachers.

Opening the Lines of Communication

Expressing the desire for communication is, perhaps, the best way to help parents feel comfortable with being open with you. Tell parents often that you value communication and that you are open to addressing their questions and concerns at any time. In addition to this, invite input from parents. Periodically, ask for feedback about a child's educational and social experience and make an effort to use this feedback as a means to improve your classroom practice. (See Figure 5–11.) Gonzalez-Mena (1994) emphasizes that feedback strengthens and enhances our lives and that parents even value feedback to assist in achieving goals for their children. Swick (1993) also mentions feedback as an essential component to successful parent-teacher partnerships.

PARENT-TEACHER CONFERENCES

When meeting with a parent for formal parent-teacher conferences, there are many strategies you can use to enhance the partnership. Begin by scheduling enough time for sharing information about the child's progress as well as allowing time for discussion and questions. Create a seating arrangement that is comfortable and engaging. Sitting behind your desk will create not only a physical barrier, but a barrier to comfortable and relationship-building communication. Prepare to share information that provides a "picture" of the child's progress. Show samples of the child's work and share personal stories of the child's interactions in the classroom and with other children. Rather than just reporting on the child's standing in comparison with other students, convey to the parent the overall progress of the child—where he or she started and the milestones reached along the way. Invite the parent to share the progress he or she has seen at home, both academically and socially, and allow the parent to share future goals for the child. Always allow time for the parent to address questions and concerns and make note of these in the parent's presence to show that you

FIGURE 5–11   Ask parents for feedback about their children's educational and social experiences and make efforts to use this feedback as a means to improve classroom practice.

value the parent's thoughts. Make time to touch base with the parent within the next few weeks and comment on the ways you have given thought to these concerns and how you have planned to address them. Your follow-up on these issues will express to the parent just how much you care about and value the issues of importance to them.

PARENTS IN THE CLASSROOM

With all of the responsibilities teachers have, parent workers in the classroom can be a great help. However, this can be stressful, as well, which is why planning for this kind of involvement is imperative. Waiting a few weeks to have parents in the classroom works very well. It gives you the chance to develop relationships and establish routines with your students. Just be sure to let parents know, from that first Back-to-School night, that you value their participation and that in a few weeks they will be free to help out in class.

Parent Jobs

There are many ways parents can help in the classroom. Prepare for this by creating a list of parent job descriptions. Before you read further about ideas for parent workers, think about the ways you might involve them in your classroom. Write your ideas on the lines below.

_____

_____

_____

_____

When planning for **parent jobs,** it is important to consider parents' comfort levels with different kinds of tasks. Some parents want to work with children. Some parents would prefer to complete tasks, such as using the copy machine, cutting out patterns for craft projects, or creating bulletin boards. Other parents can't come to class regularly and want the opportunity to participate periodically. Providing a variety of jobs to meet parents' needs is the best way to encourage participation by all parents. (See Figure 5–12.)

Below you'll find some sample job descriptions you may want to include.

Classroom Helper

This job involves coming to class on a weekly basis. As a classroom helper, your job is to work with children in the classroom. You might read to children, play games with small groups, assist children with projects, supervise learning center activities, and so on. Activities may vary, depending on whether you help in the morning or afternoon.

Preparation Helper

This job involves completing tasks for student activities. You will help me with a variety of tasks, such as using the copy machine, cutting out materials, creating bulletin boards, or setting up materials for learning centers or class projects.

FIGURE 5–12   Providing a variety of jobs to meet parents' needs is the best way to encourage participation by all parents.

Party Planners

We will have several parties during the school year. There are three different job responsibilities for planning parties.

PARTY ORGANIZER: The organizer for a party is the parent in charge. (There is only one parent in charge of each party.) It is your responsibility to organize the party, plan for parent helpers, plan decorations, call parents to ask for party donations, and so on.

PARTY HELPERS: Several parents can assist the party organizer. Your responsibility as a party helper is to assist with decorating, setting up food, supplies, and games for the party. You will also be at the party to assist the children in any way needed.

PARTY DONATORS: As a party donator, you will provide food and supplies for class parties. The party organizer will contact you about donations needed. You can be at the party, but it is not necessary for you to be there.

Guest Reader

As a guest reader, you will visit our classroom, periodically, to read to the children. The frequency of your visits will depend on the number of parents who volunteer for this job. If four parents volunteer, you will read to the children every four weeks. If 12 volunteer, you will come in once every 12 weeks. Your responsibility is to bring to class five or six picture books and spend about 30 minutes reading to the children.

Creativity Helper

Are you artistic? If so, this job is for you! The responsibility of the creativity helper is to create decorations, posters, and bulletin boards for the classroom. If you have ideas for children's craft projects, you can also facilitate such activities with the children from time to time. (See Figure 5–13.)

Chaperones

A few times during the school year, we will go on field trips. As a chaperone, you will be in charge of a small group of children. Because you will keep track of children while we're away from school, you should not bring other children along on the field trip. This is a popular job, so if too many parents sign up, we may have to have a drawing to choose the parents who can chaperone.

As you can see, there are many jobs that parents can perform. Remember that parents are there to help, rather than to take on your responsibilities as a teacher. Parents should not take your recess duties, take on your teaching responsibilities, or be left in your classroom with students when you are not there. These things can lead to liability issues that your school may frown on.

FIGURE 5-13   A parent can help children with craft projects.

Once you determine the jobs you will have in your classroom, print up a handout and send it home to parents. Allow them time to think about the jobs that will fit best with their talents and schedule. Also, create a sign-up sheet providing information about the specific days and times certain jobs will take place. For example, you may choose to have guest readers on Fridays from 2:00 to 2:30. You may decide to have classroom helpers on Tuesday and Thursday mornings from 10:00 to 11:30 and on Wednesday and Thursday afternoons from 1:00 to 2:30. (See Figure 5–14 for a sample sign-up sheet.)

Scheduling

Once you have received the sign-up sheets from parents who want to help, it's time to make a schedule. (See Figure 5–15.) It's important not to schedule too many parents in the classroom at the same time because, while parents can be great helpers, too many can create distractions for your students. Having no more than two parents in the classroom at the same time is a good rule of thumb. If you are fortunate enough to have many parents volunteer, it may be necessary to schedule

Dear Parent,

Please read the attached list of classroom jobs. Then complete the form below and return it to school by the end of the week. Be sure to indicate the days and times you are available.

Parent Name: Kathryn Gallegos

Phone Number: 712-555-8734

Student Name: Benny Gallegos

I am interested in the following jobs:
Classroom Helper
Party Planner

I am available on the following days:

Day	Morning or Afternoon
Tuesdays	Mornings
Wednesdays	Mornings
Fridays	Morning or Afternoon

FIGURE 5–14   Sign-Up Sheet Sample.

them to come in once every two weeks, rather than once a week. A calendar (see Figure 5–16) has been provided to help you create your helper schedule. Keep the calendar posted in a place where you can refer to it conveniently as you will want to be sure to have activities and tasks planned and ready to go when parent helpers arrive. Next, you'll want to notify parents of their jobs and the days/dates and times you want them to come into the classroom. Use the Helper Notification sheet (see Figure 5–17) for this purpose. Simply duplicate and cut the forms in half, complete the necessary information, and send them home to parents. A notice is also provided (Figure 5–18) for you to send home to parents to remind them of jobs that take place periodically, such as guest readers or chaperones.

Training Sessions

You may find it necessary to conduct a training session for parents who will be working with students. This helps to maintain continuity in your classroom and ease parents' anxieties about their participation. You can conduct a short training session after school. During this session, explain your

FIGURE 5–15 Scheduling parents to help in the classroom is a task worthy of time and consideration in order not to disrupt children's learning.

FAMILIES IN FOCUS

Since it is important to be completely prepared for family involvement in the classroom, you may choose not to schedule parents to come in on Mondays. Even though you may thoroughly plan lessons and activities the week before, sometimes it can just be difficult to have it altogether on a Monday. It seems there are always last-minute preparations, and planning for parent assistance adds to the responsibilities. So, from Tuesday to Friday, you can open your doors to parents, but feel free to make Monday a day for just you and "your kids."

Monday	Tuesday	Wednesday	Thursday	Friday

FIGURE 5–16   Scheduling Calendar.

philosophy of working with children, describe the kinds of activities they will be doing, where they will be working with children, and what to do to handle behavior problems. Invite parents to ask questions and address individual concerns.

MANAGING IN THE CLASSROOM

Once all of the preparations have been made, it's time to begin thinking about how to manage parent helpers when they arrive in your classroom. Some parents may show up at a time when you will be able to speak with them briefly about what they will be doing to help. At other times, parents

Dear _____,

Thank you for volunteering to help in the classroom. You have chosen the following job(s):

_____

You are invited to come to the classroom on _____

day(s) or date(s)

at _____.

time

If you are not able to help on a particular day, please call me at

_____

to let me know. Thank you!

Sincerely,

_____

- -

Dear _____,

Thank you for volunteering to help in the classroom. You have chosen the following job(s):

_____

You are invited to come to the classroom on _____

day(s) or date(s)

at _____.

time

If you are not able to help on a particular day, please call me at

_____

to let me know. Thank you!

Sincerely,

_____

FIGURE 5–17   Helper Notification.

may arrive when you are in the middle of teaching or working with students. It's nice to have a plan in place that is the least disruptive to your classroom routine. You'll want to let the students know that parents will be coming into the classroom. It is appropriate for a child to greet his or her parent upon entering the room, but the child must understand that

It's Your Turn

This is a reminder that your job as _____ is approaching.

You are invited to come to the classroom on _____
                                              day(s) or date(s)

at _____.
            time

If you are not able to attend, please call me at _____

— —

It's Your Turn

This is a reminder that your job as _____ is approaching.

You are invited to come to the classroom on _____
                                              day(s) or date(s)

at _____.
            time

If you are not able to attend, please call me at _____

FIGURE 5–18   Reminder Notice.

he or she should continue to work on projects or lessons after this initial greeting.

If a parent is scheduled to help in the classroom at a time when you will be busy with the children, it is helpful to have a folder or basket containing materials and instructions for the tasks he or she will complete. You can place a basket on a countertop containing a note describing the parent's job for the day. See the following note for an example.

Use the Parent Instructions sheet (Figure 5–19) to write instructions for working with children, completing administrative tasks, managing learning centers, and so on. The Student Progress form (mentioned in the following note.) can be found in Figure 5–20. It is helpful to have parents complete a form of this kind after working with children to give you information about the parent-child interactions. Even though you may not have time to speak with the parent immediately upon his or her arrival, it is important to make contact with the parent as soon as possible to be sure the parent feels welcome and understands the tasks you have

Welcome to class! Thanks so much for helping out. Today, I would like you to do the following: Work with Stacy, Chad, and Alicia. These students could use additional assistance with beginning addition skills. I have included a game that you can play with each of these children. You can work with each child, individually, on the carpet area at the front of the classroom. Spend about 15 minutes with each child. Please complete the Student Progress form after working with each child to let me know how things went and to indicate any problems or successes that you noticed. Let me know if you have any questions. Thanks!

planned. Remember that most parents feel a bit intimidated entering your "domain" and a quick "Hello. How are you today? Thanks for coming in," can help to break the ice.

Think about the kinds of tasks you could have parents assist with in your classroom. List your ideas below. Be sure to include some tasks that involve working with children.

Tasks with Children   Organizational Tasks

_____   _____
_____   _____
_____   _____
_____   _____
_____   _____
_____   _____

Keep in mind that parents should *assist* you in the classroom, but should not take over your responsibilities as the teacher. Remember that you should not leave the classroom, putting the parent in charge. This could lead to liability issues for you should something happen in your absence. This is also the case with asking parents to perform recess duties. It is helpful to have parents assist with duties, but they should not replace your presence on the playground. You will also need to be careful with having a parent grade papers or projects for you, as some school districts consider this to be an invasion of children's privacy. (For more information about family privacy issues, access the U.S. Department of Education's Web site concerning the Family Educational Rights and Privacy Act [FERPA] at http://www.ed.gov/policy/gen/guid/fpco/ferpa/index.html.) Compare your list of parent tasks with the following list. Are there jobs that you would like to add to your list?

Welcome to class! Thanks so much for helping in our classroom. Today, I would like you to do the following:

_____

_____

_____

_____

You can work in the following area of the room:

_____

If working with children, please complete the Student Progress Form for each child to indicate successes and/or challenges you noticed.

— —

Welcome to class! Thanks so much for helping in our classroom. Today, I would like you to do the following:

_____

_____

_____

_____

You can work in the following area of the room:

_____

If working with children, please complete the Student Progress Form for each child to indicate successes and/or challenges you noticed.

FIGURE 5–19 Parent Instructions.

Parent Tasks with Children

—reading aloud to a group of children
—listening to a child read
—playing games to reinforce skills
—assisting a child with writing
—supervising children at a learning center
—assisting you with supervising student activities
—circulating the room to assist children
—demonstrating steps for art projects

Parent Organizational Tasks

—cutting out materials for craft projects
—duplicating papers

Child's Name: _____ Date: _____

Activity:
_____

Successes:
_____
_____
_____

Challenges:
_____
_____
_____
_____

Child's Name: _____ Date: _____
Activity:
_____

Successes:
_____
_____
_____

Challenges:
_____
_____
_____
_____

FIGURE 5–20   Student Progress Form.

—sorting papers to be sent home with children
—passing out supplies or materials
—typing the class newsletter
—setting up learning centers
—gathering supplies for upcoming lessons
—taking down or creating bulletin boards
—stapling packets to go home to parents
—running errands on campus

SHOW YOUR APPRECIATION

Be sure to express your appreciation to parent helpers regularly. After a parent's first visit, send a note or make a personal phone call to say "thank you." In the future, make it a point to send a thank-you card every few months. You might also give public recognition to parents by mentioning their names and helpfulness in your weekly newsletter. This acknowledges parents' dedication to your class and also encourages other parents to get involved. After all, parents are taking time out of their busy schedules to assist you and expressions of appreciation will help to create those positive partnerships you are hoping to achieve.

■ CONCLUSION

Communication is the most important key to effective parent-teacher partnerships. In this chapter, we've addressed many strategies for building patterns of communication with parents, beginning with the first interactions and leading to regular family involvement in the classroom. These strategies take time and effort to implement so take the time to think through the ways you can build effective communication with the parents of your students. You'll find that the more time you spend preparing for family involvement in your classroom, the more comfortable you'll feel with parents, which will lead to strong partnerships.

■ SUMMARY OF IMPORTANT POINTS

- Regular communication is the key to building effective parent-teacher partnerships.
- A Back-to-School night is a great opportunity to meet parents and provide them with important information about your classroom. It also helps to convey to parents their value in their children's educational journey.
- Creating an informational presentation provides useful information to parents and gives the impression that you are prepared and that their children are in good hands.
- Sending home a weekly newsletter is an effective routine for communicating with parents.
- It is important to think through and communicate to parents jobs that they can perform in the classroom.

- Purposeful scheduling of parent helpers creates an organized plan for family involvement in the classroom.

- Creating a training session for parent helpers helps to communicate your educational philosophy and helps to build confidence in parents as they assist in the classroom.

- Showing appreciation of in-class participation expresses value to parents and encourages future participation.

CHAPTER REVIEW QUESTIONS

1. What is the key element for positive parent/teacher partnerships?
2. What forms of communication build strong partnerships?
3. What is the purpose of a Back-to-School night for parents?
4. What is the purpose of an informational presentation to parents?
5. What kinds of responsibilities should not be left to parents?
6. Why are regular expressions of appreciation important?

APPLICATION AND REFLECTION

1. Most parents feel more comfortable knowing that their children's teachers have a clear educational philosophy. Develop your educational philosophy, keeping in mind your beliefs about the education of young children, appropriate learning activities for children, optimal classroom environments, and so on. Practice expressing an abbreviated version of your philosophy using a natural, conversational style.

2. What kind of parent help would you like in your classroom? Think through the jobs parents can perform. Write a description of each job and type your list of descriptions to send home to parents.

3. Making phone calls to parents at the beginning of the school year helps to establish patterns of communication. Plan the words you will say in these initial conversations with parents. Be sure to include an encouraging word about each parent's child.

FURTHER READING

Coletta A. J. (1999). *Working together: A guide to parent involvement.* Humanics Ltd. Partners.

Mierzwik, D. (2004). *Quick and easy ways to connect with students and their parents, grades K–8: Improving student achievement through parent involvement.* Corwin Press.

 For additional information on research-based practice, visit our Web site at http://www.earlychilded.delmar.com.

Additional resources for this chapter can be found on the Online Companion™ to accompany this text at www.earlychilded.delmar.com. This supplemental material includes Web links, downloadable forms, and Case Studies with critical thinking applications. This content can be used as a study aid to reinforce key concepts presented in this chapter and to conduct additional research on topics of interest.

■ REFERENCES

Couchenour, D., & Chrisman, K. (2000). *Families, schools, and communities: Together for young children.* New York: Delmar.

Cromer, J. (1997). *Waiting for a miracle: Why schools can't solve our problems—and how we can.* New York: Dutton.

Davern, L. (May/June, 2004). School-to-home notebooks: What parents have to say. *Teaching Exceptional Children,* 22–27.

Eldridge, D. (July, 2001). Parent involvement: It's worth the effort. *Young Children,* 65–69.

Gage, J., & Workman, S. (1994). Creating family support systems: In Head Start and beyond. *Young Children, 49*(7), 74–77.

Gonzales-Mena, J. (1994). *From a parent's perspective.* Salem, WI: Sheffield.

Katz, L. (1995). *Talks on teaching.* Norwood, NJ: Ablex.

Moore, K. B. (October, 2002). Family communications: Ideas that really work. *Early Childhood Today, 17*(2), 14–15.

Noddings, N. (1995). Teaching themes of care. *Phi Delta Kappan, 76*( ), 675–679.

Orman, S. A. (February, 1993). Mathematics backpacks: Making the home-school connection. *Arithmetic Teacher, 40*(6), 306–309.

Swick, K. (1993). *Strengthening parents and families during the early childhood years.* Champaign, IL: Stipes.

Swick, K. (1997). A family-school approach for nurturing caring in young children. *Early Childhood Education Journal, 25*(2), 151–154.

Swick, K. (Summer, 2003). Communication concepts for strengthening family-school-community partnerships. *Early Childhood Education Journal, 30*(4), 275–280.

Swick, K., Grafwallner, R., Cockey, M., Roach, J., Davidson, S., Mayor, M., & Gardner, N. (1997). On board early: Building strong family-school relations. *Early Childhood Education Journal, 24*, 269–273.

CHAPTER

6

Family Involvement at Home during the Early Years

▪ CHAPTER OBJECTIVES ⎯⎯⎯⎯⎯⎯⎯⎯⎯⎯⎯⎯⎯

After reading and reflecting on this chapter, you should be able to:

- Express the importance of **family involvement at home.**
- Identify ways that parents can be involved in their children's education at home.
- Create activities for parents and children to do together at home.

▪ KEY TERMS ⎯⎯⎯⎯⎯⎯⎯⎯⎯⎯⎯⎯⎯⎯⎯⎯⎯

family involvement at home   interactive experiences

family involvement at school

FAMILIES AT HOME

We typically think of family involvement as the parent assisting at school or in school-related activities. Parents are encouraged to attend conferences, help in the classroom, come to school events, and communicate through telephone and written messages. "Essentially, parents have been invited and welcomed to be involved in the established structure of a program for their child" (McBride, 1999). And yet the majority of the research about the benefits of family involvement points to parents being involved with their children's educational experiences at home. (See Figure 6–1.)

FIGURE 6–1   Parent involvement at home brings about the greatest benefits to children.

LITERACY

In the past quarter of a century researchers have explored the question of how children learn to read and how we, as teachers and parents, can best help them in their quest. The beginnings of literacy actually are found at home. Upon entering school, most children have gained extensive knowledge about written language from their experiences with literacy in everyday life. They see print in the environment; they are often read to by family members; and they observe literacy routines in the home, such as newspaper reading, list making, and so on. They begin to construct their own ideas about the conventions of written language and imitate literacy behaviors based on their interpretations of the acts of reading and writing that they observe. They understand the "alphabetic nature" of print, how to handle books, and are aware that print is read from left to right.

The perceptions children develop at home of the function, purpose, and use of reading and writing are important factors to consider. According to Heath (1980, p. 130), it is important "to recognize that the extent to which physiologically normal individuals learn to read and write depends greatly on the role literacy plays in their families, communities, and jobs." Researchers overwhelmingly conclude that knowledge of the functions of language is equally as important as the forms of print. Children learn about the functions of print at home long before they begin to learn to read in school. (See Figure 6–2.)

The acquisition of reading skills is considered to be a constructive and interactive process (Gambrell, 1996) and often involves reading activities facilitated by other readers. These social interactions assist children in understanding the function and conventions of reading. There is also overwhelming evidence that enjoyable reading experiences with parents and others promote children's interest in literacy activities. "Children discover and invent literacy as they participate actively in a literate society" (Goodman, 1984, p. 102). This leads us to the understanding that children develop literacy skills through their life experiences.

FAMILIES AND LITERACY

Families influence the development of literacy in their children through physical environment, interpersonal interaction, and the emotional and motivational climate (Leichter, 1984). Leichter explains that the physical environment refers to economic and educational resources available, visual stimulation, and physical family arrangements. Interpersonal interaction

FIGURE 6–2   Children learn about the process of reading long before they enter formal schooling.

involves the literacy opportunities available to a child while interacting with parents and siblings. The emotional and motivational environment refers to relationships within the home that affect a child's experiences with literacy.

Homes of Early Readers

Numerous studies have focused on the homes of early readers and writers. Briggs and Elkind (1973) studied five-year-old children (readers and non-readers) to determine why some children read earlier than others. Their results revealed that the early readers had more educated mothers, and, also, fathers who read to them more frequently than the nonreaders.

In a study of 20 reading five-year-olds, Clark (1984) found similarities in the home environments that she attributes to early reading success. She concluded that many of the parents were professionals and had a wide range of books in the home. Many of the children had older siblings (also early readers) who acted as teachers and models. These homes exhibited positive adult-child interactions and the parents conveyed genuine interest in their children's experiences. Clark also found that the parents of these early readers frequented their local libraries for personal use and assisted the children in making their book selections.

Likewise, Teale (1984) describes the homes of early readers as "rich literacy environments" that very naturally include reading and writing activities, such as reading books and newspapers, writing letters, and making lists. The children living in these homes interact positively with others who model involvement with literacy materials.

The availability of reading materials in the home has also proven to be a significant factor in early reading success, according to Durkin (1966) and Morrow (2004). These homes often have library corners for children and a wide variety of books made available throughout the house. Children who are frequently read to by parents and siblings show a greater interest in books and ultimately become better readers (Briggs & Elkind, 1973; Clark, 1984).

Studies of early readers also report the significance of writing materials in the home, which leads to an increased interest in writing activities. The children are encouraged to scribble and develop writing skills naturally, which enhances the reading process (Morrow, 2004). The home environment of early readers is also characterized by interactive adults. Parents in these homes are responsive to their children's interest in literacy and provide literacy experiences and discussion. Research of the home literacy environment, overall, seems to suggest that children who bring more literacy knowledge with them to school ultimately perform better than those who do not (Yaden, Rowe, & MacGillivray, 2000).

You'll notice that most of the studies point to increased student achievement when parents expressed the value of education to their children and participated in activities with them at home, such as reading to a child and helping out with homework. "While school officials are enthusiastic about recruiting parents as volunteers, they should be aware that the cookie-baking, word-processing, candy-selling, paper-shuffling, showing-up activities traditionally associated with parent involvement are not likely to have much impact on student achievement" (Jones, 2001). It is, rather, when a parent participates in interactive experiences that a child benefits most. By participating in these kinds of activities a child is given the opportunity not only to learn along with his or her parent, but is also able to demonstrate what he or she has learned in school. (See Figure 6–3.) "Simply put, the amount of time parents spend monitoring their children's activities and assisting their children with homework has a dramatic effect on how successful their children are academically" (Peterson, 2002).

FIGURE 6–3   By participating in literacy activities with a parent, a child is given the opportunity to learn along with his or her parent and demonstrate what he or she has learned in school.

Finn (1998) states that the "home environment is among the most important influences on academic performance" (p. 20). For this reason, it is essential that we, as teachers, express to parents the value of their participation in their children's educational experiences. What's more, we need to express to them that spending time with their children at home,

FAMILIES IN FOCUS

The primary-grade teachers at Wilson Elementary School received a grant to increase the literacy development of their economically disadvantaged students. Part of the grant included doing home visits. Miss Davis was nervous at the thought of visiting the homes of her kindergarten students, but was prepared to carry out the task. News spread quickly among the families in that small town. Why did the teachers want to visit their homes? Were they planning to report them to Child Protective Services? What good could come from home visits? Miss Davis was surprised to find out that the home visits were quite pleasant and after a few uncomfortable minutes, conversations flowed easily. She left each home feeling as if she had learned about her students' families and that she had offered them a glimpse into her life.

The most resistant to the request for home visits was Jenna Bailey's father, who made it clear to others in the community that he wasn't going to let "those teachers" into his house. With a bit of coaxing, Miss Davis was able to get the father to agree to a brief visit and with anxious anticipation, she arrived at the home. As she entered the house, she noticed all five of the children and their father in the living room. Mr. Bailey was sitting in a recliner and made no attempt to get up to greet her. She chatted quietly with the children and made efforts to involve their father in the conversation. Then somehow the topic of music came up. Miss Davis mentioned that she played the guitar and, to her surprise, Mr. Bailey's face perked up and he sat forward. Before long the visit took a drastic change as Mr. Bailey got out his guitar and led the teacher and his five children in a sing-along. Miss Davis left the home that day with a smile on her face and the realization that through the singing of a few campfire songs she had gained the trust of a very reluctant parent.

whether in conversation, reading aloud, or by participating in educational activities with them, carries tremendous benefits. Many parents are at a loss for what they can do at home to assist their children academically and that's where we enter the picture. We can encourage parents by periodically providing ideas for simple, engaging, and fun activities they can do with their children. This chapter has two main sections. The first contains a series of parent letters that can be duplicated and sent home every few weeks to encourage parent-child interaction. These letters feature a variety of activities, including reading, oral language, written language, mathematics, and art. The second section contains a series of backpack activities that provide hands-on experiences with materials that you provide and allows families to borrow for a few days.

Parent-Child Activity Letters

Two kinds of letters have been provided in this chapter. There are informational letters and activity letters. The informational letters provide information to parents about the way young children learn. The activity letters focus on specific topics and provide fun ways for parents and children to work together to focus on skills related to reading, writing, mathematics, and even science, art, and communication.

You'll find that there are far more letters than you would probably send home to parents during a year. This gives you the opportunity to pick and choose the ones that best match the skill levels and needs of your children. Some of the activities are geared toward preschool and kindergarten children, while others are geared toward children in the primary grades. You can decide which activities are most appropriate to send home.

At the end of this section, you'll find a parent-child activity template. This template allows you to create your own activity letters for parents and children. You can write in your own ideas or you can select activities from different letters included in the chapter and combine them as you see fit.

ABOUT READING

Dear Parent,

At a very young age, most children understand that there is something called reading. They are aware of print and that print carries meaning. They are able to participate in the process of reading. The extent to which children learn to read and write depends greatly on the role literacy plays in their families.

Children often have a very good idea of the purpose of print. They use their experiences and the world around them to make sense of it. You have probably noticed that your child recognizes print in the environment, such as store signs, restaurant names, and even the names of their favorite cereals.

Learning is the result of experiences. Children have a wealth of knowledge about print and we need to draw on this knowledge.

Knowledge increases through interactions with adults or more-able peers (Vygotsky, 1981). The zone of proximal development focuses on the idea that when children are given opportunities to interact with adults or peers, they gain more knowledge and are challenged to higher levels.

You can assist your child in literacy development by remembering the processes of observation and collaboration.

Through observation, children learn about reading behaviors.

Through collaboration with adults and peers, children receive encouragement and motivation.

This should be encouraging to you. Simply by living life together and sharing literacy experiences together, you are assisting your child in developing beginning skills that will transfer to the process of reading.

You can add to these experiences by reading to your child regularly, discussing books and characters, and pointing out print in the environment.

I encourage you to have fun with this as you watch your child's knowledge of print grow!

ABOUT WRITTEN LANGUAGE

Dear Parent,

Your child has already learned so much about written language, just by watching you! You can share more great experiences with your child while continuing to enhance these skills. It's important that you understand the developmental processes involved in learning to write. Here's some information you might find useful.

Experimenting with writing helps to increase writing development. The more opportunities children have to experiment with writing, the more aware they are of the conventions of writing. They also increase their awareness of themselves as writers.

When young children write, they often invent the spellings of words. Many adults insist that children spell all words correctly, but invented spelling is actually a good thing. Studies tell us that children who use invented spelling are better able to read simple words. This kind of spelling also encourages children to write the words they think, rather than only writing the words they know how to spell. Don't worry about your child's writing. Conventional spelling will increase with time.

You can watch your child's writing progress over time. Below are six stages of writing development (Sulzby, 1985) that your child will likely progress through.

1. Writing via drawing

2. Writing via scribbling

3. Writing via making letter-like forms

4. Writing via reproducing letter strings

5. Writing via invented spelling

6. Writing via conventional spelling

FAMILY LITERACY

Children develop literacy skills through life experiences. This refers not only to interactions with books, but also by observing the literacy behaviors of others and being praised and motivated by family members for mimicking literacy behaviors.

Several research studies (Briggs & Elkind, 1973; Clark, 1984; Teale, 1984; Yaden et al., 2000) identify similarities in the home environments of children who read early. These homes tend to have the following materials and routines:

- lots of books in the home
- siblings who act as teachers and models
- positive adult-child interactions
- parents who show interest in the child's experiences
- frequent trips taken to the library
- library corners in the home set up with numerous children's books
- read to by parents and siblings
- opportunities to write or scribble

Encourage your child to make lists and use writing materials in play experiences. Discuss literacy experiences with your child. Ask him or her to talk about what is understood about the uses of print. Ask your child about his or her reading and writing and express to the child that these behaviors are valuable.

Try some of these things at home with your child. After all, research suggests that children with more literacy experiences at home perform better in school.

LITERACY AND PLAY

Play is necessary for social, emotional, and physical development. Froebel and Dewey both suggest that children learn best through play and through real-life experiences. Play is meaningful to children and can help to bridge the gap between home and school.

Believe it or not, encouraging play actually helps your child build skills that will assist him or her at school and in life. Here is some information that you may find useful as you encourage your child to play.

- If given the opportunity, children will use books, paper and pencil, magazines, and so on, in play. They will often label objects, write notes, make lists, or "read" to dolls.

(continues)

(*continued*)

- Through play, children can try out their understanding of reading and writing by using it in play scenarios. This helps them to understand the need for reading and writing. Providing literacy materials in play encourages children to act like readers and writers.

- Play is often symbolic. A child uses a bucket for a helmet or pretends that a block is a sandwich. Children who have high levels of symbolic play do better when it comes to reading. This is believed to be due to the fact that the child can easily understand that things represent other things.

- You can even get involved in your child's play by valuing the use of literacy materials, asking questions, and praising play ideas. Try to stay natural and in character, but make suggestions, such as, "Why don't you make a list before you go shopping?" Avoid too much involvement, though. Too much involvement interferes with play and children may stop being creative. Also, too much push for use of print materials turns kids off and they won't continue to do so in the future.

So, have some fun with your child. Play!

LITERACY ACTIVITY GUIDE FOR PARENTS

Do you ever wonder what you can do at home to promote early reading and writing? Try doing easy and fun activities using environmental print (also called EP). EP is found in the home, in stores, on television, in magazines, and on the roads. EP is print children see in their natural environments. EP includes logos, labels, road signs, billboards, and so on. We now know that young children begin to recognize environmental print at a very early age. Children usually read EP before they are able to read print in books. Parents can help children learn to read by using simple and fun EP activities. Here are some fun activities you can use with your child.

Play with Real Objects

Use real objects during dramatic play. You can use any objects for playing house, restaurant, or grocery store. Save drink bottles (milk cartons, juice boxes, soda bottles), cookie boxes, cereal boxes, restaurant boxes and bags, bandage boxes, and so on. Almost everything in the home with recognizable logos and words can be used for dramatic play. While you're playing, let your child "read" the logos and names on the containers. Encourage your child to notice the print on the boxes and bags.

Cereal Box Puzzle

Save the front panels of cereal boxes. Cut a panel into pieces to make the puzzle. Let your child assemble the puzzle. Any kind of cereal box can be turned into a wonderful and challenging puzzle. (Store the pieces in self-sealing plastic bags.)

Memory Game

Find two sets of eight different commercial logos, such as Oreo, Kmart, M&M, Goldfish, and so on. (Coupons work well for this activity.) Glue each logo onto a different index card. Place the cards face down. To play, your child turns over two cards at a time to try to make a match. If a match is found, the child keeps the pair, if not, the cards are turned face down again and play continues.

Sorting Game

Cards or coupons with logos are sorted into specified categories, such as Food/Toys, Eat/Don't Eat, Healthy/Unhealthy, and so on.

Shopping Trip

When shopping with your child, ask him or her to help you find favorite foods. You will be surprised at how many can be recognized by name.

Cereal Book

This is a book made from several cereal box covers. Cut out the front panels of several different cereal boxes. Three-hole punch the left edge of each panel and bind the "pages" together with yarn. Place the book in your child's home library.

Food Folder

Inside a file folder, glue several familiar logos. Your child will enjoy "reading" the logo names.

Important Tip: The adult is the key element in learning to read with environmental print. Be sure to have conversations with your child, not only about the logos and words, but also about the beginning letters. Ask your child if he or she recognizes any other letters in the words and if he or she knows the sounds of the letters.

Dear Parent,

Here are some great ideas for spending time with your child, while encouraging reading development.

Read, read, read! Read daily with your child. This is quite possibly the best thing you can do to enhance your child's reading development.

Make reading an interactive experience by doing the following:

- Go to the library and select books together.
- Ask your child what will happen next.
- Act out the story. Perform the story for family members.
- Read and reread. Children love to hear stories more than once. As your child becomes familiar with the text, ask him or her to read/recite portions of the story.

READING FLUENCY

Help your child increase reading fluency by asking him or her to read along with you. This is particularly helpful when reading a familiar story. As your child reads with you, he/she will hear the rhythm and expression in your voice and will mimic this as you read together.

Dear Parent,

Try these great reading activities with your child.

Reading and Drawing

The next time you read a story to your child, provide him/her with crayons and paper. Ask your child to draw a picture of an event in the story as you read.

High-Frequency Words

There are many words that appear in print over and over in a story. Recognizing common words, such as *and, the, but, then, at,* and so on, can make reading easier for your child. After reading a story, go back through the book and ask your child to identify selected words. Have fun counting the number of times a particular word appears in a book.

Story Retelling

After reading a book to your child, ask him or her to retell the story to you. Then you can take a turn retelling the story. Compare the two versions and how each of you likely added some different details to your retellings. Be sure to discuss events that happened at the beginning, middle, and end of the story.

Characters and Setting

Discuss with your child the fact that books have characters and settings. Explain that a setting is where the story happens. Read a story to your child. Identify the main characters and where the story takes place. Have your child draw a picture showing the main character(s) in the setting.

Dialogic Reading

Reading is most enjoyable when you and your child carry on conversations about the story. This is called dialogic reading—having a dialog about a story. Ask questions about the story as you read to your child. When the story is finished, ask more questions, such as:

- Who was the main character?
- What problem did the character have?
- How was the problem solved?
- What was your favorite part of the story?

Dear Parent,

Here are some great activities for encouraging reading in your home.

Reading Logs

Encourage the whole family to read. Create a reading log using a simple notebook. Designate a page of the book for each reading member of the family. Have each family member set a goal for number of books or pages to read in a month. Each time someone reads, he/she records the book or pages of the book in the reading log. Be sure to celebrate reading accomplishments as a family.

Voice Animation

When reading to your child, use an animated voice to pique your child's interest. By using different voices for the different characters in the book, your child will begin to understand the use of expression. Ask your child to make up voices for different characters, too. This is a great way to make your reading times entertaining.

What If

After you read a book to your child, ask "What if" questions. For example, after reading "Goldilocks and the Three Bears," you might ask:

"What if Goldilocks had come over when the bears were home?"

"What if Goldilocks had known the bears ahead of time?"

"What would have happened if Goldilocks had been awake when the bears returned?"

Have fun discussing other options for story events and characters.

Dear Parent,

A great way to review the parts of a story is with graphic organizers. Use the Word Web below to discuss a story you read to your child. In each of the sections, write details from the book.

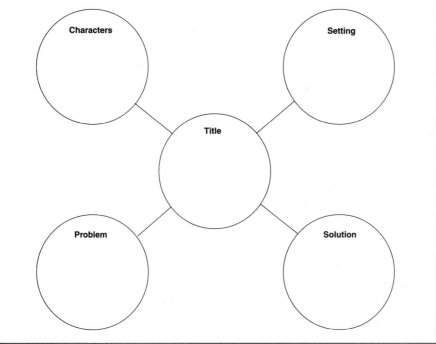

Dear Parent,

Here are some great reading activities you can do with your child. You know that reading to your child is important, so add these activities to enhance your reading time. Have fun!

Before You Read

Before reading a story to your child, take some time to discuss the book. Identify the title and the title page. Look through the pictures and identify chapter titles. Ask your child to predict what the story might be about.

While You Read

Encourage conversation as you read the book. Ask your child if his or her predictions were accurate. Identify and discuss unfamiliar words. Have your child try to determine the meanings of these words by paying attention to the ways they are used in sentences. Encourage your child to ask questions about the story if the plot is confusing in any way.

While Your Child Reads

If your child is a reader, it is still important that you read aloud to him/her on a regular basis. But, when your child reads to you, keep a few things in mind. Mistakes are okay. Remember that reading is a meaning-making process. If the mistake doesn't change the meaning of the sentence, let it go. For example, if the child substitutes the word house for home, it's okay. If the word changes the meaning, ask questions of your child to help him/her recognize the nature of the error. Be sure to have your child read text that is appropriate to his/her reading level in order to make the experience fun.

After You Read

After you read a story, be sure to take time to discuss it with your child. Ask questions, such as:

- What was your favorite part?
- Was there a part you didn't like?
- Which character was your favorite?

Ask other questions relating to the Who, What, Where, When, Why, and How of the story.

Dear Parent,

Children benefit greatly from parents who spend time with them. Here are some ideas for spending time with your child and letting the conversations flow.

Dinner Conversation

Engage your child in conversation at the dinner table. Be sure to ask specific questions that will not lead to yes/no answers. Here are some questions to get you started:

- "What was something that happened in school today?"
- "What was the best part of your day?"
- "What stories did your teacher read today?"

Be sure to allow your child to ask questions of you.

Go for a Walk

Spend time with your child by going on a walk. Use the time to talk with your child about the events of the day. Ask questions, share stories, point out interesting things seen in the neighborhood. Just enjoy being together.

Storytelling Time

Storytelling can be great fun for you and your child. First, select five objects from around the house. Then let the stories begin. Tell your child that the object of this activity is to tell a story that somehow includes all five of the selected items. Take turns telling different stories about these objects.

Story Creations

Spend time with your child making up stories. Work together to brainstorm characters, setting, and plot ideas. Begin the story with a sentence or two. Then ask your child to provide the next few sentences. Continue in this manner until the story is complete. You might want to record your story to share with other members of the family.

Dear Parent,

Here are some oral language activities that will give you the opportunity to spend time and have fun with your child.

Tongue Twisters

A tongue twister is a series of words that begin with the same letters, such as She Sells Sea Shells by the Seashore, or Peter Piper Picked a Peck of Pickled Peppers. Work with your child to create tongue twisters of your own. First, select a letter sound and then take turns using words beginning with that letter to make a silly phrase.

Back and Forth

While driving in the car or just hanging around the house, play a fun sound game. Begin by saying a word, such as *love*. Your child then says another word that begins with that sound, such as *laugh*. Continue in this manner until one of you can't think of another word. Then change to a different beginning letter sound.

Descriptions

This activity will challenge you and your child to add descriptive words to your language. To do this, begin by saying a sentence, such as "The bird chirped." Your child then repeats the sentence, adding in one descriptive word, such as "The bird chirped *sweetly*." You respond by adding another word, such as "The *blue* bird chirped sweetly." Continue in this manner until the sentence is too long to remember. Then try again with another sentence.

Nursery Rhymes

Have fun reading and reciting nursery rhymes. Once your child is familiar with a few, recite them together as you drive in the car or wait for an appointment. Make the experience a bit more challenging by introducing a new nursery rhyme, but leaving off certain rhyming words. Ask your child to add the missing words.

Dear Parent,

Try these great writing activities at home with your child.

Reading and Writing

Add a bit of writing to your story reading time. After reading a book to your child, ask your child to tell something that happened in the story. Either have your child write down the sentence on paper or have him/her dictate the sentence as you write it down. Then read the sentence aloud or have him/her read it aloud. Continue in this manner with several sentences about the story. If necessary, cut the sentences apart and work together to place them in the proper sequence.

Opportunities to Write

Giving your child a variety of ways to write will enhance his/her writing development. Here are some great ways to get your child writing at home.

- Create a family message board. Encourage family members (including your child) to write notes to one another and post them on the board.
- When your child has a special request, have him/her write it down or dictate for you to write. Post the message on the board.
- Have your child help you write items on a grocery list.
- Have your child assist you with meal planning by writing daily menus.

Remember that the use of invented spelling is okay. This encourages your child to write what is on his/her mind and not just what he/she knows how to spell. Conventional spelling will develop with time.

Family Letters

Work with your child to write letters to members of your extended family. If necessary, have your child dictate the words as you write them down. You might also want to encourage your child to write notes to family members in the house. What a joy to find a special note on the pillow or in a lunch bag!

Dear Parent,

Writing with your child can be lots of fun. Try these activities with your child.

Magazines and Newspapers

Work with your child to locate familiar words in magazines and newspapers. Cut out the words and glue them to construction paper. Then have your child re-create the words by writing them in crayon or with paint.

Write a Book

This is a great project to do with your child. Select a topic, such as My Favorite Pet or My Family. Then work together to write the story. Take turns writing sentences of the story. (If your child is in the early stages of writing development, have him or her dictate sentences as you write them down.) Finish your book by creating a cover from construction paper. Staple the book together or three-hole punch the spine and tie it together with string.

Letters

Reinforce letter recognition skills with this fun activity. Select a letter and write it in the center of a sheet of paper. Then look through magazines, newspapers, and junk mail to find words that begin with that letter. Cut out the words and glue them on the paper around the letter. Ask your child to read the words and identify the sound of the featured letter.

Dear Parent,

Here are some great written language activities to try out with your child!

Letter–Learning Fun

Play a game while driving in the car. Select an object of some kind (such as dog) and say, "I'm thinking of something that begins with the letter D." You can also say, "I'm thinking of something that begins with the /d/ sound." Allow your child to guess a word. Then give another clue, such as, "This thing is furry." Allow your child to guess. Remind him/her that it must begin with D. Continue to provide clues until your child is able to guess the selected object.

Alphabet Game

Here's a fun game that will help your child recall the letters of the alphabet. You can play this game with several people. The first person says, "I'm going on a picnic (or to the store or to the beach) and I'm bringing an apple." The next person adds on to this with something beginning with the letter B. For example, "I'm going on a picnic and I'm bringing an apple and a basket." Play continues in this manner until players are no longer able to remember the items or until you have added items A through Z.

Environmental Print

Environmental print is the print all around us on billboards, store signs, street signs, and so on. Point out this print to your child as you travel through town. Ask your child to identify the words he/she sees.

Letter Pictures

This is a fun and creative way to practice the spellings of simple words. Get out paper and crayons. Then select a simple word, such as *cat*. Ask your child to spell the word, providing assistance as needed. Then work with your child to create a picture that looks like a cat using the letters C-A-T. For example, the A could be the body; the C could be drawn above the A as the head; the T could be drawn below the A as the tail. Allow your child to add details, such as whiskers and eyes.

Dear Parent,

Have fun participating in the following activities with your child.

Vocabulary Building

Select a word for the week, such as unfathomable, and use the dictionary to define it for the family. Then challenge family members to use the word in conversation during the week. For example, "The number of books I've read this year is unfathomable." At the dinner table, ask family members to share how they have used the word in conversation.

Journaling

Keeping a journal is a great way to encourage self-expression and writing. Provide yourself and your child with a blank book or a notebook filled with paper. A few days a week, sit down to do journal writing. Just spend about five minutes writing. If your child is very young, have him/her dictate to you as you write in the journal. Then both you and your child can add drawings, photographs, or magazine cutouts to accompany the writing. Be sure to spend time sharing what you each wrote that day.

Writing Letters to Family and Friends

Select a family member or a family friend to be the recipient of a letter that you and your child write together. Talk with your child about how a letter of this kind typically begins by asking how this person is doing and how much you miss him/her. Then discuss the things the two of you might tell this person. Write the letter, taking turns with writing sentences or paragraphs. Be sure to point out the format of a letter (date, greeting, closing, etc.). Don't forget to address an envelope together and drop it in the mail!

I See

While driving in the car, play this fun alphabet game. Ask your child to look out the window to find something that begins with the letter A, such as airplane. Then look for something that begins with B, such as building. Continue in this manner identifying objects for each letter of the alphabet.

Dear Parent,

Here is some information that will help you to better understand children's development of mathematical knowledge.

First of all, people in general learn best by actively constructing their own understanding. Constructivist theory suggests the following environments for learning:

- Learners have opportunities to build on prior knowledge.

- Learners construct new knowledge and understanding from authentic experience.

- Children should have the opportunity to confront real-life problems.

- Children are encouraged to explore possibilities, invent alternative solutions, collaborate with others, try out ideas, and revise their thinking.

Passive environments that focus on the use of textbooks don't often allow children to explore as they learn math skills and don't emphasize problem solving. It is important that adults promote opportunities for children to explore and build on their mathematical understanding.

When practicing math skills at home with your child, it is important not to just drill your child with number recognition and math facts. There is so much more to understanding math skills. Instead, focus on the following:

- Engage your child in everyday mathematical experiences.

- Ask questions to determine your child's understanding.

- Explore possibilities.

- Discuss ideas.

- Allow your child to use manipulative materials to assist in mathematical understanding.

- Apply math skills to real-life situations.

According to Jean Piaget, mathematical understanding develops in stages. Keep these in mind as you work with your child and observe his/her progress:

1. Young children typically think in a forward direction, which means they can struggle with concepts that involve thinking in reverse, such as doing subtraction.

(continues)

(continued)

2. Children often have a difficult time seeing more than one point of view or more than one way of doing things. Your child may only be able to see one way of solving a problem.

3. Young children can have difficulty solving problems mentally, so it is important to provide them with hands-on materials to assist with problem solving.

4. Children learn from mistakes. The more they understand about the way math works in real life, the better able they will be to recognize their errors.

5. Learning is a social process. Children benefit from working with others.

Dear Parent,

Counting is a fun way to spend time with your child and practice math skills. Try these activities with your child.

Jellybeans

Put 10 or fewer jellybeans (or other small candies) into a dish. Have your child guess how many jelly beans are in the dish. Then count them to see if the guess was correct. Depending on the age and skill level of your child, gradually increase the number of jellybeans.

Get Physical

Have fun with counting while getting fit! Bounce a ball while counting the bounces. Jump rope while counting each jump. Try to increase the number counted over time.

Counting Cars

While you're driving around town, count cars. Select a particular color. Then count all of the cars seen in that color.

Counting around the House

There are many things to count around the house. Work with your child to count the total number of doors, windows, or closets. Count to higher numbers by counting toys, pans, or pens.

Clap Counting

Take a few minutes to do clap counting with your child. Select a number, such as 10. Then clap as you both count from 1 to 10. Increase the level of difficulty as your child becomes ready.

Dear Parent,

Have fun doing math activities with your child. Here are some activities for practicing addition and subtraction.

Bingo

Make a math fact bingo game and play it with your child. On a sheet of paper, draw a grid with three rows of three boxes. Then cut out squares of paper. On each paper square, write a math fact, such as 5 + 1, 2 + 2, 1 + 3, and so on. Then, in each square of the grid, write an answer to one of the math facts. To play, select a card with a math fact on it. Ask your child to determine the answer and find the answer on the grid. When found, it is covered with a game marker. Play until all squares on the grid are covered. (Be sure to provide manipulatives (beans, pebbles, etc.) to assist your child in determining answers.

Cereal Math

Adding and subtracting with cereal is lots of fun. First, select a cereal that is easy to use, such as Os. (Flakes won't be easy to use.) Sit at the table and work together to count out piles of 10 cereal pieces. Separate the 10 pieces to make different combinations that add up to 10. For example: 2 + 8, 1 + 9, 6 + 4, 3 + 7, and so on.

Adding to Ten

This game will help your child learn different ways to add up to 10. You'll need 10 playing cards (ace through 10). Lay the cards out on a table face up. To play, take turns picking up two cards that, when added together, add up to 10. When two matches are found, the player keeps the cards.

Math War

This game can be played in different ways, depending on the skill level of your child. Prepare by removing the face cards from a deck of regular playing cards. Divide the deck between you and your child. (1) Each player lays down one card. The person who lays down the card with the highest number keeps both cards. (2) Each player lays down two cards. Each player adds up the total of the numbers he/she put down. The player with the highest total keeps all four cards.

Dear Parent,

There are many ways to spend time with your child while practicing money-counting skills. Try these activities with your child and have fun!

Loose Change

Locate loose change around the house. Collect the money in a jar for a week. Then sit down and count the coins. First, identify each kind of coin and its value. Then work together to count them. Depending on the ability level of your child, you may want to count just a few coins at a time. Provide more assistance as the total increases.

Grocery Store Counting

Use time in the grocery store to practice counting money values. For example, ask your child to identify the cost of a box of cereal. Ask him or her to figure out how much it would cost for two boxes.

Allowance

If your child receives a weekly allowance, try this fun activity. On a table, place two piles of coins. Each pile should have a different total value. Ask your child to count the two sets of coins and agree to give him or her the pile that has the most money.

Count the Ways

How many ways can you make 10 cents? Help your child add coins and combine them in different ways, such as one nickel and five pennies, one dime, or two nickels. As your child is ready, work together to determine coin combinations that add up to 25 cents or 50 cents.

Dear Parent,

Get Creative!

Spend some creative time with your child doing the following art activities.

Sticks

You and your child can make interesting artwork using wooden craft sticks. You'll need to use thick craft glue to make the sticks adhere effectively. Just overlap the sticks to make interesting shapes and then glue the sticks together. Glue on glitter to the finished product for additional flair.

Out We Go!

Painting is always great fun, but painting outdoors is a novel experience. Pack up paper, paint, paintbrushes, and water and head to the park or even to the backyard. Use interesting items to add detail to the pictures by painting with leaves, rocks, sticks, and blades of grass. You'll be amazed at the creativity that is inspired in you and your child as you paint under a beautiful blue sky.

Finger Painting

Get messy with your child by enjoying some time doing finger painting. You can make a simple (and edible) finger paint with pudding. Prepare several kinds of pudding in different colors. You can always add food coloring to vanilla pudding (but it may stain your fingers a bit). Then sit with your child and smear the "paint" onto construction paper. Don't forget to lick your fingers to clean up!

Dear Parent,

Ready, Set, Cook!

Cooking is a great activity to do with your child. It allows you to spend quality time together and can help to teach valuable skills.

Pizza Time

Using a ready-made pizza crust, work with your child to spread on sauce and sprinkle on cheese. Have your child add all of the family's favorite toppings, such as pepperoni slices, mushrooms, and black olives. Depending on the age of your child, you can have a conversation about fractions. For example, "Let's see if you can put pepperoni on half of the pizza."

Cookies

Why not spend time with your child by making a batch of cookies together? Get out measuring cups and show your child how to measure certain ingredients. Have fun creating goodies for the family as you share precious time together.

Balanced Diet Snacks

Discuss healthy eating with your child. Then work together to create a plate of healthy snacks for you and your child to enjoy together. Ask your child to name foods that are healthy to eat. Encourage discussion about different kinds of foods—fruits and vegetables, bread, and protein. Then make a snack plate using these foods, including cut-up apples, carrot sticks, crackers, and cheese. Enjoy!

Dear Parent,

Here are some great activities to try with your child. Have fun!

Activity #1:

_____

_____

_____

_____

Activity #2:

_____

_____

_____

_____

Activity #3:

_____

_____

_____

_____

Backpack Activities

Backpack activities are great ways to motivate parents and children to work together. These are a bit more involved than the activity letters. For this kind of activity, you send home a backpack filled with specific supplies and an instruction sheet. The child gets to keep the backpack for a few days, during which time he or she completes the activity with a parent. Usually, a backpack activity includes a journal of some kind for recording family experiences.

In this section, several backpack activities are provided. You'll see a brief description of each activity for you, and instructions for preparing the backpack materials. This is followed by the instruction letter to be included in the backpack for parents. Be sure to designate a set number of days that a family can keep a particular backpack. When the backpack is returned, check to make sure that all supplies have been returned. (To assist with returning supplies, each instruction sheet contains a list of materials. This way, parents and children can be sure that all the materials on the list have been returned to the backpack before returning it to school.) In addition to this, you'll find a letter template at the end of this chapter that allows you to create your own activity instructions.

Backpack #1: Solids and Liquids

For this activity, you'll need to include a variety of supplies (see parent instructions). You can also include additional activities and additional directions by writing them on the spaces provided on the instruction sheet. Be sure to include several copies of the observation chart. That way, if a parent and child need a new observation chart or decide to complete more than one, the extras will be included. For storing solids and liquids, be sure to use containers that won't easily come open inside the backpack.

Backpack #1: Parent Instruction Letter

Have fun working with your child to learn about solids and liquids. Let the investigations begin! Please return the backpack and materials to school on the following date: _____

Materials Included:

1 container of a liquid (water)

1 container of a solid (rock)

clipboard

observation chart (several have been included)

pencil

_____

_____

_____

Directions:

1. Explain to your child that some things are solid and some are liquid. Ask your child to name any solids or liquids he or she can think of.

2. Look at the two containers. Ask your child to identify which is a solid and which is a liquid.

3. On the observation chart, make a list of all of the characteristics of a solid and those of a liquid. (You can have your child write the words or he/she can dictate the words for you to write down.)

4. Place the observation sheet on the clipboard and go through the house, looking for solids and liquids. Record these on the observation chart.

5. Return all of the materials to the backpack, including the completed chart and have your child bring it back to school by the specified date (see above).

Additional comments or directions:

_____

_____

_____

_____

Solids and Liquids Observation Chart

Write words to describe solids and liquids.

Solids   Liquids

_____   _____

_____   _____

_____   _____

_____   _____

Look through the house for solids and liquids. Write the things you find on the lines below.

Solids   Liquids

_____   _____

_____   _____

_____   _____

_____   _____

Backpack #2: Story Creations

This activity allows a parent and child to work together to write a story. As a follow-up activity, they are encouraged to spell particular words using letters cut from magazines and newspapers. Before sending the backpack home, be sure to include a new magazine and newspaper if necessary. Also, check to make sure the glue sticks don't need to be replaced.

Backpack #2: Parent Instruction Letter

It's time for you and your child to work together to write a story. Follow the directions below. Please return this backpack and supplies to school by the following date: _____

Materials Included:

paper

pencil

2 pairs of scissors

2 glue sticks

1 newspaper

1 magazine

word chart

Directions:

1. Work with your child to write a story. Take turns writing parts of the story on the paper or have your child dictate words of the story as you write.
2. After writing the story, identify words to practice spelling. Underline these words in the story.
3. Write each selected word on the word chart provided. Then look through the magazine and newspaper to find letters to use to spell each word. Glue the letters from the magazine and newspaper onto the chart.
4. Be sure to return the materials to the backpack and send it back to school by the specified date (see above).

Words to Spell	Spelled with Magazine/Newspaper Letters
1.	
2.	
3.	
4.	
5.	
6.	
7.	
8.	
9.	

Word Chart

Backpack #3: Nature

This activity encourages parents and children to observe items in nature and re-create them in drawings. Be sure that the notebook provided is filled with unlined paper for drawing pictures. When a student returns the backpack to school, allow him or her to share the pictures and sentences added to the notebook.

Backpack #3: Parent Instruction Letter

Enjoy the great outdoors with your child. Then complete this activity together. Return the backpack and supplies by the following date:

_____

Materials Included:

plastic container with lid

notebook filled with unlined paper

crayons or colored pencils

pencil

survey/feedback sheet

Directions:

1. Take a walk outside and look for interesting items in nature, such as rocks, leaves, twigs, and so on.
2. Place the items in a plastic container.
3. Take the container to a table or other flat surface and color pictures of the items in the notebook.
4. Write a sentence or two about each object. You and your child can take turns writing or have your child dictate sentences as you write.
5. Return the supplies to the backpack and have your child bring it back to school by the specified date (see above).

Backpack #4: Good Days and Bad

This activity offers a variety of experiences for parents and children. You will need to provide a copy of Judith Viorst's book *Alexander and the Terrible, Horrible, No Good, Very Bad Day*. You'll also need to include a disposable camera. Be sure to remind the children not to take more than two photographs when instructed to do so. Tell the students that after the film gets developed, they will be able to add photos to the stories they wrote about their families.

Backpack #4: Parent Instruction Letter

Try these fun activities based on a favorite children's book.

Materials Included:

Alexander and the Terrible, Horrible, No Good, Very Bad Day, by Judith Viorst

journal or notebook filled with lined paper

pencil

disposable camera

1. Begin the activity by reading the book *Alexander and the Terrible, Horrible, No Good, Very Bad Day*, by Judith Viorst to your child. Have a discussion with your child about good and bad days each of you has had.
2. Open the journal or notebook and write a story about a bad day you had. Depending on the skill level of your child, you may need to write the story as your child dictates the words.
3. Discuss a good day that your family has had together.
4. Take one or two photographs of your family together using the enclosed disposable camera.
5. Then write a story about something the family has done together. Leave space on the page for the photos to be attached after they are developed.
6. Return all of the supplies to the backpack and have your child bring it back to school by the specified date (see above).

Backpack #5: What's the Weather Like Today?

For this activity, you will need to provide a thermometer used for measuring outdoor temperatures. Be sure to use a durable thermometer that will withstand some bumping around in a backpack. This backpack should stay with the family for a little longer than the usual two or three days as the instructions ask the parent and child to monitor the weather for five days.

Backpack #5: Parent Instruction Letter

Spend time observing changes in the weather with this set of activities. Return the backpack and supplies in five days on the following date:

_____

Materials Included:

weather chart

pencil

weather thermometer

Date	Sunny? Windy? Cloudy? Rainy? Snowy?	Temperature

Comments:

_____

_____

_____

Weather Chart

1. Each day for the next five days, you and your child will track the weather.
2. At the same time each day, look outside and determine if the weather is sunny, windy, cloudy, rainy, or snowy. Record the weather on the chart.
3. Take the thermometer outside and place it in the same place each day. Let it sit for 10 minutes or so. Then read the temperature with your child. Record the temperature on the chart.
4. At the end of the week, write a few sentences at the bottom of the chart, telling what you noticed about the weather.
5. Return the materials to the backpack and have your child bring it back to school by the specified date (see above).

Backpack #6: High-Frequency Words

To prepare for this activity you will need to select about 10 high-frequency words appropriate for your students to learn. Write each word in large letters on a separate note card. Then write the same words on wooden craft sticks or tongue depressors. You'll also need to provide an empty coffee can or any other empty container tall enough to hold the wooden sticks without tipping over.

Backpack #6: Parent Instruction Letter

Many words in our language are called high-frequency words. This means that we encounter them often in print. The more high-frequency words your child knows, the easier reading will be. Try these activities to help your child learn new words.

Materials Included:

list of first 25 words

3 × 5 note cards

markers

tongue depressors

coffee can

1. You will see that each note card has a different high-frequency word on it. Review these words with your child.
2. Ask your child to create a sentence using that word.
3. Select a children's book to look through. Ask your child to locate any high-frequency words he/she can find.
4. Find the wooden sticks and the can in the backpack. You'll notice that each stick has a high-frequency word written on it.
5. Place the sticks in the can, so the words are facing the bottom of the can. Take turns selecting a stick from the can and reading the word.
6. Return the materials to the backpack and send it back to school with your child by the specified date (see above).

Backpack #7: Take a Look

For this activity, you will need to include two magnifying lenses. You may have access to these in a science kit. If the lenses are made of glass, caution your students to be very careful with them. Include a journal or a notebook filled with lined paper and pencils.

Backpack #7: Parent Instruction Letter

Children are fascinated by science, so work with your child to hone their observation skills. Return the backpack and all supplies to school on the following date: _____

Materials Included:

2 magnifying glasses

journal or notebook

pencil

Directions:

1. There are two magnifying glasses in this backpack—one for you and one for your child. Go into the yard or to a park and begin your observations.
2. Look in the dirt, in the grass, and under leaves and rocks. What do you see? Is there anything moving? Stir the dirt around or run your hand over the grass. Do you see any living things?
3. When you find something interesting invite your child to take a look, and have your child do the same with you.
4. Be sure to look for patterns on leaves and blades of grass. Look for interesting patterns and colors on insects you find.
5. Next, write in the journal or notebook about the things you observed. Depending on the writing level of your child, you may need to ask him/her to dictate as you write.
6. Take turns drawing pictures of interesting things you saw.
7. Return the supplies to the backpack and send it back to school with your child by the specified date (see above).

Backpack #8: Bubbles

This activity requires several items. See the supply list. You will also need to replenish the supplies each time the backpack is returned to school. Provide more dishwashing soap and new, unused straws for the next family to use. The type of tray you include is up to you. You can use an aluminum or a plastic tray. It should be about two inches deep. Remember, though, that a sturdier tray will be less likely to get crunched in the backpack.

Backpack #8: Parent Instruction Letter

Everyone loves bubbles! Take some time to play with bubbles with your child. Return the backpack and supplies on the following date: _____

Materials Included:

dishwashing liquid

2 drinking straws

a shallow tray

a journal or notebook

pencil

Directions:

1. Mix the dishwashing liquid with water in the aluminum tray.
2. You and your child should both take a straw. Blow into the soap mixture.
3. Blow hard through the straw. Then blow gently. Are the bubbles different when you blow in different ways?
4. Touch the bubbles. What happens to them?
5. Write in the journal or notebook about what you experienced. Depending on the writing level of your child, you may need to have him/her dictate as you write.
6. Answer the following questions:
   - What is the best way to make big bubbles?
   - What is the best way to make small bubbles?
   - What happened when you touched the bubbles?
   - What else was interesting to you?
7. Return supplies to the backpack and send it back to school with your child by the specified date (see above).

Backpack #9: Does It Dissolve?

There are many supplies needed for this backpack activity. First of all, you will need small containers, such as baby food jars or plastic tubs with lids. The coffee is supposed to be an example of a substance that will not dissolve, so be sure not to use instant coffee. Be sure to use containers whose lids will stay on securely. You will also need to include small cups. Disposable paper cups will work fine.

Backpack #9: Parent Instruction Letter

Here's a fun activity for practicing prediction skills, while learning about the kinds of things that do and don't dissolve. Return the backpack and supplies to school on the following date: _____

Materials:

5 small paper cups

plastic spoon

recording chart

pencil

small container of dirt

small container of baking soda

small container of coffee grounds

small container of salt

small container of tea leaves

Directions:

1. Fill each paper cup with water.
2. Write the name of each substance (in the containers) on the recording sheet.
3. Select a substance to begin with. Make a prediction. Will it dissolve? Write "yes" or "no" on the chart.
4. Scoop out a spoonful of the substance and stir it into a cup of water. Did the substance dissolve or not? Write the results on the recording chart.
5. Continue in this manner with each of the substances. Then try more experiments with other nontoxic substances in your home.
6. Seal the containers tightly and return the supplies to the backpack. Send it back to school with your child by the specified date (see above).

Backpack Activity: _____

Message to Parent: _____

_____

Materials Included:

_____   _____

_____   _____

_____   _____

_____   _____

Directions:

1. _____

2. _____

3. _____

4. _____

5. _____

6. _____

7. _____

8. _____

9. _____

10. _____

Return the backpack and supplies to school with your child on the following date:

_____

▦ CONCLUSION

As you can see, there are many ways to involve parents in their children's education at home. This, in fact, is the most beneficial way that parents can be involved. When parents express interest in their children and express the value of education, research shows us that these benefits to children and families are great. Use the ideas and activities in this chapter to create more activities for children and families that are motivational and appropriate to their specific needs.

▦ SUMMARY OF IMPORTANT POINTS

- Most teachers think of family involvement as engaging parents in the structure of the school by volunteering, participating in conferences, and attending school events.
- The majority of the research citing benefits of family involvement focuses on the benefits when parents are involved with their children's education at home.
- Merely involving parents within the structure of the school actually does little to benefit student/school achievement.
- Teachers must express to parents their value in the educational process and provide them with ideas for working with their children at home in fun and interactive ways.

▦ CHAPTER REVIEW QUESTIONS

1. Why is family involvement at home so important?
2. If **family involvement at school** doesn't do much to affect student achievement, can you think of reasons why this form of involvement might still be important?
3. As teachers, what can we do to engage parents in **interactive experiences** with their children's education?
4. In what kinds of ways should we encourage parents to be involved in their children's education?

▦ APPLICATION AND REFLECTION

1. Review the parent activity letters. Identify the letters that would be most appropriate for the age group you teach or will teach.

2. Review the activities in the parent letters. Are there activities in a variety of letters that you would combine differently to create a letter more appropriate to the needs of your students? Use the parent activity letter template to create your own.

3. Create a list of original parent-child activities. Record your ideas on the parent activity letter template provided.

4. Identify the backpack activities that you would most likely assemble and send home with your students.

5. Use the backpack template to create an activity of your own.

▇ FURTHER READING

Cook, D. F. (2004). *Family fun kits: Family night*. Cook Disney Editions.

Davis, L., & Keyser, J. (1997). *Becoming the parent you want to be: A sourcebook of strategies for the first five years*. Broadway.

Weidmann, J., & Bruner, K. (1998). *An introduction to family nights: Creating lasting impressions for the next generation*. Chariot Victor Publishing.

Wollman-Bonilla, J. (2000). *Family message journals: Teaching writing through family involvement*. National Council of Teachers.

For additional information on research-based practice, visit our Web site at http://www.earlychilded. delmar.com.

Additional resources for this chapter can be found on the Online Companion™ to accompany this text at www.earlychilded.delmar.com. This supplemental material includes Web links, downloadable forms, and Case Studies with critical thinking applications. This content can be used as a study aid to reinforce key concepts presented in this chapter and to conduct additional research on topics of interest.

▇ REFERENCES

Briggs, C., & Elkind, D. (1973). Cognitive development in early readers. *Developmental Psychology, 9*(2), 279–280.

Clark, M. M. (1984). Literacy at home and at school: Insights from a study of young fluent readers. In H. Goelman, A. Oberg, & F. Smith (Eds.), *Awakening to literacy* (122–130). Portsmouth, NJ: Heinemann.

Durkin, D. (1966). Children who read early. New York: Teachers College Press.

Finn, J. (1998). Parental engagement that makes a difference. *Educational Leadership, 55*(8), 20–24.

Gambrell, L. B. (1996). Creating classroom cultures that foster reading motivation. Distinguished Educator Series. *The Reading Teacher, 50,* 14–25.

Goodman, Y. (1984). The development of initial literacy. In H. Goelman, A. Oberg, & F. Smith (Eds.), *Awakening to Literacy* (102–109). Portsmouth, NJ: Heinemann.

Heath, S. B. (1980). The functions and uses of literacy. *Journal of Communication, 30,* 123–133.

Jones, R. (November, 2001). Involving parents is a whole new game: Be sure you win! *The Education Digest, 67*(3), 36–43.

Leichter, H. P. (1984). Families as environments for literacy. In H. Goelman, A. Oberg, & F. Smith (eds.), *Awakening to literacy.* Portsmouth, NJ: Heinemann.

McBride, S. (1999). Family centered practices. *Young Children, 54*(2), 74–79.

Morrow, L. (2004). *Literacy development in the early years: Helping children read and write.* Boston, MA: Allyn & Bacon.

Peterson, K. (January/February, 2002). Creating home-school partnerships. *Early Childhood News,* 39–45.

Sulzby, E. (1985). Children's emergent reading of favorite storybook. *Reading Research Quarterly, 20,* 458–481.

Teale, W. (1984). Positive environments for learning to read: What studies of early readers tell us. *Language Arts, 55,* 922–932.

Vygotsky, L. (1981). The genesis of higher mental functions. In J. J. Wertsch (Ed.), *The concept of activity.* White Plains, NY: M. E. Sharpe.

Yaden, D. B., Rowe, D. W., & MacGillivray, L. (2000). Emergent literacy: A matter (polyphony) of perspectives. In M. L. Kamil, P. B. Mosental, P. D. Pearson, & R. Barr (Eds.), *Handbook of reading research* (425–454). Mahwah, NJ: Lawrence Erlbaum Associates.

7

Family Involvement with Infant/Toddler Care and Education

▪ CHAPTER OBJECTIVES

After reading and reflecting on this chapter, you should be able to:

- Explain the growing body of research relating to parents as the first, most important teachers for infants and toddlers.
- Explain how involving the parents of infants and toddlers in early childhood care and education entails parent education.
- Expand the definition of successful family involvement to include creation of a family support system as well as a parent partnership.
- Identify the culturally sensitive practices in learning to work with diverse families of infants and toddlers.
- Outline activities and strategies for creating successful parent education and parent collaboration.

▪ KEY TERMS

attachment	family focused
critical periods	neuron

neuroscientific

parent educator

parent support

parentese

proximo-distal

psychosocial development

synapse

THE EARLY INFANT AND TODDLER YEARS

In the preceding chapters, discussion of family involvement in early childhood has focused on schools and parent involvement. Before a child goes off to school, the early infant and toddler years establish the foundation for school readiness and academic achievement. Family involvement in those crucial first three years of early childhood creates the cognitive building blocks for all learning and achievement. This chapter will focus on the importance of parent education and strategies for building family support systems and collaboration with families for infants and toddlers.

RESEARCH ON FAMILY INVOLVEMENT WITH INFANT/TODDLER CARE AND EDUCATION

As we begin this discussion of family involvement with infants and toddlers, we must emphasize that with very young children, the teacher's central role is that of **parent educator.** A major responsibility of the teacher of infants and toddlers is to disseminate a wide array of information. Whether the information is the most recent neuroscience, or helpful parenting tips, or referrals for community resources, the teacher of infants and toddlers can empower parents. If you are a parent, you understand how all-consuming and challenging parenting can be, but it is not only challenging; it is also exhausting. As the teacher of infants or toddlers, parents need your support and your solidarity to meet the challenges presented by the media, mass marketing, a changing society, and the fast and furious pace of modern society (Figure 7–1). Early childhood teachers more than any others require coaching in family involvement strategies to create and maintain successful parent partnerships.

Infants have traditionally been thought of as children up to 12 months old and toddlers 12 to 36 months old. Young children in the 0 to 3 age range are being included in child care and early childhood education programs more and more often today. Teachers and caregivers for children this young must work very closely with parents and family members for the benefit of the child's development. A wealth of research supports the

FIGURE 7–1   As the teacher of infants or toddlers, parents need your support.

commonsense notion that family involvement with infants and toddlers improves later academic performance; and that it results in higher school grades, higher scores on standardized tests, better classroom behaviors, and better attitudes toward school and learning.

The Brain Research

The most exciting and innovative research in infant and toddler cognitive development has emerged in the last two decades. Often called the "Decade of the Brain," the 1990s saw years of mounting research evidence in the neursocientific study of brain development. Brain research has affirmed the practices that early childhood practitioners have maintained for years: The first three years of human development are crucial years for learning and

Neuron

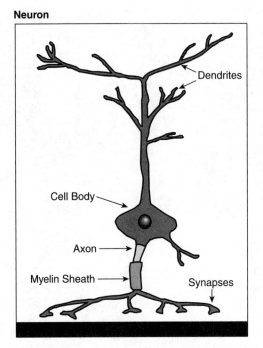

FIGURE 7–2   An infant has trillions of brain neurons that are layers of unconnected cells.

development; and parents and family members are the first, most important teachers for the infant and toddler (Shonkoff & Philips, 2000).

The most powerful neuroscienctific finding in the research on family involvement with infants and toddlers is the evidence that intellectual capacity develops after a baby is born. It is not set at birth. The wiring of a child's brain occurs *after* birth through rich experiences and interactions in the critical first three years. Traditionally, scientists have believed that brain function and IQ are determined at conception and the wiring of the brain is genetically predetermined. The role of genetics accounts for only about half of learning and intelligence while environment and experiences account for the remaining half (Bacanu, Devlin, & Roeder, 2000; Bouchard, 1988). **Neuroscientific** study of the brain has demonstrated that at birth, an infant has trillions of brain **neurons** that are layers of unconnected cells (Figure 7–2). If the neurons are used, they become integrated into the dense, interconnected web of circuitry in the brain. These connections are called **synapses.** It is during the first three years of life that most of the synapses in the infant brain are created. If neurons are not used, and synapses do not form, these neurons are killed off in a pruning process that fine-tunes the brain at about 8 to 10 years of age. Early experiences and interactions for the infant/toddler encourage the connections that develop between neurons. As the child actively investigates the world, neurons are generating massive, detailed dendrite branches (Huttenlocher & Dabholkar, 1997). Pediatric neurobiologist Harry Chugani says that the early experiences that an infant/toddler has in the critical early years "can completely change the way the person turns out" (1996). Most early experiences and interactions for an infant/toddler are the first interactions with parents and primary caregivers.

Brain development in the young child hinges on the relationship between nature and nurture. The brain is shaped by the environmental conditions of nourishment, care, stimulation, and language exposure in which each infant is bathed. The ways that parents and caregivers meet the needs of babies and the kinds of care parents and caregivers use to buffer the environment have a lifelong impact on how the baby develops, how the baby is able to learn, and how the baby is able to self-regulate (Polan & Hofer, 1999; Shore, 1997). Neuroscientists have found that emotional development, in particular, is shaped by the quality of **attachment** a parent or caregiver has with the infant. Responsive, warm caregiving has a protective, biological function that shields the infant from the stresses of daily life and allows it to adequately develop emotional "wherewithal." Rich language exposure means a rich tangle of auditory neurons for the infant. The more words spoken to a child, the faster that child develops language (Huttenlocher, et al., 1998). Adequate, proper nutrition and medical care ensure that the developing brain has the levels of protein and nutrients necessary for optimal growth and development.

The negative of these neuroscientific findings is disturbing. Early experiences of neglect and trauma can have a lasting, damaging effect on the development of the infant brain. Inadequate or neglectful care of young children results in insecure attachment and affects the emotional development and behavioral control of the child. Neglectful or abusive conditions in the earliest years can cause the developing brain to reorganize itself and consume vital energy in coping with stress. Researchers have shown that neglect, emotional detachment, social deprivation, and a lack of stimulation are the primary factors in hardwiring the brain for negative behaviors, violence, and aggression (McEwen & Schmeck, 1994; Perry, 1993). After age three the effects of abuse and neglect are extremely difficult to reverse.

Neuroscience breakthroughs have also revealed for us that the human brain is extremely "plastic." The brain is able to change and adapt in crucial ways as a response to experience (Cacioppo, Berntson, Sheridan, & McClintock, 2001). The brain can be altered; it compensates for problems and deprivation in a remarkable way (Francis, Dioro, Plotsky, & Meaney, 2002). Because of this, caregivers and teachers have the responsibility to promote and support the healthy growth and development of infants and toddlers. Optimal brain development in infants and toddlers seems to occur in "prime times" or **critical periods** when the brain is tuned to specific types of learning. Parents, caregivers, and teachers must be sensitive to these critical periods in brain development in order to contribute the best possible experiences to the healthy development of the baby. "This is an opportunity, really—one of nature's provisions for us to be able to use the environmental exposure to change the anatomy of the brain and to make it more efficient" (Chugani, 1997; see Figure 7–3).

Recent research breakthroughs in early brain development and school readiness indicate the following general guidelines for responsive care of babies and young children.

- Seek regular prenatal care for the health, safety, and good nutrition of the unborn baby.
- Breastfeed if possible for optimal nutrition and to give the baby skin-to-skin stimulation.
- Get regular well-baby checkups and timely immunizations.
- Safety proof the home and child care location of the baby.
- Always use an approved car seat whenever a baby is traveling in a car; be sure it is properly installed in the car.
- Show the baby deep care and express joy in who he or she is.
- Respond to the baby's cues and clues for interaction and care.
- Notice the baby's rhythms of wakefulness, sleepiness, hunger, alertness, and moods.
- Respond to the baby when it is first upset, so that the baby will develop a sense of dependability.
- Hold, touch, play with, and talk to the baby often, but watch for signs of overstimulation.
- Recognize that each infant is unique and will develop his/her own temperament, and at his/her own pace.
- Talk, sing, and read to your child daily. Surround the baby with the lilt of language by maintaining a running conversation with him/her.
- Toddlers can play word games and play with language as you read books, sing songs, do fingerplays, and tell stories.

FIGURE 7–3 Responsive Caregiving. *(Continues)*

Adapted from Shore, 1997.

- Provide a host of colorful toys and playthings to stimulate the baby visually.
- Allow safe exploration and play by moving around, exploring, and playing in different environments.
- Give the baby the opportunity to explore social relationships by arranging for him/her to spend time interacting with other children.
- Help the baby to begin to learn to resolve conflicts by using words.
- Use discipline as an opportunity to teach moral behavior. Teach with words, use expressions of feelings, tell the "whys" of behavior expectations.
- Tell children what they are to do as well as what they are not to do.
- Establish routines such as meal times, nap times, bedtimes, and play times so that children can depend on you.
- Be involved in child care and school environments and spend time with your child in his or her learning setting.
- Strictly limit television to those shows and videos that will help learning.
- Be sure to take care of yourself so that you can be the best parent/caregiver possible.

FIGURE 7–3   (*Continued*)

The window of opportunity for vision occurs early, within the first year of life, reaching its peak at about 10 months (Fine et al., 2003; Wilson, 1993). However, visual acuity, the ability of the eye to discriminate fine detail, develops steadily until about age eight. The window of opportunity for language begins before birth as the infant brain hears and perceives the sounds of language while still in utero. In the first six months, the individual phonemes or sounds of the language spoken by parents and caregivers register in the brain, while all other sounds are screened out (Aslin & Hunt, 2001; see Figure 7–4.) Language acquisition is strongest in the first six to seven years of life, while the ability to acquire and enlarge vocabulary continues throughout our lifetime. Parents are instrumental teachers in helping the infant to learn language by using the singsong, elongated sounds of **"parentese"** (Fernald & Kuhl, 1987). Parents in all cultures change their speech patterns to exaggerate vowel sounds, shorten their utterances, and speak in a melodious way directly into the faces of their children. Parents are teaching the brains of their infants to hear, see, and reproduce the sounds of language in this way. (See Figure 7–5.) Figure 7–6 gives teachers and parents a general timetable for language development.

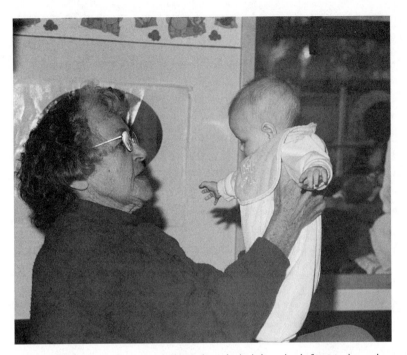

FIGURE 7–4   Parents are instrumental teachers in helping the infant to learn language by using the singsong, elongated sounds of "parentese."

The window of opportunity in motor skill development begins with large, basic motor functions. Large muscle groups are controlled by the infant in a pattern of **proximo-distal** development, that is, development which progresses from the center of the body out to the extremities of arms and legs. This critical period lasts until about age eight. Fine, delicate motor functions become differentiated at about two years old and develop over a lifetime. Beginning at about two months, the window of opportunity for emotional learning and moral development is determined by the level of distress or contentment and the level of attachment or neglect the infant experiences (Siegel, 1999). Complex feelings develop in layers in the early stages of attachment, including joy and sadness, envy and empathy, pride and shame, happiness and anger. Figure 7–7 outlines Erikson's stages of **psychosocial development,** based on the developmental concept that every child progresses through distinct stages of emotional, moral, and social growth. If there is appropriate early attachment, the conflict and crisis resolution of each stage is tempered by parents and the environment. "Experience is the chief architect of the brain" (Perry, 1996). Parents and caregivers create the environment and experiences that build the brain.

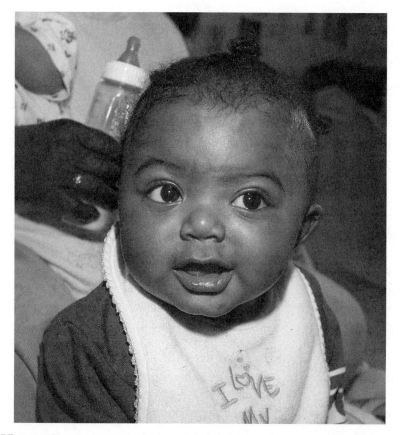

FIGURE 7–5   Parents teach the brains of their infants to hear, see, and reproduce the sounds of language.

A longitudinal study begun in 1975 by Egeland and Sroufe with 267 pregnant mothers affirms and supports the neuroscience findings. The researchers followed the mothers and their children, assessing them periodically with a series of psychological tests, interviews, questionnaires, and regular observations of mother–child interactions. The researchers paid particular attention to the children's early relationships with their primary caregivers. For 180 of the children remaining in the study, the researchers have concluded that

- attachments at one year of age predicted teacher ratings, behavior problems, and the quality of relationships with peers in preschool.

- attachments at one year of age predicted social competency at 10 years of age.

Most children will develop language skills according to this table. If a child does not demonstrate language at approximately this rate, parents need not panic but should seek medical guidance to rule out serious impairment.

Approximate Age	Language Skill
2 months	Baby cries and makes pleasure sounds in response to stimulus
3 months	Baby makes cooing, gurgling, chortling sounds
7 months	Baby makes directed, purposeful sounds such as a "raspberry"; baby plays vocally
10 months	Baby produces single-syllable babbling "ma," "pa," "ba," "da"
11 months	Baby produces multiple-syllable babbling "mama," "papa," "baba"; imitates facial expressions
14 months	Baby uses mama and dada to call parents
16 months	Baby uses other words besides mama and dada; attempts conversation
22 months	Baby may possess a vocabulary of four to six words, expresses some wants, and can be understood by others about half of the time
23 months	Baby combines two words to make short, incomplete sentences
26 months	Baby may possess a 200- to 300-word expressive vocabulary
29 months	Baby uses personal pronouns "me," "you," and "my"
34 months	Baby uses prepositions such as "by," "over," "on," can carry on a conversation, and can identify important objects, "cup," "blanket"
37 months	Can be understood by strangers most of the time
47 months	Can be easily understood by strangers

FIGURE 7–6   Typical Language Development.

Adapted from Copeland & Gleason, 1993.

- warm, responsive caregiving predicted more empathetic relationships with peers.
- warm, responsive caregiving teaches children to be socially connected.
- negative effects from poverty and environmental deprivation are cumulative and increase with age.

Stage of Basic Trust vs. Mistrust Develops approximately 0–18 months	Infants develop the capacity to trust based on whether others respond to their need for nourishment, sucking, warmth, physical contact
Stage of Autonomy vs. Shame Develops approximately 18 months–3 years	Toddlers develop self-sufficiency and independence when given freedom to test abilities in toileting, feeding, self-direction, etc.
Stage of Initiative vs. Guilt Develops approximately 3–5 years	Young children will attempt adult-like activities, misjudging their own capacities and limitations
Stage of Industry vs. Inferiority Elementary years	Children develop competence and productivity when allowed to do things on their own and praised for doing them well

FIGURE 7–7   Erikson's Stages of Psychosocial Development.
Adapted from Erikson, 1963.

- warm, responsive caregiving in poverty and environmental deprivation has buffering effects.
- abuse, trauma, and neglect have long-term, adverse effects on development.
- school achievement can be predicted by early experiences and attachments at one year of age.
- factors in resilience of infants are: responsive caregiving; early competence; well organized, predictable home environment; language exposure and capacities (Teo, Carlson, Mathieu, Egeland, & Sroufe, 1996).

Involving Parents and Families

While the brain research is compelling, there are other forms of research that support the invaluable contributions of parents to academic achievement through their involvement in the first years. Studies conducted through the past several decades have consistently demonstrated the critical importance of the home environment to later school success (Consortium for Longitudinal Studies, 1983; Hanson, 1975; Shipman et al., 1976; White et al., 1973). The findings from the Consortium for Longitudinal

---

FAMILIES IN FOCUS

Austyn is a marvelously typical baby boy (Figure 7–8). His parents are like many of today's young parents: His mother was careful to eat well, exercise, and visit her doctor during her pregnancy. She was zealous in not drinking alcohol at all while she was pregnant and avoided secondhand smoke and over-the-counter medications. Austyn's brain development began in this ideal environment. Both his mom and dad are madly in love with him. Though Austyn is breastfed, his father still actively nurtures him by holding, rocking, and singing to him each night at bedtime. Austyn is strongly attached to both parents and feels secure in their love and care.

Whether it is mealtime, bath time, or diaper-changing time, his mom holds a nonstop monologue with Austyn that fills his ears with the lilt and sounds of language. Her words are encouraging development in the centers of his brain where language functions begin. She keeps almost constant eye contact with him, and during diapering she tickles him and plays peekaboo with him. After meals, Austyn has "tummy time" on the living room floor with an array of bright, contrasting-colored toys to stimulate the visual centers of his brain. His mother shows him books filled with the pictures of animals in realistic illustrations. With each animal, she mimics the sound of the animal over and over. Austyn has begun to make the animal sounds in response to her . . . SSSSS says the snake. Baaaa says the sheep, Wooof says the doggy. Dad plays a name game with Austyn by walking with him around the house, pointing to family photos, and naming the family members. They also play peekaboo with dad's large ball cap. These games help Austyn to develop cognitively and emotionally. His mom and dad are responsive, warm parents with a securely attached baby.

Studies, an organization of researchers who examine early childhood intervention research, in particular, focused on three elements of parent involvement in early childhood. Frequent home visits, providing services to parents, and involving parents in the instruction of their young children resulted in ability gains later in school. "Closer contact between home and school and greater involvement of parents in the education of their children are probably more important" than ever realized (Lazar, 1983, p. 464).

The research evidence with infants and toddlers supports our experience that this crucial early family involvement improves academic achievement and school success in the later years. Greater parent participation in the early years has been shown to improve home behavior, school readiness, and adaptability in elementary school (Kessler-Sklar, et al., 1998; Lamb-Parker, Piotkowski, Horn, & Greene, 1995; Miedel & Reynolds,

FIGURE 7-8   Austyn is a marvelously typical baby boy.

1999; Petrie & Davidson, 1995; Reynolds, Mavrogenes, Bezruczko, & Hagemann, 1996). Henderson (1988) reports higher school grades, higher scores on standardized tests, more appropriate school behaviors, and schools that are more effective, when parents begin by participating in the education of their very young children. With active inclusion of parents by teachers and caregivers, parents report more interaction with their children at home and a sense of empowerment to help their children succeed: also, parents rate the teacher more highly (Jones, 1993). Children who grow up with their parents highly involved and genuinely concerned about schooling believe that their families value education.

An eight-year study in a "family focused" early childhood program revealed that the children in the program had highly significant gains in assessments that measure cognitive, language, vocabulary, and motor skills. The children had greater confidence levels and were significantly more capable of expressing social and emotional needs. Their families reported improved conditions in the home and children who did well and enjoyed public schooling. Parents participating in the program were expected to take part in decision making about their child's education. They participated in the center's policy council and in parenting support groups, and worked in the classroom with the teacher (Clarke, Mihata, & Frost, 1990). This study helps us to realize that families are more supportive of programs and are more involved when their participation is direct and meaningful.

Over the past four decades of research and practice, early childhood educators have redefined family involvement with very young children as the effective development of a *family support* system that functions much like an extended family might function (Powell, 1998). Parent education serves to teach parents what is best for the child and to encourage implementation of best practices at home from the perspective of the educator and the school. **Parent support,** however, views parents as equal partners in the development of best practice, and teachers work within the established family and community context to help families. Your role as teacher is to enable parents to fulfill the demands of providing sensitive, predictable, reliable care for their infants and toddlers. This includes connecting parents with resources and services in your community for prenatal care, complete nutritional care, care during and after childbirth, and immunizations and health care. Figure 7–9 is provided as a worksheet for you to begin assessing local services and recording contact information for parents. A comprehensive approach to family support goes beyond involving parents in sporadic school tasks or school processes and focuses on the family to empower, assist, and strengthen the family unit.

The National Association for the Education of Young Children accreditation criteria include expectations for parent education and family involvement in the accreditation processes of early care and education programs (1998). The National Council for the Accreditation of Teacher Education standards requires a family involvement component in certification of new teachers (2002). Quality indicators used by national organizations reflect the crucial role of family support and family involvement in the infant and toddler years. It is not an extra benefit but an important, necessary component of early care and education for you to begin planning now for the education and support of the parents of infants and toddlers.

An important element to creating good parent collaboration and effective family support is the match between the parents' view of what the child should be experiencing in his or her learning and how the teacher views the child's abilities. When parents' confidence in the caregivers and teachers of their infants and toddlers is high, they are more involved. Parent confidence

As you find the services and resources available in your community, contact each provider for brochures, flyers, or printed materials for you to have on hand at all times.

Public Assistance
Social Security
Aid to Family with Dependent Children
Food Stamps
WIC
Other_____

Legal Aid:_____
_____
_____

Prenatal Care:_____
_____
_____

Nutritional Services:_____
_____
_____

Childbirth Support:_____
_____
_____

Child Care/Day Care:_____
_____
_____

Parent Support Groups:_____
_____
_____

Immunizations:_____
_____

Counseling Agencies:_____
_____
_____

Medical Specialists for Children:
Orthopedist
Ophthalmologist
Genetic Counselor
Physical Therapist
Occupational Therapist
Speech Pathologist
Dietician
Pediatric Dentist
Oral Surgeon
Other_____

FIGURE 7–9   Worksheet of Community Services and Resources.

depends on the knowledge, skills, and level of caring they believe the caregivers and teachers possess. Parents express greater confidence if they have friendly, open communication with caregivers and teachers, if the caregivers and teachers have experience with child rearing, and if they discuss safety and discipline issues regularly with the parents (Powell, 1998). An essential ingredient to family involvement, then, for you as the teacher of an infant or toddler is excellent communication. You must talk frequently and consistently with the parents of the children you serve. Your communication must include the philosophy of your teaching and the expectations that you have for the children. You need to be available to parents. You must reinforce face-to-face communication with written communication. This also means that you must know and use the language of the families you serve. You must understand the structures, values, and traditions of the families you are striving to involve in early care and education; and your communication must be individualized. Each parent should have the opportunity to discuss his or her needs and concerns with you.

Barriers to successful parent support and family collaborations are often found in teacher perceptions of parents. Research by Dunn and Kontos (1989) revealed that teachers who believe that parents are doing a poor job of raising their infants and toddlers talk and communicate with the parents less often. Teachers communicated more frequently with parents they perceived to have higher cognitive, linguistic, or social skills. Teachers who emphasize parent support and family involvement in their classrooms tend to view parents more democratically and have more equal expectations, no matter what the family's circumstances (Epstein, 1985). As the teacher of infants and toddlers, it is important for you to be very aware of your feelings and internal reactions to parents.

ACTIVITIES AND STRATEGIES FOR INCREASING INVOLVEMENT WITH INFANTS AND TODDLERS

The research is clear: The quantity and quality of early learning experiences for the infant and toddler shapes how the brain works for a lifetime. Young children benefit enormously from increased parental involvement. Small changes create large benefits with good information and encouragement from you. What are the ways for you to support the parents of infants and toddlers? What meaningful activities and strategies can be a regular component of your classroom practice to involve parents and benefit children?

Family Home Visits

Home visits are one of the most valuable tools for early childhood caregivers and educators to use to focus on families. If you are committed to a full range of services to support families, home visits must be one of the services you offer. They are an excellent way for you to learn about families, their structure, family values, and the community context in an intimate, one-on-one fashion. The ideal arrangement is for home visits to begin during pregnancy. Home visiting nurses can offer a comprehensive model that focuses on multiple domains of growth and development at one time. Expectant families can be linked to childbirth care, prenatal care, nutritional support, and child care options during these home visits. Caregivers and educators can offer support as well as information about infant development during pregnancy.

If home visits during pregnancy are impossible, begin them as soon as the child is enrolled in your program. Your schedule as well as the parents' schedule will dictate how often you plan for home visits. Strive for a visit once a month for infants and toddlers. For your safety and for legal reasons, be sure to arrange "buddy visits" with a colleague, classroom teaching assistant, or center director accompanying you on the home visits. Careful planning for home visits means clustering them together in time and in location. For example, you may plan home visits for children who live in the same neighborhood in the same time frame. Figure 7–10 offers a record-keeping system for planning, organizing, and documenting home visits. Preplan your home visits with a simple outline of goals and objectives, keeping in mind that the ultimate purpose in your home visit is to equip parents as the first teachers of their children. (See Figure 7–11 for a follow-up self-evaluation.)

- Chat and take time to learn about family news, and events; *be approachable and get to know families in their environment.*

- Provide positive reports and observations about the child; *open up the lines of communication in a positive way.*

- Ask about and address parent concerns and questions; *demonstrate to parents that you are sincere in your desire to support the family.*

- Provide learning materials, learning games, and directions for home environment; *enhance the learning support for children in the home.*

```
┌─────────────────────────────────────────────────────────────────┐
│  Child's Name_____Age_____ │
│  Parents' Names_____Siblings_____ │
│  Address_____ │
│  Telephone_____                                      │
│  Home Visit Date_____  Time_____ │
│  Important Information Update from                                 │
│  Parents_____ │
│  Learning Materials Delivered_____ │
│  Observation Notes of Visit:                                      │
│  Environment_____ │
│  _____ │
│  Learning and Development in the                                  │
│  Home_____ │
│  _____ │
│  _____ │
│  Parental Questions or                                            │
│  Concerns_____ │
│  _____ │
│  Date and Time of Next Visit_____ │
└─────────────────────────────────────────────────────────────────┘
```

FIGURE 7–10   Home Visit Record Sheet.

- If possible, demonstrate and model learning activity with the child for the parent, reinforcing the learning and development involved in the activity; *support parents as the first teachers of their children and enhance their skills as parents.*
- Tentatively set time for the next home visit; *plan to return.*

After the visit, review your notes with your "buddy" and document the impact of the visit. Your combined perspectives on the visit will help you to understand families most clearly.

Governance and Decision Making

The family-centered approach to involving the parents of infants and toddlers in education recognizes that the entire family and the early childhood education program are interrelated. As in the Bronfenbrenner model described in Chapter 1, the caregiver or teacher acts as a bridge from home to the larger society. One important way that this bridge from home to school is made is through governance, decision making, and policy formation for the early childhood program. Parents, family members, and community members

Do you accept the parents' values about children, parenting, and education?	Yes	No
When you arrived for the visit, did you greet the parents, the child?	Yes	No
Did you include the parents in planning for the activities of the visit?	Yes	No
Was the child included in the visit, sitting beside the parent?	Yes	No
Did you model each new activity for the parent?	Yes	No
Did you identify and reinforce parent teaching strengths?	Yes	No
Did you identify and reinforce child learning strengths?	Yes	No
Did you let the parent be the primary encourager of the child?	Yes	No
Do you incorporate parent ideas into the activities as much as you can?	Yes	No
Do you think this visit was successful for the parent?	Yes	No
Do you think this visit was successful for the child?	Yes	No
Was this visit successful for you as the teacher?	Yes	No

FIGURE 7–11   Teacher Self-Evaluation of Home Visits.

should serve on committees that hire personnel, make policy for the program, and promote the school in the community. Curriculum decisions and philosophical discussions at the school level should also include parents, family members, and community members. Serving the school in these tasks helps parents come to a deeper understanding of the mission and vision of the school. Parent-teacher organizations create opportunity for parents to generate support and funds for the care and education of young children.

Communication with Parents

As we highlighted earlier in this chapter, the quality of your communication with the parents of infants and toddlers that you teach is essential to a **family-focused** program. There will be many opportunities for you to informally and casually communicate with family members of the children in your care. Each day as children are brought to your classroom or released to go home, your easy, casual conversations with parents and family are the richest source of family involvement. (Also, see Figure 7–12 for a daily record of infant care.) It is important for you to make these exchanges warm, positive, and friendly updates. Well-planned and well-executed formal communication channels will contribute much to the level of parent regard for, and involvement in, your program. The formal

```
┌─────────────────────────────────────────────────────────────┐
│                                          Date                 │
│                                          Caregiver            │
│  Arrival:_____│
│  Feedings:_____ │
│        Time                                                   │
│        Time                                                   │
│        Time                                                   │
│                                                               │
│  Diapering:_____ │
│  _____ │
│  Wakeful Time Activities:_____ │
│  _____ │
│  Observation Notes:_____ │
│  _____ │
│  Comments to Family:_____ │
│  _____ │
│  Homegoing:_____ │
│  _____ │
└─────────────────────────────────────────────────────────────┘
```

FIGURE 7–12   Daily Record of Infant Care.

communication methods we will examine more carefully are the parent handbook, newsletters and classroom activity calendars, telephone contact, electronic communication, and parent-professional conferences. Each method is invaluable for creating and cementing the connection between parents, family members, you, and the children that you care for.

Handbook

Chances are that your early care and education program has already created a family handbook. Ideally, your program or school has invested time and energy with parents, caregivers, teachers, and school administrators to write a comprehensive policy handbook that includes a mission statement or program philosophy, as well as goals and objectives for curriculum, child guidance, financial matters, health and safety concerns, and school emergency procedures. This handbook must begin with the state and local licensing guidelines and regulations for the care and nurturance of very young children. Check with your state offices for background and

```
State Agency Charged with Licensing Early Child Care and Education
Programs_____
Telephone #_____
E-mail Address_____
Street Address_____
Contact Person_____
Local Program Inspectors_____
Local Telephone #_____
E-mail Address_____
Street Address_____
Date Guidelines Requested_____
No. of Copies Requested_____
```

FIGURE 7–13   Worksheet for Information Gathering on State Licensing Guidelines.

information regarding state licensing requirements. Figure 7–13 should be used as a worksheet to gather information in your state on licensing for early childhood care and education.

If there is no handbook at your school, creating such a document need not be an overwhelming task. This can be an opportunity to build family involvement and communicate at the deepest level about children, their needs, and the goals for their development. Once you have gathered your state licensing requirements either from your administrator or from the state department charged with administration of early childhood, enlist parents and family members to meet to begin the writing process. Your handbook should build on the guidelines already in place at the state level. The handbook writing process should proceed in this general sequence:

- Give guidelines to all members of the handbook writing team for careful reading of the state licensing requirements.
- Review examples that you gathered—handbooks, policy books, etc., from other programs to help envision your handbook.
- Craft a mission and vision statement for the program if this has not been accomplished; this is the opportunity to communicate in depth with parents about their beliefs about learning and their child's needs.
- Fill in the gaps and silent places in the existing state guidelines with your program's policies; specific information about your program should be included in this step.

- Review and revise your work together over several meetings.
- Prepare the handbook for presentation; polish the document for printing.

Handbooks should be reviewed and revised on a regular basis with a parent advisory council. Revisions should go home to all families as soon as possible. Handbooks should also be easily accessible to parents and family members at all times in your classroom. Display the handbook with additional copies in an open, obvious place.

Enrollment Interview

At the time that an infant or child is enrolled in your program, you should begin a gradual process of including the child in your program. During this time period, family members and the child should visit the school several times and spend as much time as needed to become comfortable together. You might also conduct an enrollment interview at this time so that parents can tell you everything there is to know about their child. The interview should be as long as necessary for you to feel certain you understand their child's schedules and routines, likes and dislikes. Figures 7–14 and 7–15 provide a suggested format for conducting this interview. It is essential with infants and toddlers in your program that these be face-to-face interviews in order for you to connect well with parents and to help parents feel comfortable and at ease with you.

Newsletter/Activity Calendar

Your handbook should have a newsletter or activity calendar to supplement it on a consistent basis. The thought of creating and sending out a regular newsletter may feel overwhelming to you. We strongly encourage, even for very young children, that a newsletter be created to reinforce your connection to families and their connection to you. A newsletter template is provided in Chapter 5. Refer to that chapter for ideas and directions in creating your newsletter template. Most word-processing programs will allow you to customize and embellish your newsletter with attractive artwork, digital photos from your class, scans of work created by the children, and much more (Figure 7–16). Calendars can be created just as easily and can include upcoming events, important dates to remember, and your curriculum plans. Calendars can also be created on word-processing programs and embellished in the same way that your newsletter is customized (Figure 7–17). We have seen teachers and programs create newsletters with a back-to-back

Child's Name_____Date of Birth_____

Parent/Guardian_____

Home Address_____

Home Phone_____Work Phone_____

Cell Phone_____Pager_____

E-mail Address_____

2nd Parent/Guardian_____

Home Address_____

Home Phone_____Work Phone_____

Cell Phone_____Pager_____

E-mail Address_____

Authorized Persons to Pick up Child:

Name_____Name_____

Address_____

Address_____

Relationship_____

Relationship_____

Contact Phone #_____Contact Phone #_____

Family Cultural Background:_____

_____

_____

Important Family Celebrations_____

Home Language_____

Your Child_____

_____

Special Circumstances_____

Fears or Worries_____

Special Custody or Living Arrangements_____

Health History_____

Allergies_____

Food Restrictions_____

Special Dietary Needs_____

Outside Play Restrictions_____

Hearing_____Vision_____

Mobility_____

Speech/Language_____

Socialization Skills_____

Other Things to Know_____

FIGURE 7–14   Enrollment Interview.

	Comments
Parent-Child Relationships:	
Thinking and Observation Abilities:	
Emotional Concerns:	
Social Interactions:	
Organizing for School:	
Drugs, Smoking, Alcohol:	
Achievement Goals:	
Work Habits:	
School Behavior:	
Health Habits:	

FIGURE 7–15   Family Interview Needs Assessment.

calendar for parents and family members. This reduces the paper and expense involved in creating your newsletter. The easiest way for you to create your newsletter is to fill in a newsletter template as soon as you have completed your weekly plans for the children in your care. We encourage you to plan for a weekly newsletter to maintain consistency and regular written communication. If included as a regular part of your weekly planning routine, a newsletter/calendar of activities can do much to improve and enhance the family support of your program.

Electronic Communication

Electronic communication is a marvel of technology that can help you to keep in touch with parents, family members, and friends! Creating a listserv of all your parents or a program Web site makes electronic communication of general information to parents quick and easy. If you create

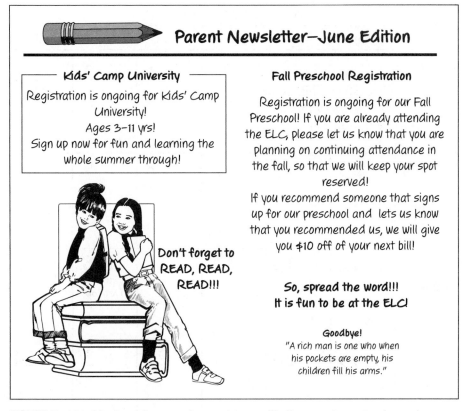

Parent Newsletter—June Edition

Kids' Camp University

Registration is ongoing for Kids' Camp University!
Ages 3–11 yrs!
Sign up now for fun and learning the whole summer through!

Don't forget to READ, READ, READ!!!

Fall Preschool Registration

Registration is ongoing for our Fall Preschool! If you are already attending the ELC, please let us know that you are planning on continuing attendance in the fall, so that we will keep your spot reserved!
If you recommend someone that signs up for our preschool and lets us know that you recommended us, we will give you $10 off of your next bill!

**So, spread the word!!!
It is fun to be at the ELC!**

Goodbye!
"A rich man is one who when his pockets are empty, his children fill his arms."

FIGURE 7–16 Most word-processing programs will allow you to customize and embellish your newsletter.

your weekly newsletter on the computer, you might simply "cut and paste" the document into an e-mail for all the parents on your listserv. Your listserv can include e-mail addresses for extended family members, or for dads who are not in the home. Links to helpful Web sites can also be a regular part of your e-mail communication. E-mail will also allow you to communicate quickly and effectively when personal, face-to-face communication is impossible. Again, you must plan to send regular, positive updates on their children. Make sure to report mostly "good stuff"!

Technology is a tremendous tool for keeping families informed and involved with their children. If taking time off for a special event is impossible, video recordings of outings, class visitors, or special projects can be copied very inexpensively to DVDs and given to family members. This is an equally effective method to keep dads who are deployed with the military involved with their infants and toddlers. DVDs can also be sent

September 2005

Sun	Mon	Tues	Wed	Thu	Fri	Sat
University of AZ South invites you to join us for *"Dining Under the Stars"* More Information Coming!				1	2	3
4 Colors & Critters "Cc"	5	6	7	8	9	10 UA South Dining *"Under The Stars!"*
11 Indians & Icky "Ii"	12	13	14	15	16 Early Bird Develop Seminar 4–5 PM	17
18 Moose, Moon, & Mice "Mm"	19	20	21	22	23	24
25 Review A, C, I, L, M	26	27	28	29	30	

FIGURE 7–17 Calendars can be created on word-processing programs and can be embellished in the same way that your newsletter is customized.

electronically. If you do not have the hardware capacity to do this, multiple copies of videotapes can be made at minimal cost. Technology can be indispensable as you keep the parents of your students involved in your classroom. An important cautionary note for you to observe at all times is to have parents sign a general release for photographing and videotaping their children in the classroom. There may be an occasion where a parent might to want to protect a child from harm. Honor the parents' wishes in

I hereby grant permission for video and photographs of my child's participation in the _____ Early Childhood Program. I understand that videos and photographs may be used with other families and with the public. I understand that these videos and photographs may appear in forms such as displays, documentation panels, books, or brochures and I agree that my family will receive no compensation. I also understand that my child's participation confers on my family no ownership rights to the photographs or negatives whatsoever. I consent that my child's work, or reproductions of his/her work may be used, exhibited, and published through any medium as part of, or in connection with, this early childhood program only. I have thoroughly read and understand the preceding paragraph.

_____

Name of Parent/Guardian– Please Print

_____

Signature of Parent/Guardian   Date

FIGURE 7–18   Release to Photograph, Videotape.

such a situation. Figure 7–18 provides a template for creating a parent release form for photographing/videotaping in your classroom.

Telephone Contact/Phone Trees

Making personal phone calls can be time-consuming but is extremely valuable when face-to-face communication is impossible. If one or more members of the family are not available for informal conversation, a phone call can maintain strong lines of communication. Touch base with the absent parent or family member in these phone calls and try to assess any needs or concerns they may have. Let these family members know how much you are enjoying their infant or toddler, and report new developments or pertinent information.

Establishing a phone tree of parents for your classroom can help build family involvement, allay fears, and provide fast, critical information. Ask if parents would be willing to take on the task of setting up the phone hotline system. The task need not be challenging. Simply give each family a name of another family that will call them in the event that the phone tree must be used. They should then in turn plan to call a family with the message or emergency information. Figure 7–19 is a simple diagram that can be used to record your classroom phone tree for copying and distributing quickly.

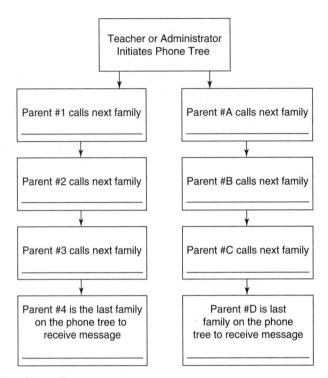

FIGURE 7–19   Phone Tree.

Conferences

Parent-professional conferences are a significant formal connection between the school or program and parents. These are critical public relations events for you, the staff in your school, and the children in your classroom. It is important that you have well-planned and well-conducted conferences.

- Be sure of the goal of your conference. What is the reason that parents and family members are meeting with you? Make careful notes of the points you want to cover in the conference.

- Take time and make the effort to get to know parents. Establish rapport with the family and put them at ease in what may be a very uncomfortable situation for them.

- Sit in a relaxed way with parents at your side to avoid any "authoritarian" positioning. Talk to parents in the mutually supportive way that you would talk with your own friends and family.

- Don't use jargon, "teacherese," or complicated explanations. Use simple language that parents will understand, without being patronizing.

_____ Collect records, documentation, notes, and artwork from the beginning of the conference period.
_____ Provide display materials for parents made of books, interesting reading, lending materials, and brochures.
_____ Arrange for refreshments, as appropriate.
_____ Prepare the room to receive families. Seat parents next to you.
_____ Welcome and engage each family member.
_____ Start on a warm, positive note.
_____ Use active listening.
_____ Avoid using educational jargon.
_____ Check your body language. Check parents' body language.
_____ Plan the educational and care objectives for the child together.
_____ Restate your decisions together.

FIGURE 7–20   Conference Checklist.

- Focus on the positive and make an effort to show and tell parents the things their child is doing well. Put problems in perspective.

- Give families adequate time to talk. Make certain the scheduling of conferences allows plenty of time for parents too. Strive for a conversation about what both you and the parents can do to help their children learn, grow, and achieve.

- Listen! Active listening means eye contact, nonverbal communication such as head nods, smiles, and hand gestures. Do not interrupt; do not argue; paraphrase back to parents what you hear them say; keep the conversation on track.

- Follow up on the conference in some way with either a phone call, a written note, or a home visit.

- Develop a plan of action and don't allow the parent to leave feeling frustrated or defeated. Let parents know what you will do next. Ask them to plan what they will do next.

Refer to Figure 7–20 as you plan your conferences.

ENVIRONMENT

Traditionally, infants and toddlers have been raised and cared for in home environments, but more and more often, infants and toddlers are included in early childhood care and education programs. Chances are that you will teach infants and toddlers in just such a program. Examine the infant and

FIGURE 7–21   An important part of environment is creating a warm, welcoming parent reception area.

toddler environment carefully for family involvement. Does the environment for your students welcome and include parents into the daily learning lives of their children? There are many components of an early childhood environment that can invite family members into the school. They include a warm parent reception area, a parent communication board, a suggestion box, family-friendly practices, and documentation of learning.

Parent Reception Area

What is it like for parents and family members to walk into your classroom or center? What greets them at the door? Look carefully at how parents and their children are received. You may want to take pictures so you can examine the situation with an objective eye. Is there a reception area to your room and does it welcome everyone who enters? If you do not have such an area, we suggest you design one that is warm and inviting. A lovely piece of art, a couple of comfortable chairs or a small sofa, an end table, a basket of picture books for parent and child to read together, a green plant, and a warm table lamp are just some of the objects to help create a welcoming parent reception area. (See Figure 7–21.)

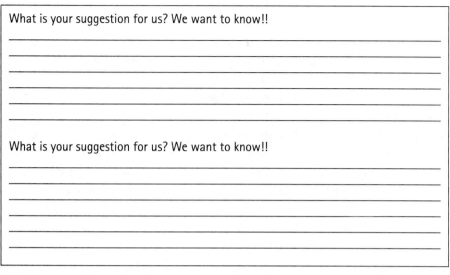

What is your suggestion for us? We want to know!!

What is your suggestion for us? We want to know!!

FIGURE 7–22   Suggestion Form.

Parent Board

Your parent reception area should include a parent communication board. Unlike other bulletin boards in your classroom, this one should be raised to eye level. It should have regular updates and information posted for parents at all times; emergency routines and phone numbers, fire escape routes, the weekly calendar, inspection certificates, menus, and meeting announcements. A nice addition to parent communication boards might be biographies of teachers and other program personnel, phone tree information, and community resources materials. This parent board can serve as an important daily reinforcment of your effort to communicate and connect with families.

Suggestion Box

Your parent reception area might also include a suggestion box. If there is inadequate time for conversation or if parents are uncomfortable, the suggestion box can be an anonymous but useful way to gather information. The box can be easily constructed out of a nicely covered cardboard box or plastic container. Figure 7–22 provides a template for a suggestion form that you might place next to the box with a few pens or pencils. Be sure to read suggestions on a regular basis.

Family Friendly

Is the classroom a family-friendly place? There are specific practices and purposeful planning that you can accomplish to make your classroom one that invites families into it. Your goal at all times should be to support the integrity of the family. Make every effort to recognize and understand the special qualities of each child. Strive to create continuity between your classroom and children's homes by learning as much as you can about the background and culture of your families. Allow children to be competent in their home language, while exposing them to English. Use their language alongside of English. Portray both genders in nurturing roles. Include fathers in your classroom. Refer to suggestions made in Chapter 4 on ways to include male role models in your classroom. Avoid gender-stereotyped toys, games, and play materials. Include dolls, books, puppets, music, and dramatic play props that reflect the culture and lifestyles of the children in your classroom. Use tapes of parents singing or reading stories whenever possible. Pictures used in your classroom should portray all kinds of family arrangements with different ethnic groups and different customs. These suggestions will transform your classroom into a family-friendly place that supports a wide range of family arrangements.

Documentation of Learning and Development

Another important way that parents and family members can stay involved in the care and education of their infants and toddlers is through documentation. Documentation refers to the ways that you as a teacher can capture and visually display the growth and learning process of young children. Careful recording of the questions, words, and dialogue of young children as they play and learn, photos that capture the process visually, and the products that children create should be displayed together in an aesthetically pleasing way. For infants and toddlers, accurate daily notes should be kept on the activities each one engages in, as well as what each child eats and drinks. You can transcribe the notes you make of children's thoughts and questions on the computer, print them out, and mount them on no-fade black paper backing for family and friends to read. Post the dialogue alongside the creations children have made. If your state has early childhood education standards, your can add the standards accomplished in the play or exploration to your documentation panel. If you use a digital camera to capture children at work, photos can be printed out on your computer and also mounted on no-fade black paper. The walls of your classroom then become

FIGURE 7–23   Family Open House. Documentation captures the process of learning for families and children.

a gallery of the children at work. This is so much more engaging for parents than store-purchased, commercially designed classroom decorations.

Documentation captures for parents, family, and the children the process of learning and development as it unfolds in your classroom. After you have taken down the documentation panels from your classroom walls, put them into binders designated for each child and begin collecting for parents a treasury of the life in your classroom. Like a portfolio, the treasury collection will house all kinds of thoughts, pictures, papers, and observations. You will have a cohesive collection to use in conferences with parents and to send home on a regular basis. (See Figure 7–23.)

CURRICULUM

You can easily include parents and family members in the curriculum for infants and toddlers if you plan ahead and take the time to get to know the parents of the children in your care. Good curriculum planning for infants and toddlers includes integrated, interactive processes with concrete, real materials and playthings in which parents and family members can participate. Infants and toddlers learn through direct experience, repetition, experimentation, and imitation. Adults must guide these learning processes. A developmentally appropriate curriculum for infants and toddlers invites play, active exploration, and movement. Relationships with caring adults are an essential element of the curriculum and parent participation can enhance the quality of these experiences. A thorough enrollment interview will help you get to know the culture and values of parents, their skills and areas of interest, and the unique ways that they can contribute to your classroom. Invite parents to participate at regular, particular times of the day. Parents should be coached to nurture self-help skills, healthy separation, problem solving, creativity, autonomy, and independence in the infants and toddlers in your classroom. Parents can fulfill many roles including reading aloud, leading music, accompanying you on outings, leading play, coaching play in centers, and completing clerical duties. There is no limit to the usefulness and learning for parents as they teach alongside you.

RESOURCES FOR PARENTS

Unlimited possibilities exist for families to be more involved with their infants and toddlers in the home. You can help facilitate this by providing a wide array of resources for parents to use and enjoy away from the school. Other resources can be provided at the school and can improve the quality of family involvement with infants and toddlers. Some of these resources can include lending libraries of toys, books, videos, DVDs, and audiotapes for home learning. Workshops, family nights, dinners, adult education courses, training sessions, and cultural events are some of the events that can enrich the learning about parenting and family learning that you can sponsor. Finally, service activities such as respite care, service exchanges, parent support groups, and committee participation can offer families invaluable, needed resources.

Lending Library of Books, Videos, and Audiotapes

Families of all types, from all cultures, can benefit from books, articles, videotapes, audiotapes, and DVDs relating to parenting. Encourage parents to use these materials regularly. We think that having the lending library in the parent reception area is ideal for advertising and encouraging the circulation of your materials. Provide a simple system for checking out and returning resource materials. We suggest a simple index card system or pocket card system. Fill in the title and bibliographic information on your resource material. Parents put their name on the index card and the date they borrowed the material. Keep the index card in a card file until the material is returned. Replace the card in the material for the next family who would like to check it out. It is crucial that, if English is not the first language for the parents of your infants and toddlers, you provide materials in their first language. Figure 7–24 lists some of basic recommendations for beginning a lending library.

Getting Ready for School Begins at Birth: How to Help Your Child Learn in the Early Years.
Claire Lerner and Lynette Ciervo.   Zero to Three 2004   ISBN 0943657873

La Preparacio Para la Escuela Empieza al Nacer: Como Ayudar a SU Hijo a Aprender en SUS Primeros Anos.
Claire Lerner and Lynette Ciervo.
                              Zero to Three 2004   ISBN 0943657881

Quirk Kids: Understanding and Helping Your Child Who Doesn't Fit In—When to Worry and When Not to Worry.
Perri Klass and Eileen
Costello.   Thomson Delmar Learning 2003   ISBN 0345451430

Take Charge! Advocating for Your Child's Education.
Jo Ann C. Shaheen and
Carolyn C. Spence.   Thomson Delmar Learning 2002   ISBN 0766842657

PKL/Creative Resources Infants/Toddlers Library Burtsing Pkg.
Judy Herr; Terri Swim.   Thomson Delmar Learning 2004   ISBN 1401896723

Supporting Play, Birth Through Age Eight.
Dorothy Justus Sluss, Ph.D.   Thomson Delmar Learning 2005   ISBN 1401851436

Positive Child Guidance.
Darla Ferris Miller.   Thomson Delmar Learning 2004   ISBN 1401812562

Guiding Children's Social Development.
Marjorie Kostelnik, Ph.D;
Alice Whiren, Ph.D.;
Anne Soderman, Ph.D.;
Laura Stein; Kara Gregory.   Thomson Delmar Learning 2006   ISBN 1401897630

Health, Safety, and Nutrition for the Young Child.
Lynn Marotz; Marie Z.
Cross; Jeanettia M. Rush.   Thomson Delmar Learning 2001   ISBN 0766809463

Families, Schools, and Communities, Together for Young Children.
Donna Couchenour;
Kent Chrisman.   Thomson Delmar Learning 2004   ISBN 140827667

FIGURE 7–24 Suggested Reading List for Lending Library. (*Continues*)

Parents Becoming Leaders: Getting Involved on Behalf of Children.
Miriam Westheimer, 2002. Families and Work Institute Pub. #C2002-01.

Ask the Children: The Breakthrough Study That Reveals How to Succeed at Work and Parenting.
Ellen Galinsky, Quill 2000. Families and Work Institute Pub. #V99-01P

Rethinking the Brain: New Insights into Early Development.   (Revised 10/03)
Rima Shore, 1997. Families and Work Institute Pub. #D97-01

FIGURE 7-24   *(Continued)*

Toy Lending Library

Like the parenting resource lending library, toys, games, and puzzles from your classroom should be available to lend out for family home use. Be certain to inventory your play materials so that parents are aware of what is available for check-out. Again, a simple system to sign out toys works best. Perhaps a signature and date line on the inventory you create will serve this purpose. Look at your classroom materials with the fresh eye of parents. Blocks, wheeled toys, trucks, airplanes and cars, dolls, carriages and strollers, nesting toys, puzzles, math manipulatives, games and puzzles, art materials and easels, music makers and tapes, children's books, dress-up clothes, sidewalk chalk, and the classroom pet should all be available for short visits home. Consider creating backpack activities as suggested in Chapter 5 using toys and activities from your classroom to rotate home for the parents and families of infants and toddlers.

Parenting Classes, Workshops, Training, and Adult Education Courses

You can make a significant difference in the parenting skills and literacy levels of the families you support through educational meetings and classes. Your assistance can forge a productive partnership with families. As families become experts in your school, they become empowered and involved. Workshops introduce families to school policies, practices, and procedures. Parenting classes focus on very specific parenting skills such as nutrition, language development, care of sick children, or child guidance and discipline. Trainings give parents and family members skills as classroom helpers, activity sponsors, curriculum planners, or policy decision makers in the school. Adult education courses are designed to give parents and family members vital skills for the job market or future success. These might include adult English literacy classes, job hunting/interview classes, functional math classes, or remedial reading and writing. Family nights or family meetings are organized for the entire family. These events bring the entire family together to actively participate in curricular activities in a station/center format involving a hands-on approach. See Chapter 7 for a detailed discussion of these school-wide events.

Service Resources

Building an effective, meaningful program for infants and toddlers at your school may entail providing support services to benefit all concerned. Child care is often reported as a barrier to family involvement in schools and class-rooms. Families may not be able to attend programs and become involved if they do not have child care for all of their children. Providing child care through the local high school, scouting organization, or city/county babysit-ting training can make family participation possible. Respite care may be needed for periodic relief for parents with chronically ill children, seniors, or children with disabilities. Service provider exchanges can help families to meet their needs. Parents may exchange child or respite care services, clean-ing or laundry services, repair or maintenance services. You simply provide the connection for parents to work with other parents in your school.

Support groups for families can serve parents and family members in a number of ways. Groups may be organized around parenting issues and provide information and guest presenters on parenting concerns. They may be organized around family concerns such as groups for fathers or noncustodial parents. It is important that the focus of support groups be information and education and not therapy.

Service Committees

A final addition to the service resources at your school might be in service committees that are designed to meet the needs of children and their fam-ilies. These service committees can be organized around particular needs. For example, you might want to organize a Welcoming Committee for new families to the school; you might consider a Benevolence Committee designed to assist families during medical emergencies, deaths in the family, or in times of crisis; consider a committee designed to send out spe-cial recognition and special occasion greetings on behalf of the school. All of these committees offer much-needed support and services to families while involving them in creating a community in your school.

CONCLUSION

It is clear from the existing research that the important contribution of family involvement begins at birth and continues throughout childhood. Parents and family members are the first, most important teachers in the lives of young children. Seeking ways to simply involve mom or dad in a school activity is painfully inadequate to the demands of modern life. Teachers must bridge the critical learning of the first three years to their classroom. Children and their families must be the focus if our involvement activities are to be meaningful, relevant activities. Early childhood teachers face a clear challenge: We must find all the possible ways to help children and their families to access and maximize the resources and benefits available to them as a community in the twenty-first century.

SUMMARY OF IMPORTANT POINTS

- Parents are the first, most important teachers for infants and toddlers.
- The research with infants and toddlers affirms that early family involvement improves academic achievement and school success.
- A major responsibility of the teacher of infants and toddlers is to disseminate a wide array of information to parents.
- Teachers must view parents as equal partners in the development of best practice with infants and toddlers.
- Teachers must work within the established family and community context to help support families.
- An important element to creating good parent collaboration and effective family support is the match between the parents' view of what the child should be experiencing in learning and how the teacher views the child's abilities.
- Parents are more confident if they have friendly, open communication with caregivers and teachers.

CHAPTER REVIEW QUESTIONS

1. Why is neuroscientific research important to supporting families and parents of infants and toddlers?
2. What activities and strategies are a component of classroom practice to involve parents of infants and toddlers?

3. What is the difference between parent education and parent support?

4. Why is a teacher's perception of the child integral to parent confidence?

5. Name the ways that technology can assist you in supporting the parents of infants and toddlers.

6. Why is sensitivity to family cultural background important in involving the entire family in education?

7. What types of lending libraries help to involve families in infant and toddler education?

▓ APPLICATION AND REFLECTION _____

1. As the teacher of infants and toddlers, it is important for you to be very aware of your feelings and internal reactions to parents. Do a quick write without stopping to erase, edit, or censor your own thoughts in response to this prompt. "When I think of the parents of my students, I feel..." Reread your entry and reflect on the feelings you have for parents.

2. The idea of conducting home visits can be scary and intimidating for teachers. Role-play a home visit with a family member, a friend, or a colleague. Make notes as to what you will say and do prior to role-playing. Self-assess and determine what part of the home visit is hardest for you.

3. Parents of infants and toddlers are most confident in teachers who have had experience raising children. Practice articulating your background experience with very young children for an imaginary parent/parents. Include all the experience you have had as a volunteer or as a young person.

4. A lending library is an integral part of a family-focused early child-hood program. Develop an inventory of the classroom materials you would like to have in order to create your own lending library.

▓ FURTHER READING _____

Couchenour, D., & Chrisman, K. (2004). *Families, Schools, and Communities, Together for Young Children.* Thomson Delmar Learning.

Galinsky, E. (2000). *Ask the Children: The Breakthrough Study That Reveals How to Succeed at Work and Parenting.* Harper Paperbacks.

Lerner, C., & Ciervo, L. (2004). *Getting Ready for School Begins at Birth: How to Help Your Child Learn in the Early Years.* Zero to Three.

 For additional information on research-based practice, visit our Web site at http://www.earlychilded.delmar.com.

Additional resources for this chapter can be found on the Online Companion™ to accompany this text at www.earlychilded.delmar.com. This supplemental material includes Web links, downloadable forms, and Case Studies with critical thinking applications. This content can be used as a study aid to reinforce key concepts presented in this chapter and to conduct additional research on topics of interest.

▮ REFERENCES

Aslin, R., & Hunt, R. (2001). Development, plasticity and learning in the auditory system. In C. Elson & M. Luciana (Eds.), *Handbook of developmental cognitive neuroscience* (205–220). Cambridge, MA: MIT Press.

Bacanu, S., Devlin, B., & Roeder, K. (2000). The power of genomic control. *American Journal Human Genetics, 66*(6), 1933–1944.

Bouchard, T. (1988). Personality similarity in twins reared apart and together. *Journal of Personality and Social Psychology, 54*(6), 1031–1039.

Cacioppo, J., Berntson, G., Sheridan, J., & McClintock, M. (2001). Multilevel analyses of human behavior: Social neuroscience and the complementing nature of social and biological approaches. In J. Cacioppo (Ed.), *Foundations in social neuroscience* (21–46). Cambridge, MA: MIT Press.

Chugani, H. (1996). Remarks at 1996 Conference: *Brain development in young children: New frontiers for research, policy, and practice.* University of Chicago, June 13–14.

Chugani, H. (1997). Neuroimaging of developmental non-linearity and developmental pathologies. In R. W. Thatcher, G. R. Lyon, J. Rumsey, & N. Krasnegor (Eds.), *Developmental neuroimaging: Mapping the development of the brain and behavior* (187–195). San Diego, CA: Academic Press.

Clarke C., Mihata, P., & Frost, M. (1990). *ECEAP longitudinal study: Summary of year two report.* Olympia, WA: Washington State Department of Community Development.

Consortium for Longitudinal Studies. (1983). *As the twig is bent.* Hillsdale, NJ: Lawrence Erlbaum Associates.

Copeland, J., & Gleason, T. (1993). *Causes of speech disorders and language delays.* Unpublished manuscript. Speech and Language Clinic, University of Arizona, Tucson, AZ.

Dunn, L., & Kontos, S. (1989, April). *Influence of family day care quality and child rearing attitudes on children's play in family day care.* Paper presented at the biennial meeting of the Society for Research in Child Development, Kansas City, MO.

Epstein, J. L. (1985). Home and school connections in schools of the future: Implications of research on parent involvement. *Peabody Journal of Education, 62,* 18–41.

Erikson, E. (1963). Childhood and society. (2nd ed.). New York, NY: Norton.

Fernald, A., & Kuhl, P. (1987). Acoustic determinants of infant preference for parentese speech. *Infant Behavior and Development, 10,* 279–293.

Fine, I., Wade, A., Brewer, A., May, M., Goodman, D., Boynton, G., Wandell, B., & MacLeod, D. (2003). Long-term deprivation affects visual perception and cortex. *Nature Neuroscience, 6*(9), 915–916.

Francis, D., Dioro, J., Plotsky, P., & Meaney, M. (2002). Environmental enrichment reverses the effects of maternal separation on stress reactivity. *Journal of Neuroscience, 22,* 787–843.

Hanson, R. (1975). Consistency and stability of home environmental measures related to IQ. *Child Development, 46,* 470–480.

Henderson, A. T. (1988). Parents are a school's best friends. *Phi Delta Kappan, 70*(2), 148–153.

Huttenlocher, J., Levine, S. C., & Vevea, J. (1998). Environmental effects on cognitive growth: A time period comparison. *Child Development, 69*(4), 1012–1029.

Huttenlocher, J., & Dabholkar, A. (1997). Developmental anatomy of the prefrontal cortex. In N. Krasnegor, G. Lyon, & P. Goldman-Rakic (Eds.), *Development of the prefrontal cortex: Evolution, neurobiology and behavior.* (69–84). Baltimore: Paul H. Brookes Publishing Company.

Jones, E. (1993). *Growing teachers: Partnerships in staff development*. Washington, DC: NAEYC.

Kessler-Sklar, S., Lamb-Parker, F., Piotkowski, C., Peay, L., & Clark, B. (1998, July). Processes by which parent involvement in Head Start improves the lives of families. Paper presented at Head Start's Fourth National Research Conference, Washington, DC.

Lamb-Parker, F., Piotkowski, C., Horn, W., & Greene, S. (1995). The challenge for Head Start: Realizing its vision as a two-generation program. In I. Sigel (Series Ed.) and S. Smith (Volume Ed.), *Advances in applied developmental psychology: Vol 9.* Two generation programs for families in poverty, pp. 135–159.

Lazar, A. & Slostad, F. (March/April, 1999). How to overcome obstacles to parent-teacher partnerships. The Clearing House, *72*(4), 206–210.

McEwen, B., & Schmeck, H. (1994). *The hostage brain*. New York: Rockefeller University Press.

Miedel, W., & Reynolds, A. (1999, July). *Parent involvement in early intervention for disadvantaged children: Does it matter?* Poster session presented at Head Start's Fourth National Research Conference, Children and Families in an Era of Rapid Change: Creating a Shared Agenda for Researchers, Practitioners, and Policy Makers, Washington, DC.

National Association for the Education of Young Children. (1998). *Accreditation criteria and procedures*. Washington, DC: Author.

National Council for the Accreditation of Teacher Education. (2002). *NCATE Standards*. Washington, DC: Author.

Perry, B. (1993). Neurodevelopment and the neurophysiology of trauma: Conceptual considerations for clinical work with maltreated children. *The Advisor 6* (Summer 1993), 1.

Perry, B. (1996). Incubated in terror: Neurodevelopmental factors in the "cycle of violence." In J. D. Osofsky (Ed.), *Children, you and violence: Searching for solutions*. New York: Guilford Press.

Petrie, A., & Davidson, I. (1995). Toward a grounded theory of parent preschool involvement. *Early Child Development and Care, 111*, 5–7.

Polan, H., & Hofer, M. (1999). Psychobiological origins of infant attachment and separation response. In J. Cassidy & P. Shaver (Eds.), *Handbook of attachment theory and research* (162–180). New York: Guilford Publishing.

Powell, D. R. (1998). Reweaving parents into the fabric of early childhood programs. *Young Children, 53*(50), 60–67.

Reynolds, A., Mavrogenes, N., Bezruczko, N., & Hagemann, M. (1996). Cognitive and family-support mediators of preschool effectiveness: A confirmatory analysis. *Child Development, 67,* 1119–1140.

Shipman, V., Boroson, M., Bidgeman, B., Gart, J., & Mikovsky, M. (1976). *Disadvantaged children and their first school experiences.* Princeton, NJ: Educational Testing Service.

Shonkoff, J., & Philips, D. (2000). *From neurons to neighborhoods: The science of early childhood development.* Committee on Integrating the Science of Early Childhood Development. Washington DC: National Academy Press.

Shore, R. (1997). *Rethinking the brain: New insights into early development.* New York: Families and Work Institute.

Siegel, D. (1999). *The developing mind.* New York: The Guilford Press.

Teo, A., Carlson, E., Mathieu, P., Egeland, B., & Sroufe, L. (1996). A prospective longitudinal study of psychosocial predictors of achievement. *Journal of School Psychology, 34*(3), 285–306.

White, B., Kaban, B., Attanucci, J., & Shapiro, B. (1973). *Experience and environment: Major influences on the development of the young child.* Vol. I. Englewood Cliffs, NJ: PrenticeHall.

Wilson, H. (1993). Theories of infant visual development. In K. Simons (Ed.), *Early visual development: Normal and abnormal* (560–572). New York: Oxford University Press.

8

Building a Comprehensive Program for Family Involvement in the Early Years

■ **CHAPTER OBJECTIVES** _____

After reading and reflecting on this chapter, you should be able to:

- Understand the importance of school-wide family involvement.
- Cite research indicating the benefits of school-wide family involvement programs.
- Identify national family involvement programs.
- Identify key components of successful family involvement programs.
- Understand the usefulness of parent education workshops.
- Implement a parent education workshop.
- Design a parent education workshop.

■ KEY TERMS

interactive experiences

parent education

school-wide plan for family
involvement

THE BENEFITS OF A SCHOOL-WIDE PLAN FOR FAMILY INVOLVEMENT

Throughout this book we have discussed the benefits and importance of family involvement and developing effective partnerships between teachers and families. While you have the ability to develop partnerships and encourage involvement in your own classroom, it isn't difficult to imagine the increase in benefits if your school were to have a school-wide plan for involving and valuing parents. In this chapter we'll look at the specific benefits of family involvement on a school-wide level. We will also discuss school-wide programs that have been successfully implemented throughout the United States. Finally, this chapter will provide materials for involving parents in at-school parent workshops to assist them in better working with their children at home.

Henderson and Berla (1997) found that in the many programs they studied, it was the schools with comprehensive and ongoing family involvement that reported increased student achievement. They go on to say that a school-wide focus on family involvement involves a complete transformation of typical relationships with families. This kind of transformation often brings about the following benefits:

- increased teacher morale
- more positive teacher ratings by parents
- increased family support
- increased student achievement
- improved reputations in the community

As early childhood educators, we have a big responsibility when it comes to involving parents. Parents of young children tend to be more receptive to participating in the school experience, but even the most involved parents tend to decrease their involvement as their children grow older. Research suggests that when parents get involved in the early years of their children's education, this involvement is more likely to continue (Henderson, 1988). But, because this involvement still has the potential to decrease somewhat over time, it is essential that a school and its faculty work together to design and put into place appropriate programs at each grade level (Epstein, 1995). Involved parents, after all, can help to improve

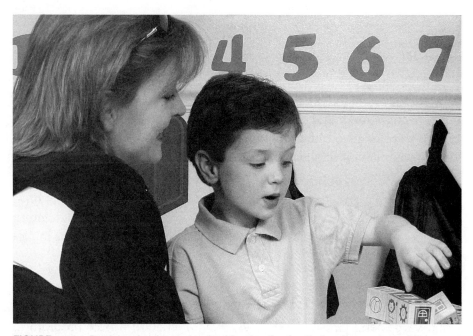

FIGURE 8–1   Participating in a school-wide plan for family involvement provides ongoing encouragement and support to parents.

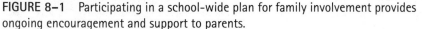

the overall school program. They can help to provide services and support to other families in the school community and assist with getting other parents involved in leadership. They can help families to connect with one another and can encourage parents to assist teachers by volunteering (Epstein, 1995). With all of these great benefits, it is still essential to remember that the main reason to involve parents is the benefits to children that come about as a result.

The difference between creating your own family involvement plan and participating in a school-wide plan lies in the ongoing encouragement and support given to parents. (See Figure 8–1.) Research suggests most families believe in the importance of parent involvement, but that many families won't pursue this involvement on their own (Epstein, 1995). They need to be encouraged by teachers and by the school as a whole.

Swick (1993) describes a school-family partnership as a shared learning process where schools invite input from families, implement strategies for developing partnerships, provide feedback to families, and focus on learning from one another. Teachers and staff members need to also communicate to families the integral role they play in their children's academic experience and encourage them to get involved and participate as equal partners with the teachers and the school (Igo, 2002).

As mentioned in Chapter 1, "the most accurate predictor of a student's achievement in school is not income or social status but the extent to which that student's family is able to:

1. Create a home environment that encourages learning.
2. Express high (but not unrealistic) expectations for their children's achievement and future careers.
3. Become involved in their children's education at school and in the community" (Henderson & Berla, 1997).

So, how does a **school-wide plan for family involvement** look? There is no one answer to this question, as these kinds of programs have been implemented successfully in many areas of the country in all different ways. Let's take a look at some of the family involvement programs implemented on a school-wide level.

RESEARCH STUDIES

Cohn-Vargas and Grose (1998) conducted a study of a pilot program in four classrooms. This home-school connections project involved such practices as regular information notices and increased communication through phone calls and mail. Parents were also provided with ideas for working with their children at home and they were invited to workshops to learn about assisting their children at home. At the end of the study the researchers noticed that the children in these pilot classrooms had the highest reading scores in the school, and they attribute this success to the impact of increased family involvement.

Henderson-Sellers (1991) reports on the success of the School Development Program created by child psychologist James Comer. The program consists of five elements:

- focus not on blame, but on what can be done
- cooperation among all adults associated with each child
- decisions made by consensus
- regular meetings with the school community
- active involvement by parents

The implementation of this program took place in many schools in the United States and, while each school reported its own benefits, many of the schools (after several years of the program's implementation) experienced higher standardized test scores, increased attendance, fewer suspensions, increased participation by parents, and more active participation by teachers.

FIGURE 8–2   Family involvement programs take on many forms and should address the needs of the community.

Bermudez and Marquez (1996) describe a parent-training program called the Parent Resource Center. This program, implemented in a low-income, urban, predominantly Hispanic area, offered parents the following:

- ESL instruction
- strategies for helping their children at home
- assistance with understanding the school system
- information about their rights and responsibilities as parents

In this study, 35 parents participated over a 12-week period. The researchers found that attendance remained high over the duration and noted that many of the parents increased their English-speaking skills, began to take on leadership roles in the school and community, and gained confidence in working with their children.

FAMILY INVOLVEMENT PROGRAMS

Family involvement programs take on many forms and must address the needs of each particular school community. (See Figure 8–2.) Many that have been implemented successfully throughout the United States are featured in this section. You might want to encourage your school to explore some of these programs or create versions of them that meet the needs of your school community.

Books and Beyond

Books and Beyond is a national program that provides incentive to instill a love of books and reading in children. This program assists teachers and schools in creating an environment where children are encouraged to read. Parents are encouraged to read to their children at home, develop literacy practices in the home that serve to increase the literacy skills of children, and monitor the television viewing habits of the family. The program has been proven successful in increasing children's reading scores on standardized tests. Other benefits of the Books and Beyond program include the increased awareness and control of the number of hours spent watching television and an increase in recreational reading in the home.

Ready to Read

Ready to Read is the preschool version of Books and Beyond and, like its predecessor, serves to instill the love of books in young children. This program encourages parents to read aloud to their children and conveys to parents that this practice is the single most beneficial activity they can do to promote later academic success.

Families and Schools Together (FAST)

Families and Schools Together, otherwise known as FAST, is a program that supports families and assists them in creating positive interactions with schools. The program involves a series of sessions that allows families to build social skills, communicate with one another, and participate in recreational activities. The sessions are run by trained facilitators representing the school, community, health professions, and parents. Attendees participate in sessions with their school-age children and are given the opportunity to interact with their children in various activities. The program facilitators attribute part of the success of attendance to a meal being provided for attendees each week and access to free child care for their younger children. FAST was originally targeted at families who were considered "at-risk," but has broadened its focus to include all families.

Family Math

Family Math is a program facilitated by trained professionals to provide opportunities for parents and children to work together to develop mathematical skills and aptitude with problem solving. A series of classes is provided over several weeks. In these classes, **interactive experiences** are provided that serve as examples of ways parents can work with their children at home to build mathematical knowledge while having fun doing it. The popularity of this program has continued for over 20 years and is now even offered for Spanish-language speakers.

Family Outreach Program of State College Area School District

State College Area School District provides numerous community education programs. This particular program was designed to provide families with effective parenting skills for the purpose of reducing stress in the home and increasing communication between parents and schools. The program provides a variety of resources to parents, including discussion groups, classes, and access to community services that seek to empower parents and help them to see their value in their roles as parents.

National Network of Partnership Schools

This partnership program combines the efforts of states, districts, schools, and Johns Hopkins University's Center on School, Family, and Community Partnerships. The program promotes school-family partnerships and focuses on six areas—parenting, communication, volunteering, at-home learning, decision making, and community collaboration. School committees of teachers, administrators, and other staff members are assembled to focus on each of the six areas. These committees develop and implement ways to involve parents and build partnerships. The success of this program is attributed to school-wide accountability, involvement of parent organizations, and involvement of the community.

Write Night

Write Night (Albee & Drew, 2001) is a school-based program that was designed and implemented by three pre-K–primary-grade teachers at Jefferson Elementary School in Missouri. These teachers recognized, first of all, that a parent is the child's first teacher and that interactions

FIGURE 8–3   Parents and children can work together on creating writing projects.

with parents and observations of caregivers serve as key components in the development of children's language and literacy skills. They believed, as Fields and Spangler (1995) report, that children gain an increased desire to learn about the conventions of written language when they know others will read their writing. Because they understood that "children learn behaviors that are modeled by significant people in their lives" (Albee & Drew, 2001), they developed a program that would capitalize on this.

Write Night involves parents and children working together at an evening workshop to create books, such as a storybook, an ABC book, and an All About Me book. (See Figure 8–3.) The attendees work their way through three stations, following the directions provided by workshop facilitators to create their books.

The facilitators have noticed the following benefits of the Write Night workshops:

- adults and children happily engaging in language and discussion
- connections between parents and children
- opportunities for teachers to model scaffolding strategies
- literacy development in children

FAMILIES IN FOCUS

It was a late spring evening and the air was warm. Curriculum Night had finally arrived. The smells of freshly mown grass and blooming trees gently blew across the school grounds. The school had a buzz of excitement that comes with children bringing their families to school. They ran ahead and urged their parents into their classrooms. Artwork of all sorts filled display boards up and down the sidewalks. Projects and creations covered desktops. This was a delightful evening when students all across the campus could show off their work to their families and include them in their classrooms. They and their teachers had been preparing all week to host families in their classroom this evening. The teachers had planned specific activities and everyone was included in the learning fun!

The PTA board members fired up the grills from the cafeteria and started cooking hamburgers. Families gathered in groups to have dinner, chat, and catch up on neighborhood events. The "grown-up" sixth-grade students had spent weeks and weeks researching a country for their World's Fair reports. They created display boards, cooked food from their country, dressed in costumes, gathered artifacts, and now they were ready to show off what they had learned. As the sun went down, the school band gathered on the lawn in the center of the campus and began to tune up for a concert. Members of the Ballet Folklorico dance troupe, dressed in bright costumes, also gathered to entertain parents and friends. Ice cream cones were served up as families drifted out of the classrooms and onto the lawns for the music and dancing.

The school-wide event was important for everyone who attended. Parents, grandparents, and younger siblings turned out to be part of the evening. PTA board members had a chance to interact with other parents in an informal way. Teachers and staff enjoyed the relaxed fun with families in the classrooms. But the students at the school benefited the most. The hard work of the last school year was proudly displayed. Their home away from home, the classroom became a family place. The sense of community and the school as the solid hub of life was strengthened and celebrated.

- parents' increased comfort level with technology
- increased communication between parents and the school

SUGGESTIONS FROM PRINCIPALS/DIRECTORS

There are numerous articles available today that contain suggestions from school principals, child care directors, and consultants, providing general suggestions for increasing family involvement and creating school environments that are welcoming to parents. In this section, we will summarize suggestions that seem to be common among experts in early childhood programs.

Consultant Kimberly Moore (2001) states that successful learning environments are based on the foundation of getting to know families. She stresses that the overall climate of the school can either draw parents in or drive them away. "In developmentally appropriate practices, this atmosphere is described as 'establishing reciprocal relationships'—actively listening and responding to families" (p. 16). She suggests involving parents through events, such as Family Night and Grandparent Night, as well as service projects and mentoring of families new to the school. She also suggests displaying photo albums of parents who participate at school activities, encouraging the school's parent organization to promote involvement in school activities, providing involvement ideas in parent newsletters, and asking for parent feedback about school programs.

Sara Wilford (2004), a literacy development specialist and educator, emphasizes that the school's principal or director sets the tone. "In a setting where trust and openness are treasured values, parents will assume equal responsibility for contributing to the vitality of children's experiences in school—alongside the director, teachers, and school support staff" (p. 9). She suggests that the director/principal keep his or her door open to welcome parents, involve faculty and staff in brainstorming ways to connect with parents, and invite parents and teachers to social gatherings. She also encourages the director/principal to connect with the president of the parent organization and create meaningful ways to involve parents through volunteerism.

PTA leader and library assistant Mary Kay Hahn makes two suggestions. First, she encourages active involvement in the Parent Teacher Association as it provides support, training, and even accountability. She also suggests that the school library is an ideal "hub" for family involvement. She says, "Library staffers are likely the only ones in contact with every student in the building on an ongoing basis and often communicating with parents across the spectrum. The library offers a gathering spot for parent and school activities, and volunteer opportunities that let parents be at school without necessarily being involved in the classroom, if they're concerned about distraction" (Faucette, 2000, p. 58).

Researchers Bermudez and Marquez (1996) make important recommendations for parent involvement, including:

1. Adequately addressing the education of children includes the involvement of parents.

FIGURE 8–4   A strategic plan is necessary in order to have effective parent involvement programs at a school.

2. A strategic plan is needed in order to have effective parent involvement programs. (See Figure 8–4.)
3. Needs assessments are necessary in order to meet the actual (rather than perceived) needs of the community.
4. Additional resources should be solicited from the community.
5. Teacher training should be provided to assist with meeting the needs of diverse parents.

PARENT EDUCATION

The information presented so far in this chapter suggests that a strategic plan of one kind or another is a key component to a successful school-wide program for family involvement. Much of the literature also suggests providing opportunities for parents to come to the school to be involved in programs designed just for them. With this in mind, the next section of this chapter focuses on the implementation of **parent education** workshops that you can use to get parents involved right away at your school. Suggest this idea to your school principal or enlist the help of your fellow teachers to organize a workshop for parents. This can be a truly school-wide endeavor or you can conduct a workshop with the parents from just a few classes in your school. The key is to start somewhere. With time and positive comments from parents, other teachers and administrators at your school are likely to "get on board."

WORKSHOPS

Conducting parent workshops at the school-wide level is a great way for parents and teachers to interact. These workshops are also helpful for connecting parents and, of course, can serve to provide excellent educational opportunities for families. This section provides the materials necessary for conducting several parent workshops at your school for parents of young children. The following is a list of the featured workshops in this chapter and brief descriptions of each.

Environmental Print Workshop

This workshop focuses on children's awareness of print in the environment and provides information to parents about how they can use this familiar print to encourage early literacy development in their children.

Enhancing Literacy Development Workshop

This adults-only workshop provides parents with activities to do with their children that increase literacy development. Parents create a rhyming activity, a phonemic awareness activity, and learn about the importance of parent/child read-aloud experiences.

Family Field Trips Workshop

Another adults-only workshop, this parent night provides ideas for fun family field trips. Parents work together to brainstorm points of interest in the community and receive information about many places they can visit with their children.

"Number One in Family Fun" Math Night

This workshop is a family affair where parents and children not only learn about fun math experiences, but also participate in them with other families.

A variety of games help parents to see that math learning is not intimidating, but fun!

Kids in the Kitchen for Nutrition IQ

Another family event, this workshop provides parents with information about good nutrition while providing interactive experiences with parents and their children.

ENVIRONMENTAL PRINT WORKSHOP

Invitation

You and your child are invited to a fun night of early reading experiences with environmental print!

Date: _____

Time: _____

Location: _____

Reminder Notice

Don't forget! We're having a fun night of early reading experiences for you and your child. We hope you'll come!

Date: _____

Time: _____

Location: _____

ENVIRONMENTAL PRINT WORKSHOP

Workshop Agenda

Activity	Time:
Sign-in and visit with other families	_____ (15 min.)
Ice Breaker Activity	_____ (15 min.)
Introduction to Environmental Print	_____ (15 min.)
Print Awareness Inventory	_____ (15 min.)
Environmental Print Games	_____ (30 min.)
Conclusion and Take-Home Materials	_____ (15 min.)

Sign-in and Visit

As parents and children arrive, have them sign in and make a nametag to wear. (Nametag templates are provided on page 301.) If possible, provide snacks or dinner for the participants and encourage them to visit with one another.

Ice Breaker Activity

Materials: index cards (one per family), pencils

Help families feel at ease and get to know one another with an activity to "break the ice." Provide each family with an index card and a pencil. Ask each parent and child to think of print on 10 signs located in the neighborhood. (These could be street signs, restaurant or store signs, billboards, etc.) List the sign print on the card. Then have them meet with other families to compare their lists. The goal is to find another family who listed the most similar sign print. Have them discuss where they have seen this print in the neighborhood.

Introduction to Environmental Print

Parents may be unfamiliar with the term *Environmental Print,* so spend a few minutes explaining what it is and how it serves to benefit children's beginning literacy development. Information is provided on page 251. This can be used to give parents a background about environmental print. After reviewing the introductory information, record the important points you want to mention to parents in your presentation.

Print Awareness Inventory

This is a fun way for parents to develop understanding about the everyday print their children already recognize. See page 253 for a complete description of materials and instructions for completing the inventory.

Environmental Print Games

Parents and children will enjoy playing games with environmental print. Create several sets of environmental print games for parents and children to play together. (See pages 255–259.)

Conclusion and Take-Home Materials

At the end of the evening, spend a few minutes summarizing the information and activities shared about environmental print and how it can be used to encourage the development of beginning literacy skills. Ask questions, such as:

1. What is your understanding of environmental print?
2. What does your child's recognition of EP reveal to you about his/her literacy development?
3. What can you do at home to encourage your child's literacy development with environmental print?

Distribute the evaluation sheet (see page 302) for parents to complete before they leave the workshop. Remember that parent input is essential to providing the kinds of workshops and interactive experiences that will build your family involvement program.

ENVIRONMENTAL PRINT WORKSHOP

Introduction to Environmental Print

Environmental print—it's the print all around us. We find it on signs, billboards, product packaging—everywhere. Most children recognize print in their surroundings at a very young age. Did you know that environmental print can be used to assist children in making connections between what they already know about written language and what they are learning in school?

Researchers have become aware of how early young children recognize a variety of print in the home environment. The logo *Cheerios,* for example, is associated with morning breakfast cereal. Later, children become aware of the names of fast-food restaurants and numerous product logos found in grocery stores. It has been found that high percentages of children between the ages of two and five can read numerous product and restaurant logos (Christie et al., 2002, 2003; Masonheimer, Drum, & Ehri, 1984). While children are typically not able to decode the actual words in the logos, they are able to use symbolic clues to read their picture meanings. Because such items carry with them rich contextualized cues, environmental print illustrates to children that print is symbolic, functional, and meaningful.

Upon entering school, most children have gained extensive knowledge about written language from their experiences with literacy in everyday life. They see print in the environment; they are often read to by family members; and they observe literacy routines in the home (newspaper reading, list making, etc.). Encounters with environmental print activities assist children in making connections between literacy experiences at home and those at school. Even before they have learned to read, children begin to relate written words to the sounds they make. By using environmental print materials in the classroom, teachers build on the literacy skills children have already developed and convey to children that reading is easy. By discussing these print items, teachers and parents can create meaningful experiences for children (Anderson & Markle, 1985; Christie et al., 2003; Duke & Purcell-Gates, 2003; Prior, 2003; Prior & Gerard, 2004). Merely spending a few minutes pointing out logos and reading them to children helps them to make valuable connections between reading and the real world (Rule, 2001) and helps to recognize that reading is everywhere.

ENVIRONMENTAL PRINT WORKSHOP

Print Awareness Inventory

Materials needed for each inventory kit:

- eight environmental print items (i.e., soda can, cereal box, etc.)
- color logo (printed on paper) for each of the eight items
- black-and-white logo (printed on paper) for each of the eight items
- typed logo word for each of the eight items
- 24 index cards
- scissors
- glue
- three rubber bands
- Print Awareness Inventory Record (page 254)
- pencil
- box or bag to store kit items

Preparation

1. Collect eight print items that will be familiar to the students, such as a Doritos bag, a Cheerios box, a Barney book, and so on.
2. Photocopy one colored copy and one black-and-white copy of each logo. Cut these out and glue each to an index card. Separate the colored logos from the black-and-white logos and rubber band each set together.
3. Type each logo word(s) on the computer using a basic, easy-to-read font. If the logo appears in all capital letters, be sure to type it this way. Print the words and cut them out. Then glue each word to an index card. Rubber band this set of cards together.
4. Place all of the items in a box or bag for convenient storage.

Directions for use

1. To conduct the inventory, each parent needs a kit and should work with only one child at a time. You might want to have parents take turns using the kits you have created and allow other parents to get snacks and visit while they wait for their turn.
2. To administer the inventory, a parent holds up one item at a time from the kit and asks the child if he or she knows the name on the item.

Print Awareness Inventory Record

EP Item	Level 1	Level 2	Level 3	Level 4
Total				

Scoring: 2 Correct
1 Category Response
0 Incorrect or No Response

3. The parent enters a score on the inventory record for each item. For example, if the child is shown a Pepsi can and says, "Pepsi," he/she receives 2 points. If the child says "soda," he/she receives 1 point (for correct category). If the child doesn't know or doesn't respond, he/she receives 0 points. The parent continues in this manner with all eight items.

4. Next, the parent shows the child each of the color logo cards and scores the child's responses in the same manner.

5. The parent continues with the black-and-white logos and the typed logos.

6. Be sure to tell parents that this activity should not frustrate the child. If the child has trouble with a particular level of the inventory, discontinue the inventory and explain that this indicates the child's print recognition level. (Later in the workshop, explain that with the use of environmental print learning activities, the child's print awareness level will increase.)

ENVIRONMENTAL PRINT WORKSHOP

Environmental Print Games: Logo Concentration

Objective

Match environmental print words to develop phonological knowledge, build vocabulary, and develop comprehension skills.

Materials: six game cards (page 257), scissors, two each of three logos, glue, rubber bands.

Preparation

Duplicate and cut out the game cards. Copy two each of four logos. Glue a logo onto each card. Laminate the cards for durability. Bundle each set of game cards using a rubber band.

Procedure

1. To play, a child and parent place the cards face down.

2. They take turns turning over two cards at a time.

3. If the cards match, the player keeps them in a stack. If the cards do not match the cards are turned face down and play continues.

Two-Piece Puzzles

Objective

Match environmental print logos to the corresponding decontextualized words to encourage transfer from contextual whole-word identification to alphabetic decoding.

Materials: two copies of page 258, cardstock, eight logos, typed form of each logo word, scissors, glue.

Preparation

Copy the puzzles on page 258 onto cardstock. Glue a logo on the lower half and the typed word on the upper half of each puzzle. Laminate the puzzles for durability and cut them apart.

Procedure

Parent and child assemble the puzzles by matching each logo to the correct typed word.

ENVIRONMENTAL PRINT WORKSHOP

Environmental Print Games: Logo Concentration Cards

ENVIRONMENTAL PRINT WORKSHOP

Environmental Print Games: Two-Piece Puzzles

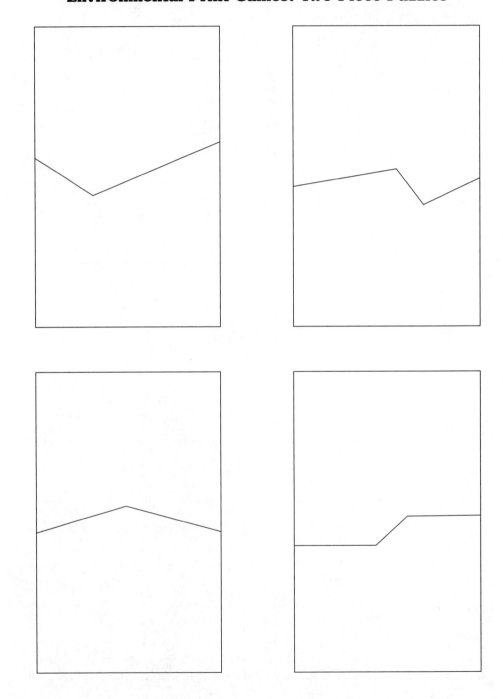

ENVIRONMENTAL PRINT WORKSHOP

Environmental Print Activities at Home

Cereal Book

Create a book of cereal box covers. Each page of the cereal book contains the cover of a familiar cereal box. Punch a hole in the top left corner of each box cover and tie the covers together with yarn or string.

Matching Product and Logo

Create a game where your child matches a logo to a picture of an item. For example, Crest is matched to a picture of a person brushing his or her teeth.

Big Puzzles

These are large puzzles featuring various products such as the cover of a cereal box, a soda pop carton, or a pizza box. The logo is cut into approximately 15 pieces for the children to assemble.

I Can Read Chart

Instead of throwing away product packaging, display this familiar print on a chart or on the front of your refrigerator. Ask your child to read the print and even encourage him/her to find familiar print items to add to the display.

Logo Writing

Have your child select a logo and glue it to a sheet of paper. Then have your child write (or dictate) a sentence for you to write using that logo. For example, "My mom took me to McDonald's."

Categorizing Logos

Collect a variety of logos. Then sit down with your child and categorize them by their beginning letters. For example, all logos beginning with the letter C are placed together.

Classifying Logos

Collect a variety of logos. Then work with your child to classify a set of logos by category—foods, drinks, and so on.

Letter Collages

Have your child select a letter to feature on his or her collage. Have him/her glue logos to the collage that correspond with the featured letter.

ENHANCING LITERACY DEVELOPMENT WORKSHOP

Invitation

You are invited to a fun night of learning to enhance your child's literacy development. This is a parents-only workshop. (Child care will be provided.)

Date: _____

Time: _____

Location: _____

Reminder Notice

Don't forget! We're having a fun night of learning to enhance your child's literacy development. We hope you'll come! (Child care will be provided.)

Date: _____

Time: _____

Location: _____

ENHANCING LITERACY DEVELOPMENT WORKSHOP

Agenda

Activity	Time:	
Sign-in and visit with other families	_____	(15 min.)
Introduction to the Workshop	_____	(15 min.)
Description of Centers	_____	(15 min.)
Center Rotation #1	_____	(15 min.)
Center Rotation #2	_____	(15 min.)
Center Rotation #3	_____	(15 min.)
Conclusion and Take-Home Materials	_____	(15 min.)

ENHANCING LITERACY DEVELOPMENT WORKSHOP

Sign-in and Visit

As parents arrive, have them sign in and make a nametag to wear. (Nametag templates are provided on page 301.) If possible, provide snacks or dinner for the participants and encourage them to visit with one another.

Introduction to the Workshop

Parents will have varying levels of understanding of literacy development, so spend a few minutes explaining the concept. Information is provided on page 263. This information should offer a brief, easy-to-understand background for parents. After reviewing the introductory information yourself, record the important points you want to mention to parents in your presentation.

Description of Centers

Explain that most of the workshop will be a make-and-take session that will allow them to create activities to use at home with their children. Take a few minutes to explain each of the centers parents will rotate through to make these activities. Be sure to show a completed project for each center, so parents can see what they will be creating.

Center Rotations

See pages 264–266 for descriptions of the make-and-take centers. These descriptions are complete with materials needed, how to conduct the activities, and what to make in the workshop for the night.

Conclusion and Take-Home Materials

At the end of the evening, spend a few minutes summarizing the information about literacy development and activities created. Ask questions, such as:

1. What did you learn about literacy experiences that assist children?
2. What do you think about the ease or difficulty of working with your child in the area of literacy?

Distribute the evaluation sheet (see page 302) for parents to complete before they leave the workshop. Remember that parent input is essential to providing the kinds of workshops and interactive experiences that will build your family involvement program.

ENHANCING LITERACY DEVELOPMENT WORKSHOP

Introduction to Literacy Development

Most children understand that there is a process of reading and they usually understand this at a very young age. They are aware of print and that print carries meaning. They are able to participate in the process of reading. Parents play an important role in their children's literacy development. The more value parents place on literacy activities, the more their children recognize this importance.

Children often have a very good idea of the purpose of print. The world around them teaches them much about reading and its purpose in our society. Research tells us that children's learning is enhanced by experiences in cooperation with the adults in their lives. The zone of proximal development focuses on the idea that when children are given opportunities to interact with adults or peers, they gain more knowledge and are challenged to higher levels.

Parents can be encouraged by this information. Simply by living life together and sharing literacy experiences together, parents can assist their children in developing beginning skills that will transfer to the process of reading.

ENHANCING LITERACY DEVELOPMENT WORKSHOP

Make-and-Take Activity #1: Finding Rhyming Words

Objective

The child will identify rhyming words in a familiar song.

Materials

Construction paper, glue, adhesive notes, markers, paper, print-out of words to a rhyming song, such as "Twinkle, Twinkle, Little Star."

Procedure

This activity involves the parent and child singing a familiar rhyming song together. The parent then sings the song again, omitting the second word in a rhyming pair. For example:

Twinkle, twinkle, little star

How I wonder what you _____.

The child is encouraged to say the rhyming word. The parent and child write each rhyming word on its own adhesive note. When all words have been written down, the parent mixes up the notes and the two work together to match up the rhyming pairs.

Preparation

At the center, each parent should take a copy of the song words and glue it to a sheet of construction paper. The parent takes several adhesive notes for conducting the activity at home. When finished, parents at that center meet to discuss other familiar children's songs they know that have rhyming words. The parents write out the words to these songs on paper using the markers provided.

ENHANCING LITERACY DEVELOPMENT WORKSHOP

Make-and-Take Activity #2: Phonemic Awareness

Objective

The child will listen for sounds heard in words.

Materials

Magazines, scissors, index cards, glue.

Procedure

Explain to parents that learning to read depends, in large part, on a child's ability to identify the individual sounds in words. (This is different from identifying only the letters.) To play this game, a child looks at pictures of various objects and identifies beginning letter sounds. (Depending on the skill level of the child, he/she could be asked to identify ending or middle sounds.)

Preparation

At this center, each parent receives 10 index cards. Each parent looks through magazines and cuts out pictures of familiar items to his/her child, such as a bike, a hamburger, or a dog. The parent glues each picture to an index card.

ENHANCING LITERACY DEVELOPMENT WORKSHOP

Make-and-Take Activity #3: Making Reading a Priority

Objective

The parent makes a schedule for reading to his/her child.

Materials

Calendar page (see page 267), pencils, highlighter pens, a collection of great children's books.

Procedure

At this center, each parent gets a calendar page and a pencil. The parent's job is to think through his or her schedule to plan for a few minutes each day to read aloud to his/her child. The parent should be sure to write on the calendar all of his/her weekly commitments. Then the parent schedules a minimum of five minutes a day to spend reading with his/her child. These reading appointments should be highlighted to draw attention to them. With available time after the schedule is created, encourage parents to peruse the collection of books for ideas on what to read with their children. Provide information to parents about checking out books from the public or school libraries.

Monday	Tuesday	Wednesday	Thursday	Friday

FAMILY FIELD TRIPS WORKSHOP

Invitation

You are invited to a fun night of learning about great family field trips in your community. This is a parents-only workshop. (Child care will be provided.)

Date: _____

Time: _____

Location: _____

Reminder Notice

Don't forget! We're having a fun night of learning about field trip opportunities in your community. We hope you'll come! (Child care will be provided.)

Date: _____

Time: _____

Location: _____

FAMILY FIELD TRIPS WORKSHOP
Agenda

Activity	Time:
Sign-in and visit with other families	_____ (15 min.)
Introduction to the Workshop	_____ (5 min.)
Ice Breaker Activity	_____ (15 min.)
Description of Centers	_____ (5 min.)
Center Rotation #1	_____ (20 min.)
Center Rotation #2	_____ (20 min.)
Center Rotation #3	_____ (20 min.)
Conclusion and Take-Home Materials	_____ (5 min.)

FAMILY FIELD TRIPS WORKSHOP

Sign-in and Visit

As parents arrive, have them sign in and make a nametag to wear. (Nametag templates are provided on page 301.) If possible, provide snacks or dinner for the participants and encourage them to visit with one another.

Ice Breaker Activity

Allow parents time to interact and introduce themselves with a brief ice breaker activity. Provide each parent with a pencil and an index card. Encourage them to mingle with other participants, asking and recording parents' names and a fun activity to do with children in town.

Introduction to the Workshop

The purpose of this workshop is to provide parents with ideas for getting them and their children involved with their community through activities and community service. Explain that these kinds of activities provide opportunities for family fun and caring for others. Because the activities and service opportunities will be specific to your area, presenters will need to research ahead of time to create a list of ideas for parents.

Description of Centers

Explain that the workshop will be consist of group "centers" related to different family field trip opportunities. Take a few minutes to explain each of the centers parents will rotate through.

Center Rotations

See pages 272–274 for descriptions of the centers. These descriptions are complete with materials needed and instructions on how to conduct the activities.

Conclusion and Take-Home Materials

At the end of the evening, spend a few minutes summarizing the information about family field trips. Ask questions, such as:

    1. What did you learn about opportunities available in the community?
    2. How realistic do you think participating in these activities will be?

Distribute the list of field trip ideas and also the Plan a Trip sheet (page 277) for parents to take home. Then, distribute the evaluation sheet (see page 302) for parents to complete before they leave the workshop. Remember that parent input is essential to providing the kinds of workshops and interactive experiences that will build your family involvement program.

FAMILY FIELD TRIPS WORKSHOP

Center Rotations: Center #1: On Being Helpful

Materials

List of ideas for volunteering in the community (see page 275), chart paper, marker, paper, and pencils for parents.

Preparation

Ahead of time, create a brief list of opportunities to volunteer in the community. Use page 275 to list and describe these ideas.

The facilitator at this center will explain that there are many opportunities to help out in the community, offering assistance to those in need as well as volunteering time at local events and organizations. Provide a few examples for the parents, such as volunteering at the humane society, visiting homes for the elderly, or picking up trash in needed locations.

Group parents together (in twos or threes) and ask them to brainstorm opportunities for volunteerism in the community. Then have the groups share their ideas as the facilitator records them on chart paper. You may want to have another facilitator at this center record the ideas and duplicate copies of them to distribute to parents before they leave the workshop.

FAMILY FIELD TRIPS WORKSHOP

Center Rotations: Center #2: Places to Go

Materials

A list of fun family field trip ideas (see page 276), paper, and pencils for parents.

Preparation

Before the workshop, list and describe activities in your community that would be appropriate for parents and children. Use page 276 to assist you in creating this list. Ideas might include visiting specific historic sites, the local zoo, a fire station, children's theater, or participating in activities offered through the local library. Be sure to include activities that are free or inexpensive.

The purpose of this center is to describe specific activities parents and children can do together in the community. Provide parents with paper and pencils for jotting down notes as the facilitator describes the activities. Also, provide parents with a detailed description of each activity and the necessary addresses and contact information for the activities/locations described.

FAMILY FIELD TRIPS WORKSHOP

Center Rotations: Center #3: Plan a Trip

Materials

Chart paper, marker, paper, and pencils for parents.

Preparation

Explain to parents that successful family field trips involve some planning. Tell them that, as a group, they will plan a simple trip. Provide an example, such as going to a local swimming pool. Remind them to think about the preparations needed before taking the trip, what will happen during the trip, and what to do afterwards.

Preparing for the Trip

Ask parents what preparations might be needed for going to a local swimming pool, such as calling ahead of time for hours of operation and admission fees. They might want to ask if it is permitted to bring pool toys and food or if a snack bar will be available. Supplies needed to bring to the pool might include bathing suits, towels, sunscreen, sandals, sunglasses, pool toys, and drinking water. List these ideas on chart paper.

During the Trip

Remind parents that this is a family trip and the idea is to spend time with their children. Ask them to think of how they might participate with their children at the swimming pool. List these ideas on the chart paper.

After the Trip

Explain to parents that follow-up activities are important for concluding a family field trip. Tell them that they might have conversations with their children on the way home to discuss the best parts of the day. Parents might also want to extend this by working with their children to create homemade books with text and illustrations describing the day. Invite parents to share their ideas for follow-up activities and record these ideas on the chart paper.

FAMILY FIELD TRIPS WORKSHOP

On Being Helpful: Ideas for Volunteerism

Use this page to list a few ideas in your community for parents and children to volunteer their time. This page will be used for your reference during the workshop.

Opportunity #1: _____

Description: _____

_____

Opportunity #2: _____

Description: _____

_____

Opportunity #3: _____

Description: _____

_____

FAMILY FIELD TRIPS WORKSHOP

Places to Go

Here are some great activities for family field trips in our area.

Activity: _____

Description: _____

_____

Contact Information: _____

Activity: _____

Description: _____

_____

Contact Information: _____

Activity: _____

Description: _____

_____

Contact Information: _____

Activity: _____

Description: _____

_____

Contact Information: _____

FAMILY FIELD TRIPS WORKSHOP

Plan a Trip

Use this page to assist with planning a family field trip.

Before the Trip

Call the site to ask important questions, such as hours of operation, admission fees, necessary supplies or attire.

Pack for the trip (clothing, food, supplies).

Notes:_____

_____

During the Trip

Remember that the purpose of the trip is to spend quality time together. Think about what you and your child will do and talk about it together in order to make it a partnership activity.

Notes: _____

_____

After the Trip

Spend time with your child after the trip, discussing the events of the day or making a project, such as a homemade book telling about the trip.

Notes: _____

_____

"NUMBER ONE IN FAMILY FUN" MATH NIGHT WORKSHOP

Invitation

Dear Family,

You and your child are invited to come and learn some ways to make math fun! You will learn some useful ideas to try at home together.

Date_____

Time_____

Place_____

Who's Invited: The Whole Family

Dress casually. We look forward to seeing everyone for "Number One in Family Fun."

Please complete and detach the form below.

_____Yes, we will attend the "Number One in Family Fun" Math Night.

_____Sorry, we are unable to attend.

Child's Name_____

Number Attending_____

If you have questions or need transportation, please call_____.

Name_____Phone_____

E-mail Address_____

"NUMBER ONE IN FAMILY FUN" MATH NIGHT WORKSHOP

Reminder

Don't Forget!

You and your family are invited to "Number One in Family Fun" Math Night

Date_____

Time_____

Place_____

Who's Invited: The Whole Family

Dress casually.

Reserve an hour and 45 minutes to participate in home math activities to teach and reinforce math concepts with your child.

To make a reservation now, please call_____.

"NUMBER ONE IN FAMILY FUN" MATH NIGHT WORKSHOP

Workshop Agenda

Activity	Time:	
Sign-in and visit with other families	_____	(15 min.)
Ice Breaker Activity	_____	(15 min.)
Introduction to Number Sense	_____	(15 min.)
Whole Group Game	_____	(15 min.)
Math Card Games Rotations	_____	(30 min.)
Conclusion and Take-Home Materials	_____	(15 min.)

CONTENT AREA: MATHEMATICS

Purpose

To provide families with home activities that will help develop number sense.

Children's Literature: *Anno's Counting Book* by Mitsumasa Anno
                        The Watering Hole by Graeme Base

Sign-in and Visit

- As parents and children arrive, have them sign in and choose a nametag to wear. Provide old, recycled playing cards from number nine of all suits and lower.
- Place tape on the front of each card to attach the card as a nametag.
- Attach a white sticky label to the lower portion of the back of the playing card to write out first names.
- Each family member receives a playing card nametag of the same suit and writes in first names on the white sticky label.

If possible, provide snacks or dinner for the participants and encourage them to visit with one another.

Ice Breaker Activity

Help families feel at ease and get to know one another with an activity to "break the ice." As families arrive, distribute the playing card nametags. Ask each family member to write his or her name on the card and use the masking tape to attach the playing card nametag to clothing. Be sure all family members have a nametag with the same card suit as this designates the game center the family will begin at. Ask the workshop participants to divide into two groups. One group forms a circle facing inward while the second group forms a circle facing out. Each participant should be facing someone else. Ring a bell or chime to signal the inner circle to begin moving counter-clockwise while the outer group moves clockwise. Ring the bell or chime again to stop the two circles. The new participants that are now facing each other introduce themselves and try to name something famous with their new partner's number. Example: The new partner has the number 3 so you call out "Three Blind Mice," or "We Three Kings," or "Three Musketeers." Move the circles again so that new participants are paired up. Allow 15 minutes for the ice breaker activity or until all of the participants have met each other.

Description of Game Rotations

Give parents the introductory material on the value of game playing for developing number sense with playing cards. Show the Anno's counting book to illustrate to parents that number sense develops at several levels simultaneously with young children. A variety of materials encourages and builds deep conceptual understanding. Explain that the workshop will consist of group games that will involve game play with playing cards for number sense development. Take a few minutes to explain each of the centers parents will rotate through.

Conclusion and Take-Home Materials

At the end of the evening, spend a few minutes summarizing the information about developing number sense with playing cards such as:

1. What did you learn about how number sense develops?
2. How realistic do you think participating in these games at home is?

GAME ROTATIONS

Introduction

This workshop is designed to show family members the ways in which one simple material found in most homes or easily obtained in drugstores or grocery stores can teach and reinforce critical math skills. Beginning with recognizing and understanding simple numbers and number names to understanding complex integers and decimal operations, playing cards are a fun material that make math come to life. Games are an invaluable teaching strategy to enrich any math curriculum. Using playing cards and card games provides a meaningful context for repetitive practice of math concepts. The games presented here are multisensory experiences that engage all learning styles. Card games teach beyond rote memorization of math facts by creating neural connections through patterns, higher-order strategizing, and mathematical language use.

Description of Activities

Whole Group Introductory Card Game: WAR

2 players

Materials

One deck of playing cards for each pair of players to divide in half.

Alternatively, index cards may be numbered and illustrated with designs to correspond to a deck of playing cards.

No other advance preparation required.

This is a traditional card game that can be simplified for number recognition or made more complex by using number operations. (If the connotation of WAR is insensitive to families or friends attending the workshop, an alternative name such as "Match" or "Traffic Jam" can be used.) Each pair of players receives a deck of cards and divides it evenly between themselves. Face cards are given the value of 10 and aces are given the value of 1.

For developing number sense: Each player then turns over a card and reads the number aloud. The highest number gets all the cards. In the event of a match, WAR is declared. Each player deals out three of his/her cards and then turns over a fourth card and reads the number aloud. The highest number gets all the cards and wins the "WAR." *For developing number operations:* Each pair of players receives a deck of cards and divides it evenly between themselves. Each player turns over two cards and either adds, subtracts, or multiplies the two numbers depending on the operation to be practiced. The player with the highest sum, difference, or product gets all of the cards. In the event of a match, WAR is declared. Each player deals out three of his/her cards and then turns over two more cards to add, subtract, or multiply. The highest sum, difference, or product gets all of the cards. Play continues until one player has collected all of the cards in the deck.

Number Concentration (Hearts Game Center)

2–4 players

Materials

One card deck for each pair or triad of players.

Alternatively, index cards may be numbered and illustrated with designs to correspond to a deck of playing cards.

Advance Preparation

Remove all face cards from the deck of playing cards.

A card deck of number cards only, no face cards, is laid out in a face-down grid of four rows and nine columns. Players take turns turning over two cards, attempting to match two numerals. To encourage number recognition in young children, numbers should be called aloud by the child. With older children, number operations can be practiced by adding, subtracting, or multiplying the two cards turned over. If the two cards match, the player keeps the two cards. If they do not match, the cards are laid face down again and the other player continues to play. When all the cards are matched, the player with the most cards wins.

Number Rummy (Spades Number Concentration)

2–5 players

Materials

One deck of cards for entire group to play Number Rummy.

The object of this card game is to make as many pairs of playing cards as possible. Each pair of players receives a deck of 52 cards. Each player is dealt 5 cards. The remaining cards make up a draw pile. The players examine the 5 cards dealt them for any pairs and lay these pairs down to start play. Each player then takes a turn and draws a card from the face-down stack. New pairs that are made are laid down. If no matches are made, a card is discarded next to the draw pile. Players may play on the pairs laid down by the other player. Play continues until one player has run out of cards. Count each player's pairs to determine who wins the game. To develop number recognition in young children, encourage the naming of the matching number.

Snap! (Diamonds Game Center)

3 players

Materials

One deck of cards for team of three players.

No other advance preparation necessary.

The object of the game is to practice speed and accuracy with number operations. Three players form a game. The card deck is divided evenly between two players while the third player is the game "caller." Ace cards have the value of 1 and face cards have the value of 10. The two players hold their partial deck face down and the caller gives the signal for each player to turn up a card and hold it at his/her forehead, out of sight. (The player will only be able to see the opponent's playing card held against his/her forehead.) The caller calls out the sum or product of the two cards, depending on the operation to be practiced. Players mentally fill in the missing card digit from the card held at their forehead. The first to correctly call the missing card digit gets both cards. Play continues until one player is out of cards.

Sum 10 (Clubs Game Center)

2 players

Materials

One deck of card for each pair of players.

Advance Preparation

Remove the cards ace through nine of just one suit for play.

The object of this game is to develop automaticity in generating sums to 10 with very young children. The cards ace through nine of a suit are taken from a deck of cards. The nine cards are laid out face down in a grid of two rows. The child picks up two cards as in the Concentration game but he/she is trying to hit the target number of 10. If the target is not hit, cards are replaced and the opponent attempts to hit the target. Example: the child turns over the two of hearts and the eight of hearts; the target sum of 10 is reached. The cards are removed from play. When play is down to a single card, check for accuracy in the sums. The number 5 playing card should be the card left. This game can be made more complex for older children by creating the sum of 20 as the target number; 18 cards are played using two suits of cards and four cards are added together to create the sum of 20. Holding the first and second sum in short-term memory in order to add up four cards encourages mental math skills. When play is down to just two cards, check for accuracy in the sums. The two remaining cards should sum to 10.

Conclusion and Take-Home Materials

At the end of the evening, spend a few minutes summarizing the information about the value of game play to develop number sense.

1. What did you learn about the value of games for learning math concepts?
2. How realistic do you think participating in these games at home will be?
3. Give parents handout copies of games directions and/or a set of playing cards for home play.

GAME PLAY DIRECTIONS FOR PARENTS

WAR

This is a traditional card game that can be simplified for number recognition or made more complex by using number operations. Each pair of players receives a deck of cards and divides it evenly between themselves. Face cards are given the value of 10 and aces are given the value of 1. *For developing number sense:* Each player then turns over a card and reads the number aloud. The highest number gets all the cards. In the event of a match, WAR is declared. Each player deals out three of their cards and then turns over a fourth card and reads the number aloud. The highest number gets all the cards and wins the "WAR." *For developing number operations:* Each pair of players receives a deck of cards and divides it evenly between themselves. Each player turns over two cards and either adds, subtracts, or multiplies the two numbers depending on the operation to be practiced. The player with the highest sum, difference, or product gets all of the cards. In the event of a match, WAR is declared. Each player deals out three of his/her cards and then turns over two more cards to add, subtract, or multiply. The highest sum, difference, or product gets all of the cards. Play continues until one player has collected all of the cards in the deck.

Number Concentration

A card deck of number cards only, no face cards, is laid out in a face-down grid of four rows and nine columns. Players take turns turning over two cards, attempting to match two numerals. To encourage number recognition in young children, numbers should be called aloud by the child. With older children, number operations can be practiced by adding, subtracting, or multiplying the two cards turned over. If the two cards match, the player keeps the two cards. If they do not match, the cards are laid face down again and the other player continues to play. When all the cards are matched, the player with the most cards wins.

Number Rummy

The object of this card game is to make as many pairs of playing cards as possible. Each pair of players receives a deck of 52 cards. Each player is dealt 5 cards. The remaining cards make up a draw pile. The players examine the 5 cards dealt them for any pairs and lay these pairs down to start play. Each player then takes a turn and draws a card from the face-down stack. New pairs that are made are laid down. If no matches are made, a card is discarded next to the draw pile. Players may play on the pairs laid down by the other player. Play continues until one player has run out of cards. Count each player's pairs to determine who wins the game. To develop number recognition in young children, encourage the naming of the matching number.

Snap!

The object of the game is to practice speed and accuracy with number operations. Three players form a game. The card deck is divided evenly between two players while the third player is the game "caller." Ace cards have the value of 1 and face cards have the value of 10. The two players hold their partial deck face down and the caller gives the signal for each player to turn up a card and hold it at his/her forehead, out of sight. (The player will only be able to see the opponent's playing card held against his/her forehead.) The caller calls out the sum or product of the two cards, depending on the operation to be practiced. Players mentally fill in the missing card digit from the card held at their forehead. The first to correctly call the missing card digit gets both cards. Play continues until one player is out of cards.

Sum 10

The object of this game is to develop automaticity in generating sums to 10 with very young children. The cards ace through nine of a suit are taken from a deck of cards. The nine cards are laid out face down in a grid of two rows. The child picks up two cards as in the Concentration game but he/she is trying to hit the target number of 10. If the target is not hit, cards are replaced and the opponent attempts to hit the target. Example: the child turns over the two of hearts and the eight of hearts; the target sum of 10 is reached. The cards are removed from play. When play is down to a single card, check for accuracy in the sums. The number 5 playing card should be the card left. This game can be made more complex for older children by creating the sum of 20 as the target number; 18 cards are played using two suits of cards and four cards are added together to create the sum of 20. Holding the first and second sum in short-term memory in order to add up four cards encourages mental math skills. When play is down to just two cards, check for accuracy in the sums. The two remaining cards should sum to 10.

KIDS IN THE KITCHEN FOR NUTRITION
IQ WORKSHOP

Invitation

Dear Family,

You and your child are invited to come and learn some ways to make cooking together fun. Come to learn some nutrition facts and take home some recipe ideas the whole family can make together.

Date_____

Time_____

Place_____

Who's Invited: The Whole Family

Dress casually. We look forward to seeing everyone for Kids in the Kitchen for Nutrition IQ.

Please complete and detach the form below.

_____Yes, we will attend the Kids in the Kitchen for Nutrition IQ.
_____Sorry, we are unable to attend.

Child's Name_____

Number Attending_____

If you have questions or need transportation, please call_____.

Name_____Phone_____

E-mail Address_____

KIDS IN THE KITCHEN FOR NUTRITION
IQ WORKSHOP

Reminder

Don't Forget!

You and your family are invited to Kids in the Kitchen for Nutrition IQ.

Date_____

Time_____

Place_____

Who's Invited: The Whole Family

Dress casually.

Reserve an hour and 45 minutes to participate in cooking and learning to improve Nutrition IQ.

To make a reservation now, please call_____.

KIDS IN THE KITCHEN FOR NUTRITION
IQ WORKSHOP

Workshop Agenda

Activity	Time:	
Sign-in and visit with other families	_____	(15 min.)
Ice Breaker Activity	_____	(15 min.)
Introduction to Nutrition	_____	(15 min.)
Cooking Rotations	_____	(45 min.)
Conclusion and Take-Home Materials	_____	(15 min.)

CONTENT AREA: HEALTH AND NUTRITION, SCIENCE

Objective

To provide families with home activities that will help develop understanding about the role of good nutrition in learning and achievement.

Sign-in and Visit

- As parents and children arrive, have them sign in and choose a nametag to wear.
- Place tape on the back of each nametag to attach the nametag.

If possible, provide snacks or dinner for the participants and encourage them to visit with one another.

Ice Breaker Activity

Help families feel at ease and get to know one another with an activity to "break the ice."

- As families arrive distribute the nametags.
- Ask each family member to write his or her name on the nametag and attach it to their clothing with a piece of masking tape.
- On the hidden side of the nametag, ask the family participant to write down his/her favorite *healthy* snack food. Families should all have the same color/shape nametag for grouping purposes during center rotations.
- Have the participants mingle by playing "20 questions" with others. Ask participants to introduce themselves and then try to guess the favorite *healthy* snack food with 20 questions such as: "Is it a fruit? Is it red? Does it keep the doctor away?"
- Allow approximately 15 minutes for all of the participants to meet.

Description of Cooking Center Rotations

Give parents the introductory information on nutrition and the importance of food in learning and academic achievement. Explain that the workshop will consist of group cooking activities so that children can learn, by preparing simple nutritious foods, that a healthy diet has value in growth and development. This workshop is designed to enhance nutrition awareness. Explain the cooking rotations.

Conclusion and Take-Home Materials

At the end of the evening, spend a few minutes summarizing the information about nutrition and cooking with children. Hand out recipe copies and copies of the USDA food pyramid. Ask families the following questions:

1. What did you learn about nutrition and cooking with your child?
2. How realistic do you think these cooking activities will be to do in your home?
3. Are there favorite kid recipes you make in your home that you can share with us?

KIDS IN THE KITCHEN FOR NUTRITION IQ

INTRODUCTION

Be aware that many children and adults may have food allergies. Some of the more common foods to which children and adults may react are wheat, milk and milk products, juice with high acid content, chocolate, eggs, and nuts. When families make reservations, be sure to ask about known food allergies. Cultural and ethnic foods influence the foods we like and eat. Different groups across America may follow different dietary patterns and have different food preferences than those that are presented here. This is information that you should have in hand from thoroughly understanding your students and their families. Inform families of the kinds of foods you will offer when they make their reservations.

These cooking activities combine snack preparation with fun and nutrition learning. Encourage the participant to try all the foods offered. In addition to the main content areas of health, nutrition, and science, young children are learning to use counting and math skills, language, small motor skills, and science process skills. A different cooking activity is made at each of the four center rotations.

COOKING TIPS FOR PARENTS SHOULD INCLUDE

- Safety first. Keep young children away from a stove and knives. Even very young children will want to put the flour in the mixing bowl or break an egg. Turn the mixer off and let them do it.
- Choose simple recipes and quick recipes for young kids. Kids love to get their hands in the dough. Consider a cookie recipe where the cookies are hand-formed. Or divide the recipe and give young children their own dough to work with.
- Praise often. Expect messes in the kitchen.
- Use the recipe to teach skills. Help the child read directions. Learning to follow written instructions is an important life skill. Help the child understand the fractions and abbreviations in most recipes.
- Have a few quick mixes on hand to cook with kids. These mixes are easily enhanced and are appropriate to a child's short attention span.

Food labels contain important nutritional information for you and your child. You can both use this information to make better choices about what you eat. Show your child how to read the basics of a food label.

My Pyramid Food Guidance System

- Look for foods with lower saturated fats.
- Sodium level is the amount of salt in a food; look for low levels of sodium.
- Look for higher fiber and lower sugar.
- Calcium is important for bones.
- Exercise is important for the amount of calories a person needs each day.

The building blocks of food are:

1. Carbohydrates: The body's main source of energy. Bread, pasta, rice, potatoes, corn, and cereals are all examples of carbohydrates.

2. Fats: Margarine, butter, lard, shortening, and cooking oil are all fats. Cheese, cream, chocolate, and some meats have a high fat content. Our bodies need just a little fat each day.

3. Proteins: This food is important for building muscles, growth, and repair of the body. Eggs, milk products, meat, dried beans, chicken, turkey, and fish are high-protein foods.

4. Minerals: These are found in small amounts in our foods. They are important to our body's functioning.

5. Vitamins: These are chemicals found in small amounts in our foods too. Like minerals, they are needed in very small quantities to help our body function well.

6. Water: This is the major component of our body and the most important part of all our food.

The U.S. Department of Agriculture and nutritional experts encourage individuals, including children, to make healthy nutritional choices for themselves. The factors to consider in making these choices are the level of physical activity, variety, proportionality, moderation, gradual improvement in diet, and personalization. Very general guidelines for making healthy food choices are:

- Eat at least 3 ounces of whole grains every day.
- Go low fat or fat free in choosing dairy products.
- Drink beverages low in added sugar.
- Choose foods closest to natural without added sugar.

(Retrieved on March 17, 2006, http://www.governmentguide.com/govsite)

Cooking Center Rotation #1 (Grapes Nametags)

Cooking Tools Needed

- mixing bowls
- large spoons
- smaller bowls for cornflake coating
- waxed paper or smaller paper plates
- mixing cups

Advance Preparation

Large-print recipe and directions at the center, plastic or disposable table covering, wet wipes for hands cleanup.

Peanut Butter Balls

Ingredients

1/2 cup peanut butter

1/2 cup honey

1 cup crushed cornflakes cereal

2 tablespoons powdered milk

Set corn flakes aside.

Mix all other ingredients well.

Roll into balls.

Then roll again in cornflakes until covered.

Refrigerate leftovers!!

Yummy snack! Great with milk!

Cooking Center Rotation #2 (Apple Nametags)

Cooking Tools Needed

- small mixing bowls for sandwich insides
- plastic knives or large tongue depressors for safe spreading
- napkins or paper towels
- wet wipes for hand cleanup

Advance Preparation

Large-print recipe and directions at the center.

Waffle Sandwich

This is so easy, kids will want to make their own breakfasts and snacks. They can even experiment to create their own signature sandwich!

Ingredients

Two waffles—frozen or homemade

Peanut butter

Jelly

Optional ingredients: marshmallow spread, bananas, chocolate chips, honey, dried fruit.

Spread peanut butter on one waffle, jelly on the other, and make a sandwich—it's that easy!

Cooking Center Rotation #3 (Banana Nametags)

Cooking Tools Needed

- blender
- rubber spatulas
- spoons for mixing
- measuring cups
- cups for serving
- napkins or paper towels
- wet wipes for hand cleanup

Advance Preparation

Large-print recipe and directions at the center.

Fruit Icee

A summer treat that older children can make alone and younger children can make with assistance.

Ingredients

2 pkg. frozen fruit in syrup

1/3 cup ice water

1/4 cup orange juice

omit water and use 3/4 cup orange juice

1/4 tsp. lemon juice

Mix all ingredients together in a blender or food processor until smooth. Turn off, scrape sides, blend again, and pour into a plastic container.

Cover and freeze until serving time.

Makes 4–6 servings

TIP: If the ice is frozen hard, let it stand at room temperature 5 minutes or so before serving.

Cooking Center #4 (Lime Nametags)

Cooking Tools Needed

- microwaveable pan
- measuring cups
- microwave
- napkins or paper towels
- wet wipes for hand cleanup

Advance Preparation

Large-print recipe and directions at the center.

Nuts and Bolts

Ingredients

1 cane cocktail nuts

1 package *Rice Chex* cereal

1 package pretzel sticks

1/2 cup peanut butter

1/2 package *Cheerios* cereal

1/2 cup oil

Mix peanut butter and oil. Heat in microwave or on stove top until smooth.

Pour all ingredients into a roasting pan. Mix well.

Bake for 15–20 minutes at 300°.

Store in airtight container.

RECIPE HANDOUT FOR PARENTS

Peanut Butter Balls

Ingredients

1/2 cup peanut butter

1/2 cup honey

1 cup crushed cornflakes cereal

2 tablespoons powdered milk

Set cornflakes aside.

Mix all other ingredients well.

Roll into balls.

Then roll again in cornflakes until covered.

Refrigerate leftovers!!

Yummy snack! Great with milk!

Waffle Sandwich

This is so easy, kids will want to make their own breakfasts and snacks. They can even experiment to create their own signature sandwich!

Ingredients

Two waffles—frozen or homemade

Peanut butter

Jelly

Optional ingredients: marshmallow spread, bananas, chocolate chips, honey, dried fruit.

Spread peanut butter on one waffle, jelly on the other, and make a sandwich—it's that easy!

Fruit Icee

A summer treat that older children can make alone and younger children can make with assistance.

2 pkg. frozen fruit in syrup

1/3 cup ice water

1/4 cup orange juice

omit water and use 3/4 cup orange juice

1/4 tsp. lemon juice

Mix all ingredients together in a blender or food processor until smooth. Turn off, scrape sides, blend again, and pour into a plastic container.

Cover and freeze until serving time.

Makes 4–6 servings.

TIP: If the ice is frozen hard, let it stand at room temperature 5 minutes or so before serving.

Nuts and Bolts

1 cane cocktail nuts

1 package *Rice Chex* cereal

1 package pretzel sticks

1/2 cup peanut butter

1/2 package *Cheerios* cereal

1/2 cup oil

Mix peanut butter and oil. Heat in microwave or on stove top until smooth.

Pour all ingredients into a roasting pan. Mix well.

Bake for 15–20 minutes at 300°

Store in airtight container.

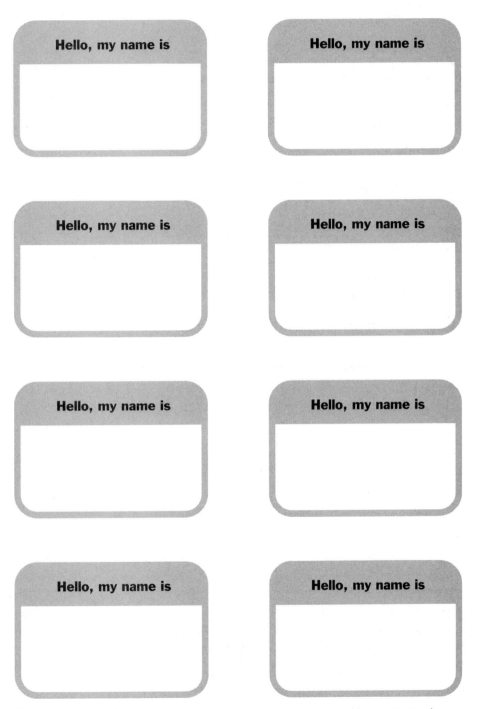

Duplicate the nametags onto adhesive paper or cut them apart and have parents pin them on as they register at the workshop.

Workshop Evaluation

Name of Workshop: _____

1. What are your thoughts about the usefulness of this workshop?

_____

_____

_____

_____

2. What was most helpful to you in this workshop?

_____

_____

_____

_____

3. What information do you wish was included?

_____

_____

_____

_____

4. How do you think you will use the information from this workshop?

_____

_____

_____

_____

5. What are your ideas for future parent workshops?

_____

_____

_____

_____

If you have questions and would like to be contacted by one of the workshop facilitators, list your questions and contact information below.

_____

_____

_____

_____

■ CONCLUSION

Recent focus on family involvement in children's educational experiences is well worth the attention, as research shows us, on both individual and school-wide levels. When emphasis is placed on involving parents, overall school achievement increases and positive perceptions are reported by children, parents, teachers, and administrators. Is it any wonder, then, that more and more family involvement programs are being implemented in schools throughout the country? As early childhood educators, we must remember that it is our responsibility to involve parents in the process, for without this involvement, we are not adequately addressing each child's educational needs to the fullest. Whether we involve parents through regular communication or through school-wide parent education workshops, we must focus on the individual needs of our school communities and help to form the most effective partnerships possible.

■ SUMMARY OF IMPORTANT POINTS

- Schools with comprehensive, ongoing family involvement report increased student achievement.
- Transformation of schools resulting from family involvement include increased teacher morale, positive parent perceptions, increased parent support, and increased student achievement.
- Parents who get involved in their children's education early on are more likely to stay involved throughout their children's school "careers."
- Involved families support schools and encourage other families to get connected with the school community.
- School-wide family involvement programs vary and should meet the needs of the school community.
- Principals/directors play integral roles in creating school environments that are welcoming to families.
- Parent education programs can serve to provide fun, interactive learning experiences for parents (and children) and can help to connect parents with other families in the school community.

■ CHAPTER REVIEW QUESTIONS

1. Why are school-wide family involvement programs beneficial?

2. What are some successful family involvement programs that have been implemented in the United States?

3. What are key components of successful family involvement programs?

4. How can parent education workshops benefit parents?

■ APPLICATION AND REFLECTION

1. Make a list of ways a school could create an overall environment that is welcoming to parents.

2. Interview a parent of school-age children. Ask this parent how he/she feels about the school his/her child attends. How does the school involve parents? Is the environment welcoming? Does the school provide opportunities for parents to interact? Are there parent education opportunities available? What does this parent think would be most helpful for creating effective home-school partnerships?

3. Create your own parent education workshop. Use the format outlined in this chapter, if necessary. Select a topic that would be beneficial or of interest to parents of young children and create the materials, activities, and handouts necessary to conduct this workshop.

■ FURTHER READING

Gordon, T. (2000). *Parent effectiveness training: The proven program for raising responsible children.* Three Rivers Press.

Taylor-Cox, J. (2005). *Family math night: Math standards in action.* Eye to Education, Inc.

For additional information on research-based practice, visit our Web site at http://www.earlychilded. delmar.com.

Additional resources for this chapter can be found on the Online Companion™ to accompany this text at http://www.earlychilded.delmar.com. This supplemental material includes Web links, downloadable forms, and Case Studies with critical thinking applications. This content can be used as a study aid to reinforce key concepts presented in this chapter and to conduct additional research on topics of interest.

■ REFERENCES

Albee, J .J., & Drew, M. (January/February, 2001). Off to the write start: A parent-teacher-child story. *Reading Horizons, 41*(3), 129–141.

Anderson, G., & Markle, A. (1985). Cheerios, McDonald's and Snickers: Bringing EP into the classroom. *Reading Education in Texas,* 30–35.

Bermudez, A. B., & Marquez, J. A. (1996). An examination of a four-way collaborative to increase parental involvement in the schools. *The Journal of Educational Issue of Language Minority Students, 16.*

Books and Beyond. http://www.booksandbeyond.org/. Retrieved June 20, 2005.

Christie, J. F., Enz, B. J., Gerard, M., Han, M., & Prior, J. (2002). Paper presented at the International Reading Association annual convention, San Francisco, CA.

Christie, J. F., Enz, B. J., Gerard, M., Han, M., & Prior, J. (2003). Paper presented at the International Reading Association annual convention, Orlando, FL.

Cohn-Vargas, & Grose, K. (1998). A partnership for literacy. *Educational Leadership, 55*(8), 45–48.

Duke, N. K., & Purcell-Gates, V. (2003). Genres at home and at school: Bridging the known to the new. *The Reading Teacher, 57*(1), 30–37.

Epstein, J. L. (May, 1995). School/family/community partnerships: Caring for the children we share. *Phi Delta Kappan, 76,* 701–712.

Family Math. http://www.lhs.berkeley.edu/equals/whatisFM.html. Retrieved June 20, 2005.

Family Outreach Program of State College Area School District. http://www.ncrel.org/sdrs/pidata/18.htm. Retrieved June 20, 2005.

Families and Schools Together. http://www.wcer.wisc.edu/fast/. Retrieved June 20, 2005.

Faucette, E. (November/December, 2000). Are you missing the most important ingredient? A recipe for increasing achievement. *Multimedia Schools, 7*(6), 56–61.

Fields, M. V., & Spangler, K. L. (1995). *Let's begin reading right.* Englewood Cliffs, NJ: PrenticeHall, Inc.

Henderson, A., & Berla, N. (1997). *A new generation of evidence: The family is critical to student achievement.* Washington, DE: Center for Law and Education.

Henderson, A. T. (October, 1988). Parents are a school's best friends. *Phi Delta Kappan,* 148–153.

Henderson-Sellers, A. (1991). Uniting schools and families. *Education Digest, 56*(8), 47–50.

Igo, S. (November, 2002). Increasing parent involvement. *Principal Leadership* (Middle School Edition), *3*(3), 10–12.

Masonheimer, P., Drum, P., & Ehri, L. (1984). Does environmental print identification lead children into word reading? *Journal of Reading Behavior, 1,* 257–271.

Moore, K. (September, 2001). Creating a family-friendly program. *Early Childhood Today, 16*(1), 16.

National Network of Partnership Schools. http://www.csos.jhu.edu/p2000/default.htm. Retrieved June 20, 2005.

Prior, J. (2003). Environmental print: Meaningful connections for learning to read. Unpublished doctoral dissertation, Arizona State University, Tempe.

Prior, J., & Gerard, M. R. (2004). Environmental print in the classroom: Meaningful connections for learning to read. Newark, DE: International Reading Association.

Ready to Read. http://www.readytoread.net/. Retrieved June 20, 2005.

Rule, A. C. (2001). Alphabetizing with environmental print. *The Reading Teacher, 54*(6), 558–562.

Swick, K. (1993). *Strengthening parents and families during the early childhood years*. Champaign, IL: Stipes.

Wilford, S. (March, 2004). Getting input from parents. *Early Childhood Today, 18*(5), 910.

Glossary

A

attachment—Bonding between an infant and a caregiver

B

Back-to-school night—Introductory meeting between teacher and families

C

chattel—The notion that children are property

cognitive development—Development of the brain and thinking capacities

constructivist—Theory of cognitive development

criminal background checks—Review of recorded history of criminal activity

critical periods—Time periods of maximum development

cultural barriers—Cultural differences that make communication difficult

D

Dad-friendly—Environment that welcomes fathers

diverse backgrounds—Varied heritage, culture, language

E

Ecological Systems Theory—Theory of layered systems

educational system—Parental understanding of the school culture

ESL—English as a Second Language

ELL—English Language Learner

Enlightenment—Period during the Renaissance when philosophers began questioning the teachings in the Catholic church

exosystem—People, settings, and institutions that indirectly touch a child's life

extended family—Family structure that includes grandparents, aunts, uncles, cousins, in-laws, etc.

F

family focused—A teacher's focus on the entire family

family involvement—Family support of a child's academic experience

family involvement at home—Home support of a child's academic experience family involvement at school—Parent participation in school activities

family structure—Any of the possible arrangements that comprise a family

father figure—Male role model

father involvement—Father support of the child's academic experience

federal poverty level—A government accounting office figure, adjusted each year for the rate of inflation, used to calculate tax liability, qualifications for aide and federal assistance, and to gauge income trends

fingerprint clearance—Procedure to register fingerprints with an official agency

G

gendered—favoring one gender over another

I

Industrial Revolution—19th century development of industry economy from an agricultural economy

interactive experiences—Activities that involve parent and child working together

J

Jean Jacques Rousseau—Enlightenment philosopher, author of *Emile*. Put forth the notion that children are born good.

John Locke—Enlightenment philosopher. Put forth the notion that children are born as "blank slates".

L

language barriers—Language differences that make communication difficult

logistical barriers—Varied issues to be considered when trying to involve parents

longitudinal study—Research conducted over a lengthy period of time

M

macrosystem—Attitudes and ideologies of the culture, such as laws, morals, values, customs, and world views

male role model—Father figure

managing parents in the classroom—Structure for including parents in the classroom

mesosystem—Linkages between two or more settings in which the child actively participates

microsystem—Relationships that most closely affect and include a child

National Association for the Education of Young Children—Professional organization of early childhood educators

N

neuron—Brain cell

neuroscience—Study of the brain's physiology

non-custodial parent—The parent not awarded custody by the court

nuclear family—Family structure consisting of mother, father, and children

O

organizational tasks—Clerical jobs

P

parent communication—Letters, notes, phone calls, conferences initiated by a teacher

parent education—Workshops and seminars provided for family support parent educator—Teacher who educates the parent as well as the child

parent jobs—Jobs parents perform in the classroom

parent presentations—Teacher talks about classroom routines and expectations

parent support—Resources provided to parents for family success

parentese—A speech register used universally by parents with their infants

pedagogical perspectives—Philosophies of teaching

proximo-distal—From the midline of the body to the extremities

psychosocial development—Development of social and emotional faculties

S

school-wide plan for family involvement—A school's strategic plan to involve families

Sociocultural theory—Theory that emphasizes social connectedness

Student-led Conferences—Alternative format of children taking the lead to present academic progress

synapse—The space between neuron connections

T

tabula rasa—The notion that children are born as "blank slates"

V

verbal-linguistic—A method of learning

Index